THE 100 BEST MUTUAL FUNDS

TO OWN IN AMERICA

FOURTH EDITION

Gene Walden

DEARBORN™
TRADE

A **Kaplan Professional** Company

Contents

100 Best Funds by Investment Objective

Aggressive Growth Funds	Ranking
Pin Oak Aggressive Stock Fund	5
INVESCO Dynamics Fund	12
Bridgeway Aggressive Growth Portfolio	13
Delaware Select Growth Fund	14
Citizens Emerging Growth Fund/Retail	17
Janus Enterprise Fund	22
Janus Mercury Fund	23
PBHG Select Equity Fund	27
Calamos Growth Fund	33
Smith Barney Aggressive Growth Fund	36
Fidelity Aggressive Growth Fund	37
IPS Millennium Fund	38
PIMCO Innovation Fund	44
Van Kampen Emerging Growth Fund	46
Phoenix-Engemann Aggressive Growth Fund	47
Strong Large Cap Growth Fund	49
Putnam New Opportunities Fund	58
SunAmerica Growth Opportunities Fund	59
Putnam Voyager Fund II	60
Dreyfus Appreciation Fund	80
Fidelity Mid Cap Stock Fund	83
PIMCO Target Fund	93
Phoenix-Engemann Focus Growth Fund	98

Balanced Funds	Ranking
Value Line Asset Allocation Fund	78

Growth and Income Funds	Ranking
Fidelity Dividend Growth Fund	42
SunAmerica Equity Growth & Income Fund	57
Vanguard Growth and Income Fund	65
Principal Preservation S&P 100 Plus Portfolio	75
SSgA Growth & Income Fund	79

Long-Term Growth Funds

International Equity Funds

	Ranking
Gabelli Global Growth Fund	25
Pilgrim International Small Cap Growth Fund	55
Oppenheimer Global Growth & Income Fund	91
Pilgrim Worldwide Growth Fund	97

Sector Funds

	Ranking
T. Rowe Price Science & Technology Fund	10
INVESCO Telecommunications Fund	11
PBHG Technology & Communications Fund	24
Fidelity Select: Electronics Portfolio	28
Fidelity Select: Computers Portfolio	29
INVESCO Technology Fund	30
Gabelli Global Telecommunications Fund	31
Fidelity Select: Technology Portfolio	51
Fidelity Select: Biotechnology Portfolio	52
Kemper Technology Fund	53
Vanguard Health Care Fund	54
First American Technology Fund	66
Alliance Technology Fund	67
Fidelity Select: Software & Computer Services Portfolio	68
Eaton Vance Worldwide Health Sciences Fund	69
John Hancock Technology Fund	70
Fidelity Select: Brokerage & Investment Portfolio	84
Seligman Communications & Information Fund	86
Fidelity Select: Telecommunications Portfolio	95
Fidelity Select: Health Care Portfolio	96
Fidelity Select: Energy Service Portfolio	99

Small-Cap Stock Funds

	Ranking
Phoenix-Engemann Small & Mid-Cap Growth Fund	15
Strong Growth Fund	21
Dreyfus Founders Discovery Fund	35
Meridian Value Fund	41
Harbor Growth Fund	50
Managers Special Equity Fund	63
GAMerica Capital Fund	73
Pilgrim MidCap Growth Fund	90

Socially Responsible Funds

	Ranking
Calvert Large Cap Growth Fund	71
Citizens Emerging Growth Fund/Retail	17

Preface

This is the 20th book I've written in the past 13 years, if you include all the editions of all the *100 Best* books. That prolific streak was no accident. The stock market has been through one of its most exciting and prosperous periods in history. And despite the market's growing volatility, stocks should continue a very robust long-term growth trend, thanks in part to the continuing growth of computer technology, telecommunications, biotechnology, the Internet, and the electronics industry.

There is no easier way to participate in the explosive growth of the American economy than to invest in mutual funds. Most of the 100 funds featured in this book have enjoyed average annual returns of 20 to 40 percent over the past five years.

Americans continue to be drawn to mutual funds for several very good reasons: Mutual funds are professionally managed by experienced investment managers; they provide instant diversification by investing in a broad range of stocks or bonds; and they provide solid performance, particularly in a good market.

The purpose of this book is to help direct you to the funds that have done the best over the past few years. With more than 8,000 funds to choose from, narrowing the field to the top performing funds is no easy task. The 100 funds in this book all have several characteristics in common: They ranked among the top 5 percent of all funds in terms of total return over the past five years; they are managed by experienced fund managers; and they are all geared to smaller individual investors.

Many of the funds from the third edition of this book have made a return visit to this fourth edition, although we've also included a number of exciting new funds that have enjoyed exceptional performance in recent years.

If you want to pick your portfolio from the cream of the crop, you've come to the right source. Choose carefully, diversify by including several different types of funds in your portfolio, and be patient. Ultimately, you should be able to enjoy the same type of investment returns that have made mutual funds the most popular form of investment ever invented. May all your picks be winners!

Acknowledgments

As they have with several of my recent books, Ed Lawler and Larry Nelson played major roles in this project. Ed, who is a talented author and professor, wrote many of the fund profiles for this book—as he has for several other *100 Best* books. Larry, who has helped with nearly every book I've written since 1990, worked from start to finish on this project, assisting with the research and fact gathering, the graphs, the fact sheets, and other key elements of the book.

I would also like to thank my editors at Dearborn Trade, including Publisher Cynthia Zigmund, Senior Managing Editor Jack Kiburz, and Senior Editorial Assistant Sandy Thomas, who have helped shape the book into an attractive, professional, user-friendly format.

Introduction

There's no easier way for individuals to cash in on the booming economy of the new millennium than to invest in mutual funds. Quick, convenient, and diversified, mutual funds have become the fast food of investing. They give investors a stake in the stock and bond markets without the hassle—no poring over stock tables, no thumbing through annual reports and corporate balance sheets, no restless nights fretting over the daily ups and downs of the markets.

The biggest obstacle, in fact, is figuring out which mutual funds are right for you. And that is no small obstacle. The selection process can be staggering. You must choose from more than 8,000 mutual funds—nearly four times the number of stocks on the New York Stock Exchange.

Despite their professional management, diversification, and finely honed trading strategies, not all funds are created equal. In fact, the vast majority of mutual funds have trailed the overall stock market the past ten years. However, there are exceptions that rise above the crowd.

The 100 Best Mutual Funds to Own in America is designed to ease your selection process by narrowing the field of choices to 100 exceptional funds. Each of these 100 funds ranks in the top 2 percent of all mutual funds in terms of total return over the past five years.

In paging through this book, you'll find a detailed overview of each fund, with helpful insights on their investment objectives and strategies, their top ten holdings, sales charges and annual fees, fund manager's experience, special shareholder services, minimum investment requirements, performance records, and asset mix. You'll also find the fund symbol, fund company address, toll-free number, and Web site—and a wealth of other vital information.

WHY MUTUAL FUNDS?

What is a mutual fund? Technically, a mutual fund is a "company" that pools investment contributions from shareholders to buy stocks, bonds, or other investments. When you invest in a mutual fund, you are buying shares of the mutual fund company, and you share in the success of that company.

But for all practical purposes, you can think of a mutual fund simply as a portfolio of investments, such as stocks and bonds. You become a part owner of that portfolio when you buy shares in the fund. With a single investment, you suddenly hold a diversified portfolio of dozens of investments. Most funds have in the range of 25 to 300 stock or bond holdings. When you own shares in a fund, your share price directly reflects the net asset value of the stocks in the fund, and the investment value of your shares fluctuates as the fortunes of the fund's holdings fluctuate.

In addition to diversification, convenience, and professional management, mutual funds offer several other benefits:

- *Liquidity.* With most funds, you can pull your money out simply by calling the company and telling them to sell your shares.
- *Low investment requirements.* It usually doesn't take a lot of money to invest in a mutual fund. Initial minimum investment requirements vary from $250 to $2,500, although a few funds require as much as $100,000 to $500,000. Once you're a shareholder, most funds allow you to contribute even smaller subsequent amounts—usually in the range of $50 to $250—so it becomes very easy even for small investors to build a position in a fund.
- *Direct purchases.* Although brokers are often helpful in recommending good mutual funds to their clients, you don't have to use a broker to buy shares in a mutual fund. You can buy shares directly from the company simply by calling the company's toll-free sales line.
- *Low (or no) sales fees.* Many companies allow you to purchase fund shares with no sales fee. These are called *no-load funds* (which mean they have no sales "load" or fee). Load funds vary in the fees they charge investors. Some *low-load funds* charge about 3 percent, although most load funds charge in the range of 4.5 to 8 percent. Some funds charge what is known as a *back-end load,* which is a sales charge you would pay when you sell your shares in the fund. Typically, back-end load funds charge 5 percent if you sell the first year, 4 percent the second year, with the fee diminishing to zero after the fifth year. Funds also charge annual expense fees that usually vary from 1 percent to 3 percent, depending on the fund.
- *Checking deduction plans.* With most funds, you can have money automatically withdrawn from your checking account and invested in the fund each month or each quarter.
- *Automatic withdrawal.* Retired investors sometimes opt for withdrawal plans that authorize the fund to pay out a set amount to the investor from his or her fund account each month or each quarter.
- *Retirement account access.* Most companies allow investors to use their funds in IRAs, SEPs, and other retirement accounts.

- *Telephone exchange.* Investors who wish to switch from one fund to another within the same family of funds are usually allowed to make that switch commission-free simply by calling the company and ordering the change.
- *Automatic reinvestment.* With most mutual funds, investors can have their dividends and capital gains distributions automatically reinvested in additional shares of the fund with no additional sales fee.

FUNDS FOR EVERY TASTE

There are a wide variety of mutual funds to meet the tastes and risk thresholds of nearly everyone who invests. The original mutual funds were designed to produce a combination of growth and income by investing in a diversified portfolio of dividend-paying blue chip stocks. Many such "growth and income" funds are still offered today, along with a host of other types of funds.

Growth and income funds.   These funds are appropriate for investors who want a steady stream of income along with some appreciation. They are not appropriate for high-income investors who want to minimize their taxes, because the additional income adds to the investors' tax burden. Because they invest in more well-established companies, growth and income funds are among the least risky types of mutual funds.

Long-term growth funds.   These funds invest primarily in stocks of fast-growing companies in order to provide long-term appreciation (with minimal current income) for shareholders. While growth funds tend to be more volatile in the short term than income-oriented funds, they tend to provide better long-term returns. Because of their diversification, long-term growth funds are among the least risky types of funds.

Aggressive growth funds.   These stock funds come in many forms. Some invest in depressed stocks that have turnaround potential. Others look for trendy stocks. Most of the top aggressive growth funds in recent years have had large positions in high-tech stocks. Other funds look for good start-up companies that could blossom into major corporations. And still others invest in potential takeover stocks that could experience a sharp run-up in prices. With aggressive growth funds, the portfolio managers play a numbers game. Some of their picks pan out; others fall flat. Their hope is to make enough money on the winners to more than compensate for the losers. In truth, the label "aggressive growth" applies more to the types of stocks that these funds invest in than to their overall performance. Although a large share of the top-ranked funds in this book are aggressive growth funds, many aggressive growth funds have proven to be no more profitable than other stock funds—just more volatile. These funds tend to be riskier than growth funds, particularly over the short term.

International and global funds.   These funds give investors a stake in the international market. Global funds invest in both U.S. and foreign stocks, whereas international funds invest strictly in foreign stocks. Because they invest in foreign stocks, international funds can be somewhat riskier than U.S. growth stock funds. However, by investing in an international fund as part of a diversified portfolio, you add foreign diversification, which actually reduces the overall risk of your portfolio.

Sector funds.   These specialty funds invest strictly in stocks of a single industrial sector. There are funds for almost any market sector you could name—precious metals, utilities, high-tech, medical technology, financial services, and others. If you think gas and oil stocks are ready to take off, you might invest in an energy fund. If you want a hedge against inflation, you might invest in a gold fund that buys the stocks of gold mining companies. While specialty funds have broad stock holdings within a specific sector, they lack the diversity and safety of traditional stock funds. If the sector is faring poorly, so will the fund. For instance, medical funds experienced phenomenal growth in 1991 when the medical sector was hot, but when medical stocks cooled off amid political discussions of medical cost containment, health care sector funds became the worst-performing funds of 1992. Sector funds are the riskiest of all funds. Another example is Internet stock funds. They were on fire in 1999, with the growth of some funds exceeding 200 percent. But in 2000, with the Internet market in the tank, Internet mutual funds were among the worst performers in the market.

Index funds.   These are funds designed to mirror the overall market. By buying an index fund, you can expect to achieve a return similar to the growth of the overall market. While that may not seem particularly adventuresome, index funds do tend to outperform about 80 percent of all mutual funds, simply because index funds are 100 percent invested in stocks at all times. Some index funds are tied to the Dow Jones Industrials, while others are designed to reflect the Standard and Poor's 500 Index.

Money market funds.   Although money market funds are a form of mutual fund, they are considered a separate class. Brokerage firms use money market fund accounts for clients who want to continue drawing interest on the money in their account when it is not invested in securities or other investments. Banks also offer money market accounts for clients who want to get a slightly higher return than they would get through a standard savings account. These are the safest of all funds, but generally provide the lowest long-term return.

Bond funds.   Bond funds first became popular in the 1970s, when investors began opting for managed portfolios of corporate bonds rather than individual bonds. An offshoot of the traditional bond fund was the *high-yield bond fund*—portfolios of low-rated *junk bonds* that pay interest rates three or four points higher than those paid by many of the AAA-rated bonds. With individual junk bonds, safety is a major concern because of the risk of default, although the diversification of a portfolio of bonds reduces the risk substantially. In reality, all bond funds—even government bond funds— carry a great deal more risk than most investors expect. Bond values rise and fall as interest rates fluctuate. When interest rates rise, bond values drop. A 2 percent rise in market interest rates can push the value of a bond fund down by 10 percent or more. Conversely, when market rates are falling, bond funds enjoy excellent appreciation, although the best bond funds generally fall far short of the best stock funds over the long term. This book covers bond funds—both high quality and high yield—in the honorable mention section.

Tax-exempt bond funds.   These funds invest in municipal bonds, which provide a tax break for investors. The dividends they pay are exempt from federal taxes, and in the case of funds that comprise tax-exempt bonds from the investor's state, they are also exempt from state taxes. The problem, however, is that the returns these funds provide are among the lowest in the industry—even after taking the tax break into account. Municipal bonds also carry a degree of risk. It is possible for bond issuers to default, creating major losses for bondholders, as was the case in Orange County, California, in 1994.

Closed-end funds.   A closed-end fund is a professionally managed, diversified portfolio that is closed to new investors. As with stock offerings, investment companies underwrite such funds to raise a limited amount of money. Once the cutoff point has been reached, no new investments are accepted, and the fund begins trading on the open market like a stock. Some of the best-known closed-end funds include the Mexico Fund, the Korea Fund, the Brazil Fund, and the Taiwan Fund, all of which trade on the New York Stock Exchange. By contrast, open-end funds can continue to issue new shares as shareholders contribute new investment dollars. Investors buy shares directly from the mutual fund company rather than through a stock exchange. (Closed-end funds are not covered in this book; only the traditional open-end funds are featured.)

RATING THE TOP 100 FUNDS

From 8,000 funds, my objective was to sift out the 100 best. I began by focusing on the top 2 percent of all funds based on total return over the past five years. Of those top-ranking funds, I eliminated from consideration all funds that were closed to new shareholders, all funds with excessive minimum investment requirements (anything over $10,000 was eliminated), and funds with new fund managers. (I made an exception for some Fidelity funds, because the company has a policy of shifting fund managers from fund to fund every few years. It is a policy that has worked well for Fidelity, because the funds are all managed more or less on a team basis anyway.) Then I looked at the track histories of the funds and eliminated funds that had been particularly volatile over the past few years.

I also eliminated one well-performing fund because of inexcusably poor service. The Prudential Target Large Cap Growth Fund was dropped from the list when representatives answering the 800 phone line were unable to answer our questions on the tenure of the fund managers, fund purchase requirements, the fund's track history, and other routine questions regarding the fund. There are too many other good funds available to settle for a fund family that can't even answer the most basic questions on their products.

Once I had assembled the list of 100, the next step was to rank the funds from 1 to 100. The ranking system revolved around the following three categories, each worth a maximum of 5 points (for a maximum total of 15 points).

Performance.   Each fund was graded based on its five-year total return record (through late 2000). It is important to note that the system ranks the funds relative to other funds from the top 100—not relative to all mutual funds. If I had graded them relative to all funds, then all 100 of the funds in this book would have scored a perfect five because they all rank in the top 2 percent of all mutual funds over the five-year period. Instead, I graded on a curve, with roughly the top 25 funds receiving a perfect five, the next 25 receiving a four, and so on down to two points.

Consistency.   Rather than look at day-to-day volatility, I graded each fund's consistency on a year-to-year basis. I compared the performance of each fund to the Dow Jones Industrial Average each year over a five-year period from 1995 through 1999 (and part of 2000). A fund would score a perfect five if it outperformed the Dow (or ended the year virtually even with the Dow) each of the five years. Generally, if it trailed the Dow one of the five years, the fund would score a four; if it trailed the Dow two of the five years, it would score three points; if it trailed the Dow three of the five years, it would score a two for the category; and if it trailed four of the five years, it would score a one, although all funds earned at least two points in this category.

Fees/Services/Management.   This is the most subjective of the three categories — with certain guidelines. With this category, it was more a matter of deducting points than awarding them. To receive a perfect five, a fund would need to (1) be a true no-load fund (with no sales fee to buy or sell); (2) have a fund manager who had been with the fund at least four years; (3) offer the full range of standard services that most funds offer (checking account deduction, automatic withdrawal, retirement account availability, instant telephone redemption, and free switching between funds within the family by telephone); and (4) have reasonable minimum investment requirements (of no more than $5,000 initial investment minimum and $500 subsequent investment minimum).

A load fund — with a front-end or back-end sales fee of 4 percent or above — would automatically lose two points in this category. If the fund manager had been with the fund less than three years, another point would normally be deducted — with rare exception. (The only exceptions would be for a veteran fund manager who established an impressive track record with another fund.) If a fund didn't offer most of the standard mutual fund services mentioned previously, another point was deducted. If its minimum investment requirement was excessive (for instance, a couple of funds in the book require a $10,000 minimum investment), yet another point would be subtracted.

BREAKING TIES

With 100 funds graded on a 15-point rating system, many funds scored the same. How did I break the ties? I looked at several factors:

- *Asset size.* I prefer smaller funds of under $1 billion in assets over the behemoth funds with assets of $10 billion to $25 billion. The smaller funds have much greater flexibility in moving in and out of stocks.
- *Consistency.* I prefer funds that provide consistent performance year in and year out rather than funds that have one great year and a few average years.
- *Diversification.* A fund that is well diversified across industry lines would generally rank above the sector funds, which invest exclusively in a specific industry. The reason is that the risk factor is much higher with sector funds. Although they may have done well over the most recent five-year period, if their sector should suddenly fall out of favor, they would stand to fall much faster than the broadly diversified funds.
- *Five- and ten-year total return.* Funds that have provided great returns for a full decade look like solid bets, but five-year returns are also important.
- *Management.* For funds with identical five-year returns, I looked at the fund manager. A fund with a manager who had been with the fund five to ten years would be rated above a fund with a relatively new manager.

MUTUAL FUNDS AND TAXES

There's no question that mutual funds are an investment conceived in convenience: you get diversity, professional management, and a host of special services all for a simple investment. But the convenience ends when the taxes begin. Unless you invest strictly in tax-exempt municipal bond funds or tuck your mutual funds safely away in a tax-sheltered retirement plan, you're likely to encounter some confusing twists when calculating your taxes.

Each year most stock and bond funds pay out interest, dividends, and capital gains distributions (from profits made on trades within the fund). As a shareholder, you are liable for taxes on those gains, even if you had those distributions automatically reinvested in additional shares. Your fund will send you a Form 1099-DIV (or similar form) annually that details your taxable gains for the year.

You are also liable for taxes on the appreciation of your fund shares when you sell out your holdings. But take special care in calculating your gains, particularly if you have your fund distributions automatically reinvested. The tendency among investors is to *overpay,* because they forget they've already paid taxes on the reinvested share of their holdings.

For instance, if your total holdings went from $1,000 when you bought the fund to $2,000 when you sold, that doesn't mean you owe taxes on the full $1,000 gain. Part of that gain came from reinvested dividends and capital gains for which you already paid taxes.

To determine your true taxable total:

1. Add up all the dividends and distributions from the fund that you have had reinvested in additional shares.
2. Subtract the total value of your holdings when you bought the shares from the total value when you sold the shares to determine your total gain.
3. Then subtract your reinvested distributions from your total gain. That is your taxable income. For example, you paid $1,000 and reinvested $100 in distributions. If you sold at $2,000:

Value at sale	$2,000
Initial investment	– 1,000
Reinvested distribution	– 100
Taxable income	$ 900

For investors who have accumulated shares over time, the IRS offers several options for calculating taxable gains on the sale of a portion of those shares:

- *First in, first out (FIFO).* You sell the first fund shares you purchased and pay taxes on the gains. The best circumstance to use FIFO would be if your fund shares have declined recently. That means you may have paid the most for your earliest shares and therefore would represent the smallest taxable gain.
- *Average cost.* Your taxes would be based on the average price you paid for shares you accumulated over time. To calculate the average, divide your total investment in the fund (including reinvested gains) by the number of shares you own. That works best when share prices have surged over time, because you probably paid the least for your earliest shares and would show the biggest gain for those shares if you used FIFO. By using cost averaging, you can push up the average purchase and cut down the total taxable gain.

- *Specific identification.* This allows you to identify the specific shares you are selling, which enables you to select the shares that will give you the smallest taxable gain.
- *Tax-averse investors may prefer municipal bond funds.* The dividends they pay are exempt from federal taxes, and in the case of funds that comprise tax-exempt bonds from your state, they may also be exempt from state taxes. But you are still subject to taxes on any capital gains those funds earn by selling bonds at a profit.

Despite the tax breaks, it would probably be a mistake to put too much of your money in municipal bond funds. They tend to be among the worst-performing funds on the market over the long term. Even with the tax savings, their total after-tax return is likely to trail that of most taxable stock and bond funds over the long term.

TAKING ACTION

This book is designed to help you reduce your universe of choices from the roughly 8,000 funds currently on the market to the much more manageable level of 100. But ultimately, it is you who must take action if you are to profit from the information in this book.

How should you select the fund or funds that are right for you? Here is a simple action plan:

1. Skim through the book to find a few funds that look promising to you.
2. Once you've selected a handful of good funds, try to do a little more research. You could go to the fund's Web site (listed at the top of the fund profile along with the address), where there may be a wealth of information about the fund and the fund family. Or you can call the fund's toll-free number (also listed with the address in the fund profile) and request the most recent annual or semiannual report and prospectus.
3. Read through the fund information, then weigh all the factors that are important to you. Consider the fund's long-term performance, sales loads, annual fees, minimum investment requirements, services, type of fund, fund manager, asset size, and any other factors you consider important.
4. Decide which fund (or funds) you want to buy.
5. Call the fund's toll-free number and place your order.

6. To go one step further, you can track the progress of your fund each day in the mutual fund section of the *Wall Street Journal, Investor's Business Daily, USA Today,* and many major metropolitan daily newspapers. You may also want to check out our Web site, where we may post occasional articles or updates on these funds. The Web site is <www.allstarstocks.com>.

THE COMPLETE PORTFOLIO

For a diversified approach, you will probably want to invest in several different funds, depending on your investment objectives. For instance, you should consider buying a broadly diversified stock growth fund, an aggressive growth fund, an international stock fund, perhaps a growth and income fund, and a sector fund such as a high-tech fund. This book helps you choose from the best of each category.

Here are several factors to consider in making your selection—and several ways this book can help you assess those factors:

- *Investment objectives.* Do you want income, capital appreciation, safety, or aggressive growth? Look for funds that meet your objectives.
- *Performance.* You want a fund that has provided superior long-term performance. Good performance in a single year means very little. Very often, the best-performing funds one year become the worst-performing funds the next. This book takes a long-term perspective, featuring funds based on superior five-year performance records.
- *Consistency.* Are you willing to put up with some volatility in hopes of getting better long-term returns? Or would you rather have a fund that tends to match the market year in and year out but may not offer quite the long-term potential of some other more volatile funds? This book rates funds on year-to-year consistency.
- *Fees.* If you plan to hold a fund for years to come, the initial sales load won't make a lot of difference. But if you expect to move in and out of various funds from year to year, then the 4 to 8 percent fee that most load funds charge would make a significant difference in your total return. Investors who do a lot of buying and selling of mutual funds should seriously consider using only no-load or low-load funds. Also, take a look at the fund's annual expense ratio. Those fees can vary from as little as 0.7 percent to as high as 3 percent, which can make a big difference over time. This book lists all the fees associated with each of the 100 featured funds.
- *Management.* A fund is truly a reflection of its manager. A fund with a great track record may not be such a great fund if the manager leaves.

If you are selecting a fund based on its past performance, make sure the manager responsible for that performance is still running the fund.

• *Services.* As mentioned earlier, mutual funds offer a variety of services such as automatic checking account deduction, periodic fund withdrawal plans, and IRA accounts. Make sure the fund you are interested in offers the services you need.

WORDS FOR THE WISE

Chances are as you read this book, you'll run into some terms you may not fully understand. Here is a glossary of some of the key terms you may need to know:

American depositary receipt (ADR). An ADR is a foreign stock sponsored by a U.S. bank and reissued on a U.S. stock exchange. Although ADRs do not trade at the same price in the United States as they do at home (because the sponsoring bank issues them at a different price), their prices move exactly in concert with the price movements of the original stock.

annual expense ratio. This is a yearly mutual fund fee assessed to cover the fund's expenses, including management fees, transaction fees, and marketing expenses. Annual expense ratios usually vary from 0.6 percent to about 3 percent of the fund's net asset value. The expense ratio is deducted directly from each shareholder's holdings.

assets. Assets are the amount of money invested in a mutual fund by shareholders. The largest mutual fund is Fidelity Magellan, which boasts about $30 billion in total assets. Most funds are in the range of $25 million to $3 billion.

back-end load. This is a fee charged by some mutual funds to investors when they sell their shares in the fund. The fees, which range from about 1 to 6 percent, typically diminish about 1 percent each year the investor holds the fund. For instance, a fund with a maximum 5 percent back-end load will charge the full 5 percent the first year. But the fee normally drops to 4 percent the second year, 3 percent the third, 2 percent the fourth, 1 percent the fifth, and zero after the fifth year. There are two types of back-end loads: *deferred sales charges* and *redemption fees.* Deferred are definitely the preferred. Funds with deferred sales fees base the charges on the net asset value of the shares when you bought them, while redemption fees are based on the price of your shares at the time you sell. So if your fund has a strong gain, you'll pay much more in redemption fees than you would in deferred sales charges. (See also *load, no-load fund, front-end load, redemption fee,* and *deferred sales charge.*)

bottom-up investment approach. This is an investment method in which an investor selects stocks based on the merits of each individual stock without regard to the overall economy. It is the opposite of a top-down approach in which an investor looks at broad economic patterns to determine which investment sectors would make the most timely investments. Most stock mutual fund managers use a bottom-up approach, although some use a blend of both. (See also *top-down investment approach.*)

cash equivalent. Cash equivalent refers to an investment that has a monetary value equal to a specified sum.

cash equivalent investments. These are interest-bearing securities of high liquidity and safety, such as commercial paper, certificates of deposit, and Treasury bills, which are considered virtually as good as cash. Money market funds invest almost exclusively in cash equivalents. When stock mutual fund managers sense a looming downturn in the market, they often lighten their stock portfolios and move more assets to cash equivalents. That provides safety and a little income for the short term.

classes of mutual fund shares. Mutual fund companies often issue fund shares of several classifications. The shares, which normally are referred to as A, B, C, D, and so on, usually have the same asset mix but different investor requirements. For instance, A shares may have a front-end sales load and a low annual expense ratio, whereas B shares may have a back-end load and a slightly higher annual expense ratio. C shares may have no sales load but a very high annual expense ratio, and D shares may be geared to institutional and affluent investors and may require a minimum investment of $100,000 or more.

deferred sales charge. This is a sales fee or back-end load charged by some mutual funds to shareholders when they sell their fund shares. (See *back-end load.*)

dividend. A dividend is a portion of a company's earnings that is paid to its shareholders. Funds holding dividend-paying stocks pass those dividends onto shareholders in lump payments either quarterly, semi-annually, or annually, depending on the fund. Investors in most funds may have dividends automatically reinvested in additional shares.

dividend yield. The dividend yield is the annual dividend payment divided by its market price per share. If a stock is trading at $100 a share, and it pays a $10 dividend, the dividend yield is 10 percent.

equity investment. An equity investment is a security (usually common stock or preferred stock) that represents a share of ownership in a business entity (usually a corporation).

front-end load. This is the sales fee a mutual fund charges investors to buy shares of the fund. The fee (usually in the range of 3 to 8.5 percent) is deducted directly from the investor's contribution. For instance, a $1,000 investment in a fund with a 5 percent front-end load would result in $50 in load fees and $950 in actual fund shares. (See also *load, no-load fund,* and *back-end load.*)

load. A fund's load is a sales fee charged to the investors. Loads normally vary from about 3 percent to 8.5 percent of the total purchase amount. (See also *no-load fund, front-end load, back-end load,* and *redemption fee.*)

money market fund. This is a mutual fund that invests in high-quality, short-term debt instruments such as Treasury bills or certificates of deposit. Money market fund investors earn a steady stream of interest income that varies with short-term interest rates. Generally, investors may cash out at any time.

net asset value (NAV). The NAV is the total worth of all the investments of a mutual fund. It changes daily to reflect fluctuations in the price of the fund's stock and bond holdings.

no-load fund. A no-load fund is a mutual fund that charges no sales fee to buy or sell its shares. (See also *load, front-end load,* and *back-end load.*)

open-end mutual fund. This is a mutual fund that allows investors to buy shares directly from the mutual fund company and stands ready to redeem shares whenever shareholders are ready to sell. Open-end funds may issue new shares any time there is a demand for more shares from investors. Shareholders buy and sell shares at the fund's net asset value (plus sales fees). Rather than selling at net asset value, closed-end fund shares trade like stock on a stock exchange at whatever price the market is willing to pay.

price-earnings ratio (PE). Specifically, a company's PE is its stock price divided by its earnings per share over the past 12 months. PE is Wall Street's most commonly used ratio to determine a stock's value to investors. They are a lot like golf scores: the lower the better. For instance, a company with a stock price of $20 and earnings per share of $1 has a 20 PE ($20 divided by $1), while a company with a stock price of $10 and the same $1 earnings per share has a 10 PE. The higher a stock's PE, the more expensive the stock is relative to its earnings.

redemption fee.   This is a sales fee or back-end load charged by some mutual funds to shareholders when they sell their shares. (See *back-end load.*)

top-down investment approach.   This is an investment strategy in which the investor looks at broad economic trends to decide which types of investments appear to be best positioned for growth and then selects individual investments based on that economic assessment. It is the opposite of a bottom-up strategy, in which an investor assesses an individual investment strictly on its own merits, irrespective of the overall economy. (See also *bottom-up investment approach.*)

12b-1 fee.   A 12b-1 fee is a small fee assessed annually by some mutual funds to cover advertising and marketing expenses. The fee is deducted directly from each sharcholder's holdings and usually represents less than 1 percent of net asset valuc.

For investors with patience and persistence, mutual funds can be a simple and effective way to enjoy a lifetime of success in the investment market.

White Oak Growth Fund

Oak Associate Funds
3875 Embassy Parkway, Suite 250
Akron, OH 44333
888-462-5386
www.oakassociates.com
Ticker symbol: **WOGSX**

Fund managers: James D. Oelschlager, Donna L. Barton, and
Douglas S. MacKay
Fund objective: Long-term growth

Performance	★ ★ ★ ★ ★
Consistency	★ ★ ★ ★ ★
Fees/Services/Management	★ ★ ★ ★ ★
Total	**15 Points**

The White Oak Growth Fund concentrates its investment eggs in just three baskets, but they are three of the market's best-performing baskets—technology, health care, and financial services.

Fund manager James Oelschlager, who has been at the helm since the fund was founded in 1992, and his team look for fast-growing companies within those sectors that have market caps of at least $5 billion. The fund strategy is to buy quality stocks and hold for the long term.

The portfolio turnover rate is a paltry 6 percent, and the average holding period is about three years. But knowing when to sell a stock is considered a key to the success of the fund. Oelschlager looks for downward revisions in earnings estimates, changes in long-term earnings projections, analyst contacts, valuation, and balance sheet issues in determining whether a stock should be sold.

The $4.5 billion fund holds only about 25 stocks in the portfolio. Such concentration certainly has its risks, but the fund's recent performance demonstrates the strategy's upside. A $10,000 investment in the fund five years ago would now be worth nearly $50,000. Even more impressive, the fund has outperformed the Dow Jones Industrial Average each of the past five years.

Among the fund's largest holdings are both high-tech stocks, such as Applied Materials, Cisco Systems, and EMC, and medical blue chips, such as Merck and Eli Lilly. Discount broker Charles Schwab is also among the top ten holdings. Technology stocks make up about 47 percent of the portfolio, followed by financial companies, 24 percent, and health care, 18 percent.

"We continue to believe that the health care, technology, and financial services sectors offer the average investor the best opportunities for growth," says Oelschlager.

The fund stays more than 90 percent invested in stocks under normal conditions.

PERFORMANCE

The fund has enjoyed outstanding growth over the past five years. Including dividends and capital gains distributions, the White Oak Growth Fund has provided an average annual return the past five years (through late 2000) of 37.7 percent.

A $10,000 investment in 1995 would have grown to nearly $50,000 five years later.

CONSISTENCY

The fund has been very consistent, outperforming the Dow Jones Industrial Average for five consecutive years through 1999 (and again through most of 2000). Its biggest gain came in 1995, when it moved up 52.7 percent (compared with a 33.5 percent rise in the Dow).

FEES/SERVICES/MANAGEMENT

The fund is a pure no-load fund, with no fees to buy or sell shares. The fund's total annual expense ratio of 1.00 percent (with no 12b-1 fee) compares favorably with other funds.

The fund offers all the standard services such as retirement account availability, automatic withdrawal, and automatic checking account deduction. Its minimum initial investment of $2,000 and minimum subsequent investment of $50 are in line with other funds.

Fund manager James Oelschlager, who guides the fund along with Donna Barton and Douglas MacKay, has been with the fund since its inception in 1992. The Oak Associates fund family includes just three funds.

Top Ten Stock Holdings

1. Applied Materials	6. Sun Microsystems
2. Cisco Systems	7. Merck
3. Charles Schwab	8. CIENA
4. EMC	9. Microsoft
5. Intel	10. Eli Lilly

Fund inception: 1992
Asset mix: Common stocks, 96%; cash/equivalents, 4%
Total net assets: $4.5 billion

Load

Front-end load	*None*
Redemption fee (max.)	*None*

Annual Fees

12b-1 fee	*None*
Management fee	0.67%
Other expenses	0.33
Total annual expense	1.00%

Minimum initial investment	$2,000
Minimum subsequent investment	$50

Services

Telephone exchanges	*Yes*
Automatic withdrawal	*Yes*
Automatic checking deduction	*Yes*
Retirement plan/IRA	*Yes*
Instant redemption	*Yes*
Portfolio manager (years)	8
Number of funds in family	3

The fund has grown at nearly 20 percent per year for the past ten years. A $10,000 investment in the fund ten years ago would now be worth about $60,000.

Reynolds takes a conservative buy-and-hold approach, with just a 6 percent annual portfolio turnover ratio. The fund stays almost 100 percent invested in stocks under normal circumstances.

PERFORMANCE

The fund has enjoyed outstanding growth over the past five years. Including dividends and capital gains distributions, the Reynolds Blue Chip Growth Fund has provided an average annual return the past five years (through late 2000) of 33 percent.

A $10,000 investment in 1995 would have grown to about $41,500 five years later.

CONSISTENCY

The fund has been fairly consistent, outperforming or matching the Dow Jones Industrial Average the past five years through 1999 (and was about even with the Dow through most of 2000). Its biggest gain came in 1999, when it moved up 51 percent (compared with a 25.2 percent rise in the Dow).

FEES/SERVICES/MANAGEMENT

The fund is a pure no-load fund, with no fees to buy or sell shares. The fund's total annual expense ratio of 1.50 percent (with a 0.25 percent 12b-1 fee) is in line with other funds.

The fund offers all the standard services such as retirement account availability, automatic withdrawal, and automatic checking account deduction. Its minimum initial investment of $1,000 and minimum subsequent investment of $100 are in line with other funds.

The fund has been managed by Fred Reynolds since its inception in 1988. The Reynolds fund family includes only five funds and allows shareholders to switch from fund to fund by telephone.

Top Ten Stock Holdings

1. America Online
2. Cisco Systems
3. Microsoft
4. Intel
5. IBM

6. Wal-Mart
7. Nokia
8. Pfizer
9. Merck
10. Johnson & Johnson

Fund inception: 1988
Asset mix: Common stocks, 100%
Total net assets: $633 million

Load

Front-end load	*None*
Redemption fee (max.)	*None*

Annual Fees

12b-1 fee	0.25%
Management fee	1.00
Other expenses	0.25
Total annual expense	1.50%
Minimum initial investment	$1,000
Minimum subsequent investment	$100

Services

Telephone exchanges	*Yes*
Automatic withdrawal	*Yes*
Automatic checking deduction	*Yes*
Retirement plan/IRA	*Yes*
Instant redemption	*Yes*
Portfolio manager (years)	12
Number of funds in family	5

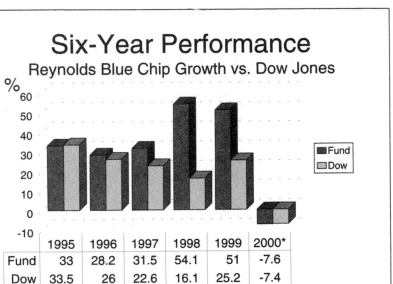

Six-Year Performance
Reynolds Blue Chip Growth vs. Dow Jones

	1995	1996	1997	1998	1999	2000*
Fund	33	28.2	31.5	54.1	51	-7.6
Dow	33.5	26	22.6	16.1	25.2	-7.4

% Avg. Annual Total Return   *2000 returns through 10/1/00
Fund vs. Dow Jones Industrial Avg.   (5-year avg. annual return: 29.4%)

3

Janus Growth and Income Fund

Janus Investment Funds
100 Fillmore Street
Denver, CO 80206-4928
800-525-3713
www.janusfunds.com
Ticker symbol: **JAGIX**

Fund manager: David Corkins
Fund objective: Growth and income

Performance	★ ★ ★ ★
Consistency	★ ★ ★ ★ ★
Fees/Services/Management	★ ★ ★ ★ ★
Total	**14 Points**

Many mutual fund managers look for companies with strong management, a healthy earnings outlook, and a good business plan. David Corkins, manager of the Janus Growth and Income Fund, considers those elements plus one additional factor.

"I'm looking for a catalyst, an intangible, something that will spark growth that others might miss," he says. Since taking over the fund in 1997, he has demonstrated a good eye for companies sparked by catalysts. The average annual rate of return on his watch has been about 32 percent.

The Janus Growth and Income Fund invests about 75 percent of its assets in companies with strong growth potential, while the remaining 25 percent is invested in companies with income potential. Because of that investment strategy, the $9 billion fund is not designed for investors who need consistent income. There are about 110 stocks in the fund.

The fund is heaviest in technology stocks, which account for 44 percent of assets. Other leading sectors include cyclical consumer goods, 23 percent; financials, 7 percent; consumer staples, 4 percent; utilities, 3 percent; and energy, 3 percent. The portfolio is loaded with well-known companies, such as Cisco Systems, Nokia, Sun Microsystems, General Electric, and Time Warner.

The fund has had a modest 43 percent annual portfolio turnover ratio.

PERFORMANCE

The fund has enjoyed outstanding growth over the past five years. Including dividends and capital gains distributions, the Janus Growth and Income Fund has provided an average annual return the past five years (through late 2000) of 29.9 percent.

A $10,000 investment in 1995 would have grown to about $37,000 five years later.

CONSISTENCY

The fund has been very consistent, outperforming or matching the Dow Jones Industrial Average for five consecutive years through 1999 (and again through most of 2000). Its biggest gain came in 1999, when it moved up 51.2 percent (compared with a 25.2 percent rise in the Dow).

FEES/SERVICES/MANAGEMENT

The fund is a pure no-load fund, with no fees to buy or sell shares. The fund's total annual expense ratio of 0.9 percent (with no 12b-1 fee) compares favorably with other funds.

The fund offers all the standard services such as retirement account availability, automatic withdrawal, and automatic checking account deduction. Its minimum initial investment of $2,500 and minimum subsequent investment of $100 are a little higher than most other funds.

David Corkins has managed the fund since 1997. The Janus fund family includes 38 funds and allows shareholders to switch from fund to fund by telephone.

Top Ten Stock Holdings

1. Cisco Systems
2. Nokia
3. AT&T-Liberty Media
4. Sun Microsystems
5. Enron

6. Time Warner
7. Texas Instruments
8. General Electric
9. EMC
10. Comcast

Fund inception: 1991
Asset mix: Common stocks, 77%; cash/equivalents, 20%; preferred stocks, 2%; corporate bonds, 1%
Total net assets: $9.2 billion

Load

Front-end load	*None*
Redemption fee (max.)	*None*

Annual Fees

12b-1 fee	*None*
Management fee	0.66%
Other expenses	0.24
Total annual expense	0.90%
Minimum initial investment	$2,500
Minimum subsequent investment	$100

Services

Telephone exchanges	*Yes*
Automatic withdrawal	*Yes*
Automatic checking deduction	*Yes*
Retirement plan/IRA	*Yes*
Instant redemption	*Yes*
Portfolio manager (years)	3
Number of funds in family	38

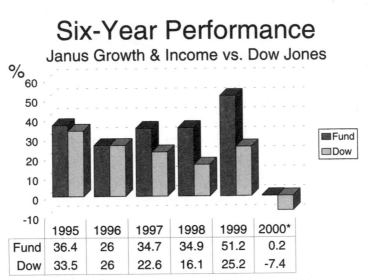

Six-Year Performance
Janus Growth & Income vs. Dow Jones

	1995	1996	1997	1998	1999	2000*
Fund	36.4	26	34.7	34.9	51.2	0.2
Dow	33.5	26	22.6	16.1	25.2	-7.4

% Avg. Annual Total Return   *2000 returns through 10/1/00
Fund vs. Dow Jones Industrial Avg.   (5-year avg. annual return: 29.1%)

Alger Retirement Fund: Capital Appreciation

Alger Funds
429 N. Pennsylvania Street
Indianapolis, IN 46204
800-992-3362
www.algerfunds.com
Ticker symbol: **ALARX**

Fund managers: David Alger, Seilai Khoo, and Ronald Tartaro
Fund objective: Aggressive growth

Performance	★ ★ ★ ★ ★
Consistency	★ ★ ★ ★
Fees/Services/Management	★ ★ ★ ★ ★
Total	**14 Points**

Everything is fair game for the Alger Capital Appreciation Retirement Portfolio. The fund managers look for companies of all sizes that offer the potential for solid growth. Its leading holdings include a number of high-tech and Internet stocks, such as Cisco Systems, Sun Microsystems, Amgen, and eBay, although Citigroup is also among the leading holdings.

Fund founder David Alger says he prefers stocks "from the fastest growing companies in America."

The $300 million fund was opened in 1993 and has posted an average annual return of about 31 percent since its inception. Not only has the no-load fund had strong returns, but it also has been very consistent, outperforming the Dow four of the past five years.

Technology stocks account for about 74 percent of assets, followed by communication services, 6 percent; health care, 5 percent; consumer staples, 3 percent; financials, 2 percent; consumer cyclicals, 2 percent; energy, 2 percent; and capital goods, 1 percent.

The fund managers take a fairly aggressive approach, with a 155 percent annual turnover ratio. The fund stays 90 to 100 percent invested in stocks under normal circumstances.

PERFORMANCE

The fund has enjoyed outstanding growth over the past five years. Including dividends and capital gains distributions, the Alger Capital Appreciation Retirement Portfolio has provided an average annual return the past five years (through late 2000) of 30.8 percent.

A $10,000 investment in 1995 would have grown to about $38,000 five years later.

CONSISTENCY

The fund has been very consistent, outperforming the Dow Jones Industrial Average four of the past five years through 1999 (and was about even with the Dow through most of 2000). Its biggest gain came in 1999, when it moved up 88.7 percent (compared with a 25.2 percent rise in the Dow).

FEES/SERVICES/MANAGEMENT

The fund is a true no-load fund, with no fees to buy or sell shares. It has an annual expense ratio of 1.28 percent (with no 12b-1 fee), which compares favorably with other funds.

The fund offers all the standard services such as retirement account availability, automatic withdrawal, and automatic checking account deduction. Its minimum initial investment of $1 and minimum subsequent investment of $25 compare very favorably with other funds.

The fund has been managed since its inception by David Alger, who runs the fund along with comanagers Seilai Khoo and Ronald Tartaro. The Alger fund family includes 21 funds and allows shareholders to switch from fund to fund by telephone.

Top Ten Stock Holdings

1. Sun Microsystems
2. Cisco Systems
3. Citigroup
4. Amgen
5. Ariba

6. Oracle
7. eBay
8. Nortel Networks
9. Pfizer
10. Hewlett-Packard

Fund inception: 1993
Asset mix: Common stocks, 95%; cash/equivalents, 4%; preferred stocks, 1%
Total net assets: $287 million

Load

Front-end load	*None*
Redemption fee (max.)	*None*

Annual Fees

12b-1 fee	*None*
Management fee	0.85%
Other expenses	0.43
Total annual expense	1.28%

Minimum initial investment	$1
Minimum subsequent investment	$25

Services

Telephone exchanges	*Yes*
Automatic withdrawal	*Yes*
Automatic checking deduction	*Yes*
Retirement plan/IRA	*Yes*
Instant redemption	*Yes*
Portfolio managers (years)	7
Number of funds in family	21

The fund managers look for several important factors in selecting stocks for the portfolio. The price-earnings ratio (PE) is a key consideration. The managers look for companies with a low PE relative to both the overall market and to the stock's historical levels. They also compare the PE with the company's growth rate. The stocks that make it into the portfolio tend to be the fast-growing companies that appear to be attractively priced. The fund managers will sell out a stock if its financials weaken, or if they uncover another stock they like better.

PERFORMANCE

The fund has enjoyed very outstanding growth over the past five years. Including dividends and capital gains distributions, the Pin Oak Aggressive Stock Fund has provided an average annual return the past five years (through late 2000) of 36.8 percent.

A $10,000 investment in 1995 would have grown to about $48,000 five years later.

CONSISTENCY

The fund has been fairly consistent, outperforming the Dow Jones Industrial Average three of the past five years through 1999 (and again through most of 2000). Its biggest gain came in 1999, when it moved up 99 percent (compared with a 25.2 percent rise in the Dow).

FEES/SERVICES/MANAGEMENT

The fund is a pure no-load fund, with no fees to buy or sell shares. The fund's total annual expense ratio of 1.00 percent (with no 12b-1 fee) is in line with other funds.

The fund offers all the standard services such as retirement account availability, automatic withdrawal, and automatic checking account deduction. Its minimum initial investment of $1,000 and minimum subsequent investment of $100 are in line with other funds.

James D. Oelschlager, who has been with the fund since its inception in 1992, manages the fund along with Donna Barton and Douglas MacKay. The Oak fund family includes only four funds.

Top Ten Stock Holdings

1. Brocade Communications
2. CacheFlow
3. Cisco Systems
4. JDS Uniphase
5. Network Appliance

6. Foundry Networks
7. Linear Technology
8. Applied Materials
9. Maxim Integrated Products
10. Vitesse Semiconductor

Fund inception: 1992
Asset mix: Common stocks, 93%; cash/equivalents, 7%
Total net assets: $771 million

Load

Front-end load	*None*
Redemption fee (max.)	*None*

Annual Fees

12b-1 fee	*None*
Management fee	0.74%
Other expenses	0.26
Total annual expense	1.00%

Minimum initial investment	$1,000
Minimum subsequent investment	$100

Services

Telephone exchanges	*Yes*
Automatic withdrawal	*Yes*
Automatic checking deduction	*Yes*
Retirement plan/IRA	*Yes*
Instant redemption	*Yes*
Portfolio manager (years)	8
Number of funds in family	4

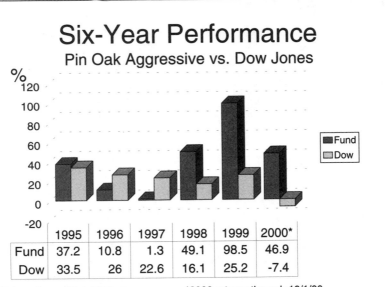

Six-Year Performance
Pin Oak Aggressive vs. Dow Jones

	1995	1996	1997	1998	1999	2000*
Fund	37.2	10.8	1.3	49.1	98.5	46.9
Dow	33.5	26	22.6	16.1	25.2	-7.4

% Avg. Annual Total Return   *2000 returns through 10/1/00
Fund vs. Dow Jones Industrial Avg.   (5-year avg. annual return: 36.7%)

Managers Capital Appreciation Fund

Managers Funds
40 Richards Avenue
Norwalk, CT 06854-2325
800-835-3879
www.managersfunds.com
Ticker symbol: **MGCAX**

Fund managers: Joseph McNay and Kevin Riley
Fund objective: Long-term growth

Performance	★ ★ ★ ★ ★
Consistency	★ ★ ★
Fees/Services/Management	★ ★ ★ ★ ★
Total	**13 Points**

The Managers Capital Appreciation Fund is run by two managers who bring their own investment philosophies to the stock selection process for this blue chip portfolio.

Kevin Riley of Roxbury Capital Management looks for growing companies that are leaders in their sector and that appear to have sustainable growth potential in earnings and cash flow. He diversifies across industry groups and invests in companies that are in different phases of their business cycle.

Joseph McNay looks for companies with accelerating earnings growth that have a dominant product or service. Although he is not a value investor, McNay looks for stocks that are "underowned" or attractively priced relative to his growth projections.

The mix of investment styles has been good for the growth of the fund, which was opened in 1984. A $10,000 investment in the fund ten years ago would now be worth about $85,000—a 24 percent average annual return.

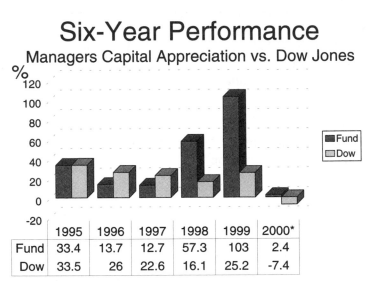

Six-Year Performance
Managers Capital Appreciation vs. Dow Jones

	1995	1996	1997	1998	1999	2000*
Fund	33.4	13.7	12.7	57.3	103	2.4
Dow	33.5	26	22.6	16.1	25.2	-7.4

% Avg. Annual Total Return   *2000 returns through 10/1/00
Fund vs. Dow Jones Industrial Avg.   (5-year avg. annual return: 33.9%)

7

Harbor Capital Appreciation Fund

Harbor Funds
One Seagate
Toledo, OH 43666
800-422-1050
www.harborfund.com
Ticker symbol: **HACAX**

Fund manager: Spiros Segalas
Fund objective: Long-term growth

Performance	★ ★ ★ ★
Consistency	★ ★ ★ ★
Fees/Services/Management	★ ★ ★ ★ ★
Total	**13 Points**

Fund manager Spiros Segalas takes a bottom-up approach in selecting blue chip stocks for the Harbor Capital Appreciation Fund. He is looking for solid growth stocks that meet his rigid set of criteria. He wants companies with superior earnings and revenue growth, with improving sales momentum and high levels of unit growth. And he wants high or improving profitability and a strong balance sheet.

Launched in 1988, this large-cap stock fund has provided an average annual return the past ten years of about 23 percent. A $10,000 investment in the fund ten years ago would now be worth about $80,000.

The $10 billion fund invests across several industries, although technology is the dominant sector at about 53 percent of the portfolio. Consumer staples accounts for 27.5 percent of the portfolio; financials, 11 percent; capital goods, 3 percent; and utilities, 2 percent.

The fund is loaded with familiar names, such as Microsoft, Cisco Systems, Intel, Home Depot, and Hewlett-Packard.

Fund manager Segalas is fairly active in his trading approach, with a 68 percent annual portfolio turnover ratio. The fund stays 90 to 100 percent invested in stocks under normal circumstances.

PERFORMANCE

The fund has enjoyed strong growth over the past five years. Including dividends and capital gains distributions, the Harbor Capital Appreciation Fund has provided an average annual return the past five years (through late 2000) of 28.5 percent.

A $10,000 investment in 1995 would have grown to about $35,000 five years later.

CONSISTENCY

The fund has been very consistent, outperforming the Dow Jones Industrial Average four of the past five years through 1999 (and again through most of 2000). Its biggest gain came in 1999, when it moved up 45.8 percent (compared with a 25.2 percent rise in the Dow).

FEES/SERVICES/MANAGEMENT

The fund is a pure no-load fund, with no fees to buy or sell shares. The fund's total annual expense ratio of 0.66 percent (with no 12b-1 fee) is lower than most other funds.

The fund offers all the standard services such as retirement account availability, automatic withdrawal, and automatic checking account deduction. Its minimum initial investment of $2,000 and minimum subsequent investment of $500 are in line with other funds.

The fund has been managed by Spiros Segalas since 1990. The Harbor fund family includes nine funds and allows shareholders to switch from fund to fund by telephone.

Top Ten Stock Holdings

1. Microsoft
2. Cisco Systems
3. Vodafone AirTouch
4. Intel
5. Nokia

6. Home Depot
7. Citigroup
8. Hewlett-Packard
9. Qwest Communications
10. Texas Instruments

Fund inception: 1988
Asset mix: Common stocks, 97%; cash/equivalents, 3%
Total net assets: $9.5 billion

Load

Front-end load	*None*
Redemption fee (max.)	*None*

Annual Fees

12b-1 fee	*None*
Management fee	0.60%
Other expenses	0.06
Total annual expense	0.66%

Minimum initial investment	$2,000
Minimum subsequent investment	$500

Services

Telephone exchanges	*Yes*
Automatic withdrawal	*Yes*
Automatic checking deduction	*Yes*
Retirement plan/IRA	*Yes*
Instant redemption	*Yes*
Portfolio manager (years)	10
Number of funds in family	9

The fund stays at least 90 percent invested in stocks under normal circumstances. Fund manager Black is fairly aggressive in her investment approach, with a 144 percent annual portfolio turnover ratio.

PERFORMANCE

The fund has enjoyed outstanding growth over the past five years. Including dividends and capital gains distributions, the Warburg Pincus Capital Appreciation Fund has provided an average annual return the past five years (through late 2000) of 28.7 percent.

A $10,000 investment in 1995 would have grown to about $35,000 five years later.

CONSISTENCY

The fund has been very consistent, outperforming the Dow Jones Industrial Average four of the past five years through 1999 (and again through most of 2000). Its biggest gain came in 1999, when it moved up 48.4 percent (compared with a 25.2 percent rise in the Dow).

FEES/SERVICES/MANAGEMENT

The fund is a pure no-load fund, with no fees to buy or sell shares. The fund's total annual expense ratio of 1.01 percent (with no 12b-1 fee) is in line with other funds.

The fund offers all the standard services such as retirement account availability, automatic withdrawal, and automatic checking account deduction. Its minimum initial investment of $1,000 and minimum subsequent investment of $100 are in line with other funds.

The fund has been managed by Susan Black since 1994. The Warburg Pincus fund family includes more than 35 funds and allows shareholders to switch from fund to fund by telephone.

Top Ten Stock Holdings

1. Citigroup
2. Intel
3. Nortel Networks
4. Pfizer
5. Cisco Systems

6. General Electric
7. Pharmacia
8. Lehman Brothers Holdings
9. Viacom
10. Sun Microsystems

Fund inception: 1987
Asset mix: Common stocks, 92%; cash/equivalents, 8%
Total net assets: $1.5 billion

Load

Front-end load	*None*
Redemption fee (max.)	*None*

Annual Fees

12b-1 fee	*None*
Management fee	0.70%
Other expenses	0.31
Total annual expense	1.01%
Minimum initial investment	$1,000
Minimum subsequent investment	$100

Services

Telephone exchanges	*Yes*
Automatic withdrawal	*Yes*
Automatic checking deduction	*Yes*
Retirement plan/IRA	*Yes*
Instant redemption	*Yes*
Portfolio manager (years)	6
Number of funds in family	over 35

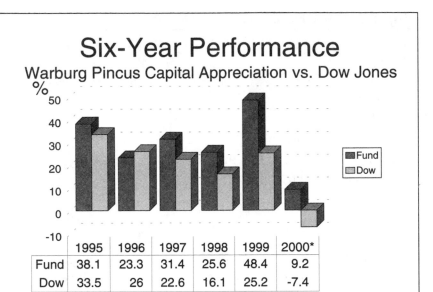

Six-Year Performance
Warburg Pincus Capital Appreciation vs. Dow Jones

	1995	1996	1997	1998	1999	2000*
Fund	38.1	23.3	31.4	25.6	48.4	9.2
Dow	33.5	26	22.6	16.1	25.2	-7.4

% Avg. Annual Total Return   *2000 returns through 10/1/00
Fund vs. Dow Jones Industrial Avg.   (5-year avg. annual return: 28.6%)

9

PBHG Large Cap Growth Fund

PBHG Funds
P.O. Box 419534
Kansas City, MO 64141-6534
800-433-0051
www.pbhgfunds.com
Ticker symbol: **PBHLX**

Fund manager: Michael Sutton
Fund objective: Long-term growth

Performance	★ ★ ★ ★ ★
Consistency	★ ★ ★ ★
Fees/Services/Management	★ ★ ★ ★
Total	**13 Points**

The PBHG Large Cap Growth Fund invests in some of the leading blue chip stocks across a broad range of industries. Citigroup, Wal-Mart, Tyco International, Nortel Networks, Pfizer, General Electric, Microsoft, Juniper Networks, and JDS Uniphase are among the fund's largest holdings.

The fund is geared to investors who want a stake in a diversified selection of America's fastest-growing large-cap stocks.

Fund advisor Michael Sutton looks for companies with strong business momentum, solid earnings growth, and the potential for sustained capital appreciation. The fund invests in companies in excess of $1 billion in market capitalization.

The fund was founded in 1995 and has posted an average annual return of 36.7 percent since its inception.

The fund invests across a variety of industries, including technology, 43 percent of assets; consumer cyclicals, 12 percent; industrial, 11 percent; health care, 10 percent; and financial, 9 percent.

The $300 million fund stays 85 to 95 percent invested in stocks under normal circumstances. The fund manager is aggressive in his management approach, with a 184 percent annual portfolio turnover ratio.

PERFORMANCE

The fund has enjoyed very outstanding growth over the past five years. Including dividends and capital gains distributions, the PBHG Large Cap Growth Fund has provided an exceptional average annual return the past five years (through late 2000) of 36 percent.

A $10,000 investment in 1995 would have grown to about $46,500 five years later.

CONSISTENCY

The fund has been very consistent, outperforming or matching the Dow Jones Industrial Average four of the past five years through 1999 (and again through most of 2000). Its biggest gain came in 1999, when it jumped up 67.1 percent (compared with a 25.2 percent rise in the Dow).

FEES/SERVICES/MANAGEMENT

The fund is a pure no-load fund, with no fees to buy or sell shares. The fund's total annual expense ratio of 1.17 percent (with no 12b-1 fee) is in line with other funds.

The fund offers all the standard services such as retirement account availability, automatic withdrawal, and automatic checking account deduction. Its minimum initial investment of $2,500 and minimum subsequent investment of $1 are a little higher than most other funds.

The fund has been managed by Michael Sutton only since 1999. The PBHG fund family includes 17 funds and allows shareholders to switch from fund to fund by telephone.

Top Ten Stock Holdings

1. Cisco Systems
2. General Electric
3. Clear Channel Communications
4. Wal-Mart Stores
5. Nokia
6. Nortel Networks
7. Lucent Technologies
8. Gemstar International Group
9. Texas Instruments
10. QUALCOMM

Fund inception: 1995
Asset mix: Common stocks, 89%; cash/equivalents, 11%
Total net assets: $300 million

Load

Front-end load	*None*
Redemption fee (max.)	*None*

Annual Fees

12b-1 fee	*None*
Management fee	0.75%
Other expenses	0.42
Total annual expense	1.17%

Minimum initial investment	$2,500
Minimum subsequent investment	$1

Services

Telephone exchanges	*Yes*
Automatic withdrawal	*Yes*
Automatic checking deduction	*Yes*
Retirement plan/IRA	*Yes*
Instant redemption	*Yes*
Portfolio manager (years)	1
Number of funds in family	17

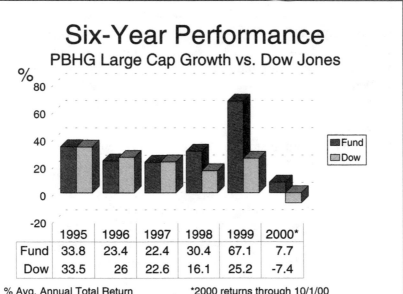

Six-Year Performance
PBHG Large Cap Growth vs. Dow Jones

	1995	1996	1997	1998	1999	2000*
Fund	33.8	23.4	22.4	30.4	67.1	7.7
Dow	33.5	26	22.6	16.1	25.2	-7.4

% Avg. Annual Total Return   *2000 returns through 10/1/00
Fund vs. Dow Jones Industrial Avg.   (5-year avg. annual return: 34%)

10

T. Rowe Price Science & Technology Fund

T. Rowe Price Funds
100 East Pratt Street
Baltimore, MD 21202
800-638-5660
www.troweprice.com
Ticker symbol: **PRSCX**

Fund manager: Charles Morris
Fund objective: Sector

Performance	★ ★ ★ ★ ★
Consistency	★ ★ ★
Fees/Services/Management	★ ★ ★ ★ ★
Total	**13 Points**

This was the number-one ranked fund in the very first edition of *The 100 Best Mutual Funds to Own in America,* published in 1995. A $10,000 investment in the fund at that time would have grown to nearly $40,000 five years later—a 31 percent average annual return.

Founded in 1987, the T. Rowe Price Science and Technology Fund invests in a diversified selection of technology-related stocks. Leading sectors include communications, 33 percent; semiconductors, 26 percent; software, 20 percent; hardware, 13 percent; and information services, 6 percent. The fund stays almost fully invested in stocks under normal circumstances.

"Because the fund's scale and diversification make it unlikely to be the top performer in any particular quarter," says fund manager Chip Morris, "we manage the fund with the objective of generating consistent absolute and superior relative performance over a longer-term horizon."

Among the fund's leading holdings are such well-known high-tech leaders as Cisco Systems, Analog Devices, Oracle, Maxim Integrated Products, Xilinx, and Dell Computer.

In structuring the $14 billion portfolio, Morris follows seven key principles: stay exposed to long-term, secular investment themes; diversify among the most attractive sectors; invest in companies with significant intellectual property; concentrate on companies with sustainable business models; emphasize companies embarking on meaningful new product cycles; focus on strong management; and "keep the portfolio fresh."

Morris takes a fairly aggressive management approach, with a 128 percent annual portfolio turnover ratio.

PERFORMANCE

The fund has enjoyed outstanding growth over the past five years. Including dividends and capital gains distributions, the T. Rowe Price Science and Technology Fund has provided an average annual return the past five years (through late 2000) of 31 percent.

A $10,000 investment in 1995 would have grown to about $38,500 five years later.

CONSISTENCY

The fund has been fairly consistent, outperforming the Dow Jones Industrial Average three of the past five years through 1999 (and was about even with the Dow through most of 2000). Its biggest gain came in 1999, when it moved up 101 percent (compared with a 25.2 percent rise in the Dow).

FEES/SERVICES/MANAGEMENT

The fund is a pure no-load fund, with no fees to buy or sell shares. The fund's total annual expense ratio of 0.87 percent (with no 12b-1 fee) compares very favorably with other funds.

The fund offers all the standard services such as retirement account availability, automatic withdrawal, and automatic checking account deduction. Its minimum initial investment of $2,500 and minimum subsequent investment of $100 are a little higher than most other funds.

The fund has been managed by Chip Morris since 1991. The T. Rowe Price fund family includes more than 80 funds and allows shareholders to switch from fund to fund by telephone.

Top Ten Stock Holdings

1. Cisco Systems	6. Xilinx
2. Oracle	7. Microsoft
3. Analog Devices	8. Texas Instruments
4. Vodafone AirTouch ADR	9. Dell Computer
5. Maxim Integrated Products	10. Nokia

Fund inception: 1987
Asset mix: Common stocks, 97%; cash/equivalents, 2%; preferred stocks, 1%
Total net assets: $14 billion

Load

Front-end load	*None*
Redemption fee (max.)	*None*

Annual Fees

12b-1 fee	*None*
Management fee	0.67%
Other expenses	0.20
Total annual expense	0.87%

Minimum initial investment	$2,500
Minimum subsequent investment	$100

Services

Telephone exchanges	*Yes*
Automatic withdrawal	*Yes*
Automatic checking deduction	*Yes*
Retirement plan/IRA	*Yes*
Instant redemption	*Yes*
Portfolio manager (years)	9
Number of funds in family	82

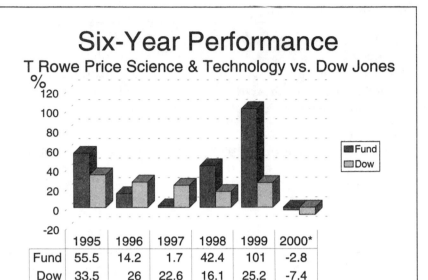

Six-Year Performance
T Rowe Price Science & Technology vs. Dow Jones

	1995	1996	1997	1998	1999	2000*
Fund	55.5	14.2	1.7	42.4	101	-2.8
Dow	33.5	26	22.6	16.1	25.2	-7.4

% Avg. Annual Total Return   *2000 returns through 10/1/00
Fund vs. Dow Jones Industrial Avg.   (5-year avg. annual return: 26.9%)

INVESCO Telecommunications Fund

INVESCO Funds
7800 East Union Avenue
Denver, CO 80237
800-525-8085
www.invescofunds.com
Ticker symbol: **ISWCX**

Fund manager: Brian Hayward
Fund objective: Sector

Performance	★ ★ ★ ★ ★
Consistency	★ ★ ★
Fees/Services/Management	★ ★ ★ ★ ★
Total	**13 Points**

The recent boom in the telecommunications industry—fueled by rapid growth in the demand for cell phones, fax machines, and the Internet—has helped make the INVESCO Telecommunications Fund one of the fastest-growing mutual funds in America. The fund has been growing at about 43 percent per year for the past five years.

The fund has been investing in some of the telecommunications industry's leading performers. JDS Uniphase, a maker of fiber optics, has been one of several fast-growing telecommunications manufacturers to contribute to the fund's recent success.

Brian Hayward, who has managed the $3 billion fund since 1997, has also invested in some of the international telecoms, such as Nokia, the Finnish maker of wireless handsets that seem to be ringing everywhere. Other leading holdings in the fund include EchoStar, Cisco Systems, Gemstar International Group, and Nortel Networks. There are about 100 stocks in the portfolio.

Hayward notes that the high-growth, highly valued firms in which the fund invests bear little resemblance to the dot-coms with little or no revenue growth. Communications company stocks are not a bet on the future but an investment in a large and lucrative industry already enjoying an impressive financial performance.

Founded in 1994, the fund's portfolio turnover is a modest 62 percent. The fund stays at least 90 percent invested in stocks under normal circumstances.

PERFORMANCE

The fund has enjoyed outstanding growth over the past five years. Including dividends and capital gains distributions, the INVESCO Telecommunications Fund has provided an average annual return the past five years (through late 2000) of 43.3 percent.

A $10,000 investment in 1995 would have grown to about $60,000 five years later.

CONSISTENCY

The fund has been fairly consistent, outperforming the Dow Jones Industrial Average three of the past five years through 1999 (and again through most of 2000). Its biggest gain came in 1999, when it moved up 144.3 percent (compared with a 25.2 percent rise in the Dow).

FEES/SERVICES/MANAGEMENT

The fund is a pure no-load fund, with no fees to buy or sell shares. The fund's total annual expense ratio of 1.24 percent (with a 0.25 percent 12b-1 fee) is in line with other funds.

The fund offers all the standard services such as retirement account availability, automatic withdrawal, and automatic checking account deduction. Its minimum initial investment of $1,000 and minimum subsequent investment of $50 are in line with other funds.

The fund has been managed by Brian Hayward since 1997. The INVESCO fund family includes 32 funds and allows shareholders to switch from fund to fund by telephone.

Top Ten Stock Holdings

1. EchoStar Communications
2. SDL, Inc.
3. Applied Micro Circuits
4. PMC-Sierra
5. JDS Uniphase

6. Cisco Systems
7. Nokia
8. Gemstar International Group
9. Comverse Technology
10. Nortel Networks

Fund inception: 1994
Asset mix: Common stocks, 93%; cash/equivalents, 7%
Total net assets: $3.6 billion

Load

Front-end load	*None*
Redemption fee (max.)	*None*

Annual Fees

12b-1 fee	0.25%
Management fee	0.62
Other expenses	0.37
Total annual expense	1.24%
Minimum initial investment	$1,000
Minimum subsequent investment	$50

Services

Telephone exchanges	*Yes*
Automatic withdrawal	*Yes*
Automatic checking deduction	*Yes*
Retirement plan/IRA	*Yes*
Instant redemption	*Yes*
Portfolio manager (years)	3
Number of funds in family	32

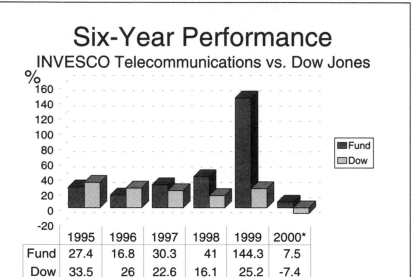

Six-Year Performance
INVESCO Telecommunications vs. Dow Jones

	1995	1996	1997	1998	1999	2000*
Fund	27.4	16.8	30.3	41	144.3	7.5
Dow	33.5	26	22.6	16.1	25.2	-7.4

% Avg. Annual Total Return
Fund vs. Dow Jones Industrial Avg.

*2000 returns through 10/1/00
(5-year avg. annual return: 42.5%)

INVESCO Dynamics Fund

INVESCO Funds
Mutual Fund Services
P.O. Box 701
Milwaukee, WI 53201-0701
800-525-8085
www.invescofunds.com
Ticker symbol: **FIDYX**

Fund managers: Timothy Miller and Thomas Wald
Fund objective: Aggressive growth

Performance	★ ★ ★ ★
Consistency	★ ★ ★ ★
Fees/Services/Management	★ ★ ★ ★ ★
Total	**13 Points**

The dynamic changes in the economy brought on by the Internet have been more pronounced in business than they have for individual computer users.

Medium-sized companies that are helping to build the Internet backbone are among the key focus areas for the INVESCO Dynamics Fund. A top holding in the $8 billion, 170-issue fund is Network Appliance, a leading supplier of file servers and Internet cache systems used by companies for quick access to large amounts of data.

Another favorite is Siebel Systems, maker of customer relationship software to help companies manage orders and inventory. Other top holdings include EchoStar, VeriSign, VERITAS Software, and JDS Uniphase. Technology companies represent about 43 percent of the total portfolio.

Founded in 1967 and managed since 1993 by Timothy Miller and Thomas Wald, the fund's portfolio turnover rate is a modest 23 percent.

In addition to its Internet and computer focus, the fund has also been moving some of its investments into the biotechnology sector where Miller and Wald look for companies with promising new-product pipelines.

The fund's average annualized total return over ten years has been about 24.4 percent. A $10,000 investment in the fund ten years ago would now be worth about $87,000. The fund stays at least 90 percent invested in stocks under normal circumstances.

PERFORMANCE

The fund has enjoyed outstanding growth over the past five years. Including dividends and capital gains distributions, the INVESCO Dynamics Fund has provided an average annual return the past five years (through late 2000) of 29 percent.

A $10,000 investment in 1995 would have grown to about $36,000 five years later.

CONSISTENCY

The fund has been fairly consistent, outperforming the Dow Jones Industrial Average four of the past five years through 1999 (and again through most of 2000). Its biggest gain came in 1999, when it moved up 71.8 percent (compared with a 25.2 percent rise in the Dow).

FEES/SERVICES/MANAGEMENT

The fund is a pure no-load fund, with no fees to buy or sell shares. The fund's total annual expense ratio of 1.03 percent (with a 0.25 percent 12b-1 fee) compares favorably with other funds.

The fund offers all the standard services such as retirement account availability, automatic withdrawal, and automatic checking account deduction. Its minimum initial investment of $1,000 and minimum subsequent investment of $50 are in line with other funds.

The fund has been managed by Timothy Miller and Thomas Wald since 1993. The INVESCO fund family includes 32 funds and allows shareholders to switch from fund to fund by telephone.

Top Ten Stock Holdings

1. EchoStar Communications	6. Harrah's Entertainment
2. VeriSign	7. BroadVision
3. VERITAS Software	8. Gemstar International Group
4. JDS Uniphase	9. Siebel Systems
5. Exodus Communications	10. Network Appliance

Fund inception: 1967
Asset mix: Common stocks, 93%; cash/equivalents, 7%
Total net assets: $8 billion

Load

Front-end load	*None*
Redemption fee (max.)	*None*

Annual Fees

12b-1 fee	0.25%
Management fee	0.52
Other expenses	0.26
Total annual expense	1.03%

Minimum initial investment	$1,000
Minimum subsequent investment	$50

Services

Telephone exchanges	*Yes*
Automatic withdrawal	*Yes*
Automatic checking deduction	*Yes*
Retirement plan/IRA	*Yes*
Instant redemption	*Yes*
Portfolio manager (years)	7
Number of funds in family	32

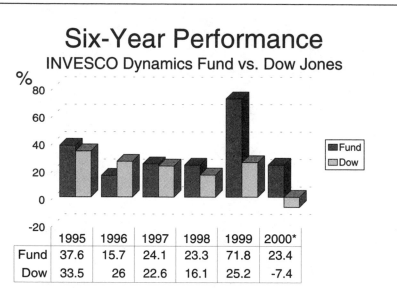

Six-Year Performance
INVESCO Dynamics Fund vs. Dow Jones

	1995	1996	1997	1998	1999	2000*
Fund	37.6	15.7	24.1	23.3	71.8	23.4
Dow	33.5	26	22.6	16.1	25.2	-7.4

% Avg. Annual Total Return   *2000 returns through 10/1/00
Fund vs. Dow Jones Industrial Avg.   (5-year avg. annual return: 31.9%)

Bridgeway Aggressive Growth Portfolio

Bridgeway Funds
5650 Kirby Drive, Suite 141
Houston, TX 77005-2443
800-661-3550
www.bridgewayfund.com
Ticker symbol: **BRAGX**

Fund manager: John Montgomery
Fund objective: Aggressive growth

Performance	★ ★ ★ ★ ★
Consistency	★ ★ ★
Fees/Services/Management	★ ★ ★ ★
Total	**12 Points**

The Bridgeway Aggressive Growth Portfolio is a tiny fund with just $45 million in assets, but that number could grow quickly if the fund continues to perform as it has the past five years. During that period, the fund has posted an average annual return of nearly 40 percent.

The fund invests in a number of little-known companies, such as Esterline Technologies, JLG Industries, Gleason, and Atlantic Coast Airlines. In fact, most of its holdings have a market capitalization of under $1 billion, although there are a few bigger names among the top holdings, including Sun Microsystems and CompUSA.

The fund is weighted heavily in technology stocks, which account for about 41 percent of total assets. Other leading sectors include consumer cyclicals, 13 percent; capital goods, 12 percent; consumer staples, 9 percent; transportation, 8 percent; financials, 5 percent; basic materials, 5 percent; health care, 4 percent; and energy, 3 percent.

Fund manager John Montgomery takes a very aggressive trading approach, with a 211 percent annual portfolio turnover ratio.

PERFORMANCE

The fund has enjoyed exceptional growth over the past five years. Including dividends and capital gains distributions, the Bridgeway Aggressive Growth Portfolio has provided an average annual return the past five years (through late 2000) of about 40 percent.

A $10,000 investment in 1995 would have grown to about $54,000 five years later.

CONSISTENCY

The fund has been fairly consistent, outperforming the Dow Jones Industrial Average three of the past five years through 1999 (and again through most of 2000). Its biggest gain came in 1999, when it moved up 120.6 percent (compared with a 25.2 percent rise in the Dow).

FEES/SERVICES/MANAGEMENT

The fund is a pure no-load fund, with no fee to buy or sell shares. The fund's total annual expense ratio of 1.04 percent (with a 0.25 percent 12b-1 fee) compares favorably with other funds.

Investors cannot buy the fund directly from the company but must go through a broker. The fund offers all the standard services such as retirement account availability, automatic withdrawal, and automatic checking account deduction. Its minimum initial investment of $2,000 and minimum subsequent investment of $500 are in line with many other funds.

The fund has been managed by John Montgomery since its inception in 1994. The Bridgestone fund family includes only six funds and allows shareholders to switch from fund to fund by telephone.

Top Ten Stock Holdings

1. Esterline Technologies	6. Sun Microsystems
2. CompUSA	7. Raychem
3. JLG Industries	8. Bio-Rad Lab
4. Gleason Corp.	9. Roanoke Electric Steel
5. Atlantic Coast Airlines	10. C-Cube Microsystems

Fund inception: 1994
Asset mix: Common stocks, 93%; cash/equivalents, 5%; other, 2%
Total net assets: $45 million

Load

Front-end load	*None*
Redemption fee (max.)	*None*

Annual Fees

12b-1 fee	0.25%
Management fee	0.47
Other expenses	0.32
Total annual expense	1.04%
Minimum initial investment	$2,000
Minimum subsequent investment	$500

Services

Telephone exchanges	*Yes*
Automatic withdrawal	*Yes*
Automatic checking deduction	*Yes*
Retirement plan/IRA	*Yes*
Instant redemption	*Yes*
Portfolio manager (years)	6
Number of funds in family	6

Six-Year Performance
Bridgeway Aggressive Growth vs. Dow Jones

	1995	1996	1997	1998	1999	2000*
Fund	27.1	32.2	18.3	19.3	120.6	34.8
Dow	33.5	26	22.6	16.1	25.2	-7.4

% Avg. Annual Total Return
Fund vs. Dow Jones Industrial Avg.

*2000 returns through 10/1/00
(5-year avg. annual return: 42.7%)

15

Phoenix-Engemann Small & MidCap Growth Fund

Phoenix-Engemann Funds
625 Second Street
Petaluma, CA 94952
800-814-1897
www.phoenixfunds.com
Ticker symbol: **PAMAX**

Fund managers: Lou Abel and Yossi Lipsker
Fund objective: Small-cap stocks

Performance	★ ★ ★ ★ ★
Consistency	★ ★ ★ ★
Fees/Services/Management	★ ★ ★
Total	**12 Points**

The Phoenix-Engemann Small & MidCap Growth Fund avoids the land of the giants. Fund managers Lou Abel and Yossi Lipsker prefer to pluck their issues from the ranks of companies with market caps of about $1.5 billion or less.

Founded in 1994, the fund is designed for investors with a time horizon of five years or more who seek the performance advantages of small stocks, which have historically had an advantage over larger stocks. Small and midcap stocks with a record of substantial growth, financial strength, and a favorable long-term outlook are the kinds of companies selected for the 100-issue, $200 million portfolio.

About half the portfolio is derived from the nation's most buoyant sector—technology. Other leading sectors in the portfolio are consumer cyclicals, 15.7 percent; health care, 9.7 percent; and financial services, 7.2 percent.

You won't find any household names among its leading holdings, although many of them could become blue chips in the years ahead.

Among its largest holdings are companies such as Applied Micro Circuits, Metris, Advanced Energy, and Ortel.

The fund managers are fairly active in their management approach, with a 105 percent annual portfolio turnover ratio. The fund stays about 90 percent invested in stocks under most circumstances.

PERFORMANCE

The fund has enjoyed outstanding growth over the past five years. Including dividends and capital gains distributions, the Phoenix-Engemann Small & MidCap Growth Fund has provided a load-adjusted average annual return the past five years (through late 2000) of 34.1 percent.

A $10,000 investment in 1995 would have grown to about $43,000 five years later.

CONSISTENCY

The fund has been very consistent, outperforming or nearly matching the Dow Jones Industrial Average four of the past five years through 1999 (and again through most of 2000). Its biggest gain came in 1999, when it moved up 84.6 percent (compared with a 25.2 percent rise in the Dow).

FEES/SERVICES/MANAGEMENT

The fund has a front-end load of 5.75 percent. The fund's total annual expense ratio of 1.73 percent (with a 0.25 percent 12b-1 fee) is in line with other funds.

The fund offers all the standard services such as retirement account availability, automatic withdrawal, and automatic checking account deduction. Its minimum initial investment of $500 and minimum subsequent investment of $25 compare favorably with other funds.

The fund has been managed by Lou Abel and Yossi Lipsker since its inception in 1994. The Phoenix-Engemann fund family includes 45 funds and allows shareholders to switch from fund to fund by telephone.

Top Ten Stock Holdings

1. Applied Micro Circuits
2. Ortel
3. Peregrine Systems
4. BEA Systems
5. Metris Companies

6. Kansas City South Industries
7. Micrel
8. Cost Plus
9. Pinnacle Oil International
10. London Pacific Group

Fund inception: 1994
Asset mix: Common stocks, 89%; cash/equivalents, 11%
Total net assets: $202 million

Load

Front-end load	5.75%
Redemption fee (max.)	*None*

Annual Fees

12b-1 fee	0.25%
Management fee	0.94
Other expenses	0.54
Total annual expense	1.73%

Minimum initial investment	$500
Minimum subsequent investment	$25

Services

Telephone exchanges	*Yes*
Automatic withdrawal	*Yes*
Automatic checking deduction	*Yes*
Retirement plan/IRA	*Yes*
Instant redemption	*Yes*
Portfolio manager (years)	6
Number of funds in family	45

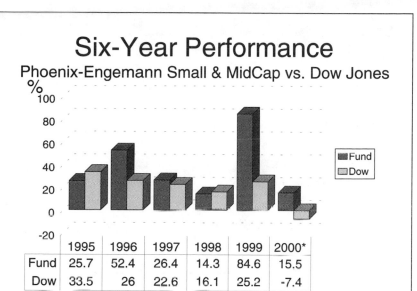

Six-Year Performance
Phoenix-Engemann Small & MidCap vs. Dow Jones

	1995	1996	1997	1998	1999	2000*
Fund	25.7	52.4	26.4	14.3	84.6	15.5
Dow	33.5	26	22.6	16.1	25.2	-7.4

% Avg. Annual Total Return
Fund vs. Dow Jones Industrial Avg.

*2000 returns through 10/1/00
(5-year avg. annual return: 36.3%)

16

Legg Mason Value Fund/Primary

Legg Mason Funds
100 Light Street
P.O. Box 1476
Baltimore, MD 21203-1476
800-368-2558
www.leggmasonfunds.com
Ticker symbol: **LMVTX**

Fund manager: William Miller
Fund objective: Long-term growth

Performance	★ ★ ★ ★
Consistency	★ ★ ★ ★ ★
Fees/Services/Management	★ ★ ★
Total	**12 Points**

Fund manager William Miller of the Legg Mason Value Fund/Primary likes to buy shares of first-rate large-cap companies before the market recognizes them as blue chip companies.

Miller, who has managed the $12 billion fund since 1990, holds on to his discoveries for the long haul. Portfolio turnover in the 40-stock portfolio is less than 20 percent per year.

A $10,000 investment in the fund ten years ago would now be worth about $67,000—a 21 percent average annual return.

Miller is particularly fond of stocks from the financial and technology sectors, which represent 29 and 27 percent of the portfolio, respectively. Top holdings from the financial sector include Citigroup and Chase Manhattan. Top holdings from the technology sector include America Online—one of Miller's early favorites—Gateway, Dell, and IBM.

Other top sectors of the fund are communications services at 13 percent; consumer cyclicals, 10.5 percent; health care, 6 percent; consumer staples, 6 percent; and capital goods, 3 percent.

Finding diamonds in the technology rough will be much tougher in the next few years now that everyone has figured out the game, says Miller, who will continue to look for stocks of companies that appear undervalued in relation to their long-term earning power. The fund stays almost 100 percent invested in stocks under normal circumstances.

PERFORMANCE

The fund has enjoyed excellent growth over the past five years. Including dividends and capital gains distributions, the Legg Mason Value Fund/ Primary has provided an average annual return the past five years (through late 2000) of 30.5 percent.

A $10,000 investment in 1995 would have grown to about $37,500 five years later.

CONSISTENCY

The fund has been very consistent, outperforming the Dow Jones Industrial Average for five consecutive years through 1999 (and again through most of 2000). Its biggest gain came in 1998, when it moved up 48 percent (compared with a 16.1 percent rise in the Dow).

FEES/SERVICES/MANAGEMENT

The fund is a pure no-load fund, with no fees to buy or sell shares. The fund's total annual expense ratio of 1.69 percent (with a 0.70 percent 12b-1 fee) is in line with other funds.

The fund offers all the standard services such as retirement account availability, automatic withdrawal, and automatic checking account deduction.

The company's ability to provide assistance for investors requesting information leaves much to be desired. Of the dozens of fund families we called, this was by far the worst. We were cut off, transferred, and put on hold many times before finally reaching a representative who was able to answer some very routine questions about the fund.

The fund's minimum initial investment of $1,000 and minimum subsequent investment of $100 are in line with other funds.

The fund has been managed by William Miller since 1990. The Legg Mason fund family includes 24 funds and allows shareholders to switch from fund to fund by telephone.

Top Ten Stock Holdings

1. America Online	6. MCI WorldCom
2. Dell Computer	7. Citigroup
3. Gateway	8. Nokia
4. NEXTEL Communications	9. United Health Group
5. WPP Group	10. Chase Manhattan

Fund inception: 1982
Asset mix: Common stocks, 97%; cash/equivalents, 3%
Total net assets: $12 billion

Load

Front-end load	*None*
Redemption fee (max.)	*None*

Annual Fees

12b-1 fee	0.70%
Management fee	0.66
Other expenses	0.33
Total annual expense	1.69%

Minimum initial investment	$1,000
Minimum subsequent investment	$100

Services

Telephone exchanges	*Yes*
Automatic withdrawal	*Yes*
Automatic checking deduction	*Yes*
Retirement plan/IRA	*Yes*
Instant redemption	*Yes*
Portfolio manager (years)	10
Number of funds in family	24

Six-Year Performance

Legg Mason Equity Trust Value vs. Dow Jones

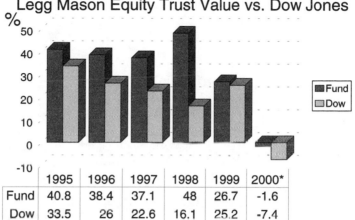

	1995	1996	1997	1998	1999	2000*
Fund	40.8	38.4	37.1	48	26.7	-1.6
Dow	33.5	26	22.6	16.1	25.2	-7.4

% Avg. Annual Total Return
Fund vs. Dow Jones Industrial Avg.

*2000 returns through 10/1/00
(5-year avg. annual return: 29.6%)

17

Citizens Emerging Growth Fund/Retail

Citizens Funds
1 Harbor Place
Portsmouth, NH 03801
800-223-7010
www.citizensfunds.com
Ticker symbol: **WAEGX**

Fund manager: Richard Little
Fund objective: Aggressive growth

Performance	★ ★ ★ ★ ★
Consistency	★ ★ ★
Fees/Services/Management	★ ★ ★ ★
Total	**12 Points**

The Citizens Emerging Growth Fund/Retail invests aggressively in socially responsible companies.

The fund, which has under $400 million in assets, has been one of the most successful socially responsible funds in the industry, with an average annual return of more than 30 percent the past five years. All Citizens funds screen stocks for such issues as environmental stewardship, equal opportunity, employee and community relations, weapons, tobacco, gambling, and other issues.

Fund manager Richard Little looks for companies that are in the early stage of their life cycle and that offer the potential for accelerated earnings, revenue growth, or share price appreciation. The fund invests in small, midcap, and large blue chip stocks, with a target market capitalization range of $243 million to $12.6 billion.

The fund is heavily invested in technology stocks, including such leading holdings as Mercury Interactive, VERITAS Software, PMC-Sierra, and Xilinx.

Telecommunications equipment and services account for about 17 percent of total assets, followed by retail, 11 percent; semiconductors, 10 percent; software, 9 percent; computers, 5 percent; electronics, 5 percent; hand and machine tools, 4 percent; insurance, 4 percent; diversified financial services, 4 percent; and health care, 3 percent.

The fund manager takes an aggressive buy-and-sell approach, with an annual portfolio turnover ratio of 209 percent.

PERFORMANCE

The fund has enjoyed outstanding growth over the past five years. Including dividends and capital gains distributions, the Citizens Emerging Growth Fund/Retail has provided an average annual return the past five years (through late 2000) of 33.7 percent.

A $10,000 investment in 1995 would have grown to about $43,000 five years later.

CONSISTENCY

The fund has been fairly consistent, outperforming the Dow Jones Industrial Average three of the past five years through 1999 (and again through most of 2000). Its biggest gain came in 1999, when it moved up 68.1 percent (compared with a 25.2 percent rise in the Dow).

FEES/SERVICES/MANAGEMENT

The fund is a true no-load fund, with no fee to buy or sell fund shares. The fund's total annual expense ratio of 1.82 percent (with a 0.25 percent 12b-1 fee) is a little higher than most other funds.

The fund offers all the standard services such as retirement account availability, automatic withdrawal, and automatic checking account deduction. Its minimum initial investment of $2,500 is a little bit on the high side as compared with other funds.

Fund manager Richard Little has been part of the fund's management team since 1996. The Citizens fund family includes only six funds and allows shareholders to switch from fund to fund by telephone.

Top Ten Stock Holdings

1. Mercury Interactive
2. Tandy
3. VERITAS Software
4. PMC-Sierra
5. Gemstar International Group

6. Intuit
7. SPX Corp.
8. KLA-Tencor Corp.
9. Adaptec
10. Xilinx

Fund inception: 1994
Asset mix: Common stocks, 92%; cash/equivalents, 8%
Total net assets: $381 million

Load

Front-end load	*None*
Redemption fee (max.)	*None*

Annual Fees

12b-1 fee	0.25%
Management fee	1.00
Other expenses	0.57
Total annual expense	1.82%

Minimum initial investment	$2,500
Minimum subsequent investment	$1

Services

Telephone exchanges	*Yes*
Automatic withdrawal	*Yes*
Automatic checking deduction	*Yes*
Retirement plan/IRA	*Yes*
Instant redemption	*Yes*
Portfolio manager (years)	4
Number of funds in family	6

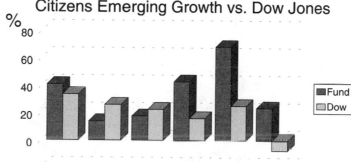

Six-Year Performance
Citizens Emerging Growth vs. Dow Jones

	1995	1996	1997	1998	1999	2000*
Fund	40.7	13.9	17.7	42.7	68.1	23.7
Dow	33.5	26	22.6	16.1	25.2	-7.4

% Avg. Annual Total Return   *2000 returns through 10/1/00
Fund vs. Dow Jones Industrial Avg.   (5-year avg. annual return: 33.8%)

18

Vanguard Growth Equity Fund

Vanguard Funds
P.O. Box 419805
Kansas City, MO 64141-6805
800-662-2739
www.vanguard.com
Ticker symbol: **VGEQX**

Fund manager: Robert E. Turner
Fund objective: Long-term growth

Performance	★ ★ ★ ★ ★
Consistency	★ ★ ★
Fees/Services/Management	★ ★ ★ ★
Total	**12 Points**

The Vanguard Growth Equity Fund invests in a diversified selection of large and midsized stocks that are reasonably priced and have strong earnings growth potential. The fund is geared toward investors interested in owning a stake in some of America's leading blue chip and high-tech stocks.

Many of the top holdings are well-known companies from the technology, health care, and consumer sectors, including General Electric, Cisco Systems, Pfizer, EMC, Sun Microsystems, America Online, and Oracle.

About 40 percent of the fund's $450 million in assets are invested in technology stocks. Other leading sectors include health care, 17 percent; consumer services, 16 percent; consumer staples, 9 percent; financial services, 5.5 percent; and utilities, 5 percent.

The fund was opened in 1992 and has posted a 23 percent average annual return since its inception.

Fund manager Robert Turner, who has managed the fund from the beginning, tries to stock his portfolio with big-name companies that have a history of strong growth. But he doesn't hold for long. He takes a very aggressive trading approach, with a 328 percent annual portfolio turnover ratio. The fund stays 90 to 100 percent invested in stocks under normal circumstances.

PERFORMANCE

The fund has enjoyed outstanding growth over the past five years. Including dividends and capital gains distributions, the Vanguard Growth Equity Fund has provided an average annual return the past five years (through late 2000) of 32 percent.

A $10,000 investment in 1995 would have grown to about $40,000 five years later.

CONSISTENCY

The fund has been fairly consistent, outperforming the Dow Jones Industrial Average three of the past five years through 1999 (and again through most of 2000). Its biggest gain came in 1999, when it moved up 53.6 percent (compared with a 25.2 percent rise in the Dow).

FEES/SERVICES/MANAGEMENT

The fund is a pure no-load fund, with no fees to buy or sell shares. The fund's total annual expense ratio of 0.92 percent (with no 12b-1 fee) compares favorably with other funds.

The fund offers all the standard services such as retirement account availability, automatic withdrawal, and automatic checking account deduction. Its minimum initial investment of $10,000 and minimum subsequent investment of $50 are much higher than most other funds.

Robert E. Turner has managed the fund since its inception in 1992. The Vanguard fund family includes over 120 funds and allows shareholders to switch from fund to fund by telephone.

Top Ten Stock Holdings

1. General Electric
2. Cisco Systems
3. Pfizer
4. EMC
5. Sun Microsystems

6. America Online
7. Oracle
8. Corning
9. Nortel Networks
10. CIENA

Fund inception: 1992
Asset mix: Common stocks, 97%; cash/equivalents, 3%
Total net assets: $450 million

Load

Front-end load	*None*
Redemption fee (max.)	*None*

Annual Fees

12b-1 fee	*None*
Management fee	0.75%
Other expenses	0.17
Total annual expense	0.92%

Minimum initial investment	$10,000
Minimum subsequent investment	$50

Services

Telephone exchanges	*Yes*
Automatic withdrawal	*Yes*
Automatic checking deduction	*Yes*
Retirement plan/IRA	*Yes*
Instant redemption	*Yes*
Portfolio manager (years)	8
Number of funds in family	over 120

Six-Year Performance

Vanguard Growth Equity vs. Dow Jones

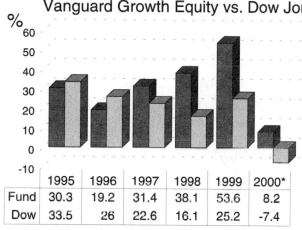

	1995	1996	1997	1998	1999	2000*
Fund	30.3	19.2	31.4	38.1	53.6	8.2
Dow	33.5	26	22.6	16.1	25.2	-7.4

% Avg. Annual Total Return
Fund vs. Dow Jones Industrial Avg.

*2000 returns through 10/1/00
(5-year avg. annual return: 30.4%)

19
INVESCO Blue Chip Growth Fund

INVESCO Funds
7800 East Union Avenue
Denver, CO 80237
800-525-8085
www.invescofunds.com
Ticker symbol: **FLRFX**

Fund manager: Trent May
Fund objective: Long-term growth

Performance	★ ★ ★ ★
Consistency	★ ★ ★
Fees/Services/Management	★ ★ ★ ★ ★
Total	**12 Points**

Blue chips don't come cheap, but when a fund manager picks the right ones it can make all the difference in a fund's growth.

Picking the most promising blue chips is the underlying strategy for Trent May, who has managed the $2 billion INVESCO Blue Chip Growth Fund since 1996. Founded in 1935, the fund is one of the graybeards of the industry.

May is willing to pay a premium for the high-quality large-cap companies that dominate the fund. That may explain the sky-high average price-earnings ratio of most of the fund's roughly 60 stock holdings. Technology stocks command nearly half the portfolio at 48 percent. Other top sectors are health care at 17 percent; financials, 12 percent; consumer staples, 8 percent; and consumer cyclicals, 7.5 percent.

Blue chips from the technology sector include Cisco Systems, America Online, Nokia, Microsoft, and Intel. Other leading holdings include health care blue chip Warner-Lambert and financial services blue chip Charles Schwab.

The turnover ratio in the portfolio is about 134 percent. A $10,000 investment in the fund ten years ago would now be worth about $57,000—an average annual return of about 19 percent.

The fund stays nearly 100 percent invested in stocks under normal circumstances.

PERFORMANCE

The fund has enjoyed very strong growth over the past five years. Including dividends and capital gains distributions, the INVESCO Blue Chip Growth Fund has provided an average annual return the past five years (through late 2000) of 29 percent.

A $10,000 investment in 1995 would have grown to about $36,000 five years later.

CONSISTENCY

The fund has been fairly consistent, outperforming the Dow Jones Industrial Average three of the past five years through 1999 (and again through most of 2000). Its biggest gain came in 1998, when it moved up 41.7 percent (compared with a 16.1 percent rise in the Dow).

FEES/SERVICES/MANAGEMENT

The fund is a pure no-load fund, with no fees to buy or sell shares. The fund's total annual expense ratio of 1.03 percent (with a 0.25 percent 12b-1 fee) compares favorably with other funds.

The fund offers all the standard services such as retirement account availability, automatic withdrawal, and automatic checking account deduction. Its minimum initial investment of $1,000 and minimum subsequent investment of $50 are in line with other funds.

The fund has been managed by Trent May since 1996. The INVESCO fund family includes 32 funds and allows shareholders to switch from fund to fund by telephone.

Top Ten Stock Holdings

1. Warner-Lambert	6. Citigroup
2. Charles Schwab	7. Nokia
3. Cisco Systems	8. Maxim Integrated Products
4. Dell Computer	9. Intel
5. America Online	10. Microsoft

Fund inception: 1935
Asset mix: Common stocks, 98%; cash/equivalents, 2%
Total net assets: $2 billion

Load

Front-end load	*None*
Redemption fee (max.)	*None*

Annual Fees

12b-1 fee	0.25%
Management fee	0.55
Other expenses	0.23
Total annual expense	1.03%

Minimum initial investment	$1,000
Minimum subsequent investment	$50

Services

Telephone exchanges	*Yes*
Automatic withdrawal	*Yes*
Automatic checking deduction	*Yes*
Retirement plan/IRA	*Yes*
Instant redemption	*Yes*
Portfolio manager (years)	4
Number of funds in family	32

Six-Year Performance
INVESCO Blue Chip Growth vs. Dow Jones

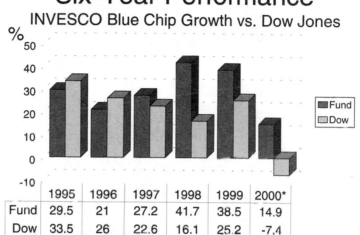

	1995	1996	1997	1998	1999	2000*
Fund	29.5	21	27.2	41.7	38.5	14.9
Dow	33.5	26	22.6	16.1	25.2	-7.4

% Avg. Annual Total Return   *2000 returns through 10/1/00
Fund vs. Dow Jones Industrial Avg.   (5-year avg. annual return: 29.6%)

20

Fidelity Growth Company Fund

Fidelity Funds
82 Devonshire Street
Boston, MA 02109
800-544-8544
www.fidelity.com
Ticker symbol: **FDGRX**

Fund manager: Steven Wymer
Fund objective: Long-term growth

Performance	★ ★ ★ ★
Consistency	★ ★ ★
Fees/Services/Management	★ ★ ★ ★ ★
Total	**12 Points**

Fund manager Steven Wymer continues to scour the stock market for large companies with above-average prospects for earnings growth.

That strategy has helped Wymer land some large technology companies that are still experiencing rapid growth, such as Cisco Systems, National Semiconductor, JDS Uniphase, and Agilent Technologies.

Technology stocks account for about 46 percent of the fund's total assets, followed by health care, 15 percent; financials, 8 percent; utilities, 5 percent; nondurables, 5 percent; industrial machinery and equipment, 4 percent; media and leisure, 3 percent; and retail and wholesale, 3 percent.

A massive fund with $34 billion in assets, the Fidelity Growth Company Fund has more than 250 stock holdings. The fund, founded in 1983, has had solid growth the past decade, with a 23 percent average annual return since 1990. A $10,000 investment in the fund ten years ago would now be worth about $75,000.

Wymer is relatively aggressive in managing the fund, with an 86 percent annual portfolio turnover ratio. The fund stays almost 100 percent invested in stocks under most circumstances.

PERFORMANCE

The fund has enjoyed outstanding growth over the past five years. Including dividends and capital gains distributions, the Fidelity Growth Company Fund has provided an average annual return the past five years (through late 2000) of 28 percent.

A $10,000 investment in 1995 would have grown to about $34,000 five years later.

CONSISTENCY

The fund has been fairly consistent, outperforming the Dow Jones Industrial Average three of the past five years through 1999 (and again through most of 2000). Its biggest gain came in 1999, when it moved up 79.5 percent (compared with a 25.2 percent rise in the Dow).

FEES/SERVICES/MANAGEMENT

The fund is a pure no-load fund, with no fees to buy or sell shares. The fund's total annual expense ratio of 0.74 percent (with no 12b-1 fee) compares very favorably with other funds.

The fund offers all the standard services such as retirement account availability, automatic withdrawal, and automatic checking account deduction. Its minimum initial investment of $2,500 and minimum subsequent investment of $250 are a little high compared with other funds.

Steven Wymer has been managing the fund since 1997. The Fidelity fund family includes more than 300 funds and allows shareholders to switch from fund to fund by telephone.

Top Ten Stock Holdings

1. Cisco Systems
2. PE Corp.-Celera Genomics Group
3. Network Appliance
4. Agilent Technologies
5. Texas Instruments
6. JDS Uniphase
7. National Semiconductor
8. PE Corp.-PE Biosystems Group
9. Microsoft
10. Research in Motion

Fund inception: 1983
Asset mix: Common stocks, 98%; cash/equivalents, 2%
Total net assets: $34 billion

Load

Front-end load	*None*
Redemption fee (max.)	*None*

Annual Fees

12b-1 fee	*None*
Management fee	0.51%
Other expenses	0.23
Total annual expense	0.74%

Minimum initial investment	$2,500
Minimum subsequent investment	$250

Services

Telephone exchanges	*Yes*
Automatic withdrawal	*Yes*
Automatic checking deduction	*Yes*
Retirement plan/IRA	*Yes*
Instant redemption	*Yes*
Portfolio manager (years)	3
Number of funds in family	over 300

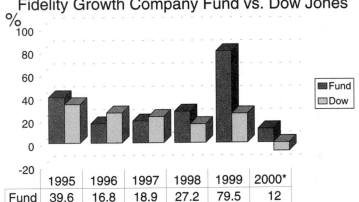

Six-Year Performance
Fidelity Growth Company Fund vs. Dow Jones

	1995	1996	1997	1998	1999	2000*
Fund	39.6	16.8	18.9	27.2	79.5	12
Dow	33.5	26	22.6	16.1	25.2	-7.4

% Avg. Annual Total Return
Fund vs. Dow Jones Industrial Avg.

*2000 returns through 10/1/00
(5-year avg. annual return: 29%)

Strong Growth Fund

Strong Funds
P.O. Box 3863
Milwaukee, WI 53201
800-368-3863
www.strongfunds.com
Ticker symbol: **SGROX**

Fund manager: Ronald Ognar
Fund objective: Small-cap stocks

Performance	★ ★ ★ ★
Consistency	★ ★ ★
Fees/Services/Management	★ ★ ★ ★ ★
Total	**12 Points**

Strong Growth Fund manager Ronald Ognar stays ahead of the curve — and the competition — by keeping his ear to the ground. "Wherever there's a great growth story, we're on it," says Ognar. "We invest in companies of all sizes that dominate their markets, lead the way with innovation, and show strong earnings growth."

Ognar is quick to seize on a trend. For example, when he determined that taxpayers were getting refunds that were 14 percent higher than the year before, he invested in the stocks of such consumer electronics companies as Best Buy, Circuit City, and Tandy.

He also believes that the suppliers and builders of the Internet infrastructure will ride that techno-trend toward long-term success. The top three sectors in the 108-issue Strong Growth Fund portfolio are telecommunications equipment, 15 percent; semiconductors, 11 percent; and networking equipment, 6 percent. Other sectors include energy, 4 percent; financials, 4 percent; health care, 3 percent; utilities, 3 percent; and capital goods, 3 percent.

The $4 billion fund is aggressively managed to seize on opportunities presented by growth companies of all sizes. The portfolio turnover rate is a whooping 324 percent. The fund stays at least 90 percent invested in stocks under normal circumstances.

PERFORMANCE

The fund has enjoyed excellent growth over the past five years. Including dividends and capital gains distributions, the Strong Growth Fund has provided an average annual return the past five years (through late 2000) of 29.5 percent.

A $10,000 investment in 1995 would have grown to about $36,500 five years later.

CONSISTENCY

The fund has been fairly consistent, outperforming the Dow Jones Industrial Average three of the past five years through 1999 (and again through most of 2000). Its biggest gain came in 1999, when it moved up 75.1 percent (compared with a 25.2 percent rise in the Dow).

FEES/SERVICES/MANAGEMENT

The fund is a pure no-load fund, with no fees to buy or sell shares. The fund's total annual expense ratio of 1.20 percent (with no 12b-1 fee) is in line with other funds.

The fund offers all the standard services such as retirement account availability, automatic withdrawal, and automatic checking account deduction. Its minimum initial investment of $2,500 is a little high as compared with other funds.

The fund has been managed by Ronald Ognar since its inception in 1994. The Strong fund family includes 51 funds and allows shareholders to switch from fund to fund by telephone.

Top Ten Stock Holdings

1. Cisco Systems
2. Juniper Networks
3. Kohl's
4. JDS Uniphase
5. VERITAS Software

6. Applied Micro Circuits
7. E-Tek Dynamics
8. SDL, Inc.
9. PE Corp. Biosystems Group
10. Home Depot

Fund inception: 1994
Asset mix: Common stocks, 93%; cash/equivalents, 7%
Total net assets: $3.8 billion

Load

Front-end load	*None*
Redemption fee (max.)	*None*

Annual Fees

12b-1 fee	*None*
Management fee	0.75%
Other expenses	0.45
Total annual expense	1.20%

Minimum initial investment	$2,500
Minimum subsequent investment	$50

Services

Telephone exchanges	*Yes*
Automatic withdrawal	*Yes*
Automatic checking deduction	*Yes*
Retirement plan/IRA	*Yes*
Instant redemption	*Yes*
Portfolio manager (years)	7
Number of funds in family	51

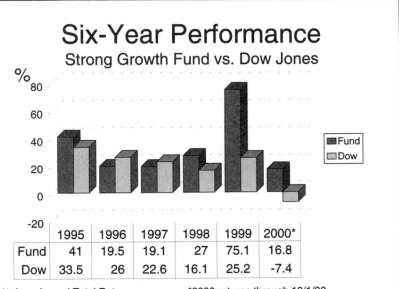

	1995	1996	1997	1998	1999	2000*
Fund	41	19.5	19.1	27	75.1	16.8
Dow	33.5	26	22.6	16.1	25.2	-7.4

% Avg. Annual Total Return   *2000 returns through 10/1/00
Fund vs. Dow Jones Industrial Avg.   (5-year avg. annual return: 30.8%)

22
Janus Enterprise Fund

Janus Investment Funds
100 Fillmore Street
Denver, CO 80206-4928
800-525-3713
www.janus.com
Ticker symbol: **JAENX**

Fund manager: James Goff
Fund objective: Aggressive growth

Performance	★ ★ ★ ★ ★
Consistency	★ ★
Fees/Services/Management	★ ★ ★ ★ ★
Total	**12 Points**

Enterprising investors willing to tolerate a few bumps along the road to solid returns should consider the Janus Enterprise Fund.

The $9 billion fund seeks long-term capital growth by investing in small to midsized companies that have strong potential for growth. James Goff, who has managed the fund since its inception, has a taste for technology and media stocks with relatively high price-earnings ratios, including such issues as Metromedia Fiber Network, Inktomi, AT&T Canada, and PSINet.

Goff focuses on solid, well-run businesses with products that he believes have staying power with their target market, and that may remain profitable no matter how the economy is performing.

The sometimes-volatile technology sector represents about two-thirds of the portfolio. The leading tech sectors include semiconductors, 15 percent; cellular telecommunications, 9 percent; radio, 9 percent; fiber optics, 7 percent; medical, 6 percent; telecommunications services, 5.5 percent; computer data security, 5 percent; and wireless equipment, 4 percent.

Other significant sectors in the portfolio include consumer staples, 15 percent, and consumer cyclicals, 14 percent.

Launched in 1992, the fund has posted about a 29 percent average annual return since its inception.

The fund has about 90 stock holdings in all. Goff is fairly aggressive in his management style, with a 98 percent annual portfolio turnover ratio. The fund stays almost 100 percent invested in stocks under normal circumstances.

PERFORMANCE

The fund has enjoyed outstanding growth over the past five years. Including dividends and capital gains distributions, the Janus Enterprise Fund has provided an average annual return the past five years (through late 2000) of 35 percent.

A $10,000 investment in 1995 would have grown to about $45,000 five years later.

CONSISTENCY

The fund has been somewhat inconsistent, outperforming the Dow Jones Industrial Average only two of the past five years through 1999 (and again through most of 2000). Its biggest gain came in 1999, when it moved up 121.9 percent (compared with a 25.2 percent rise in the Dow).

FEES/SERVICES/MANAGEMENT

The fund is a pure no-load fund, with no fees to buy or sell shares. The fund's total annual expense ratio of 0.95 percent (with no 12b-1 fee) compares favorably with other funds.

The fund offers all the standard services such as retirement account availability, automatic withdrawal, and automatic checking account deduction. Its minimum initial investment of $2,500 and minimum subsequent investment of $100 are a little higher than most other funds.

James Goff has managed the fund since the fund's inception in 1992. The Janus fund family includes 38 funds and allows shareholders to switch from fund to fund by telephone.

Top Ten Stock Holdings

1. Metromedia Fiber Network
2. Paychex
3. AMFM
4. McLeod USA
5. Inktomi

6. AT&T Canada 'B'
7. Vitesse Semiconductor
8. Network Solutions
9. PSINet
10. SDL, Inc.

Fund inception: 1992
Asset mix: Common stocks, 99%; cash/equivalents, 1%
Total net assets: $9 billion

Load

Front-end load	*None*
Redemption fee (max.)	*None*

Annual Fees

12b-1 fee	*None*
Management fee	0.69%
Other expenses	0.26
Total annual expense	0.95%
Minimum initial investment	$2,500
Minimum subsequent investment	$100

Services

Telephone exchanges	*Yes*
Automatic withdrawal	*Yes*
Automatic checking deduction	*Yes*
Retirement plan/IRA	*Yes*
Instant redemption	*Yes*
Portfolio manager (years)	8
Number of funds in family	38

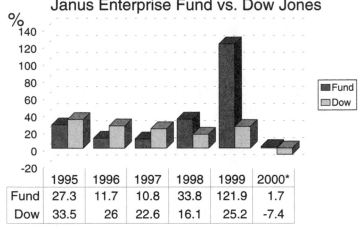

Six-Year Performance
Janus Enterprise Fund vs. Dow Jones

	1995	1996	1997	1998	1999	2000*
Fund	27.3	11.7	10.8	33.8	121.9	1.7
Dow	33.5	26	22.6	16.1	25.2	-7.4

% Avg. Annual Total Return
Fund vs. Dow Jones Industrial Avg.

*2000 returns through 10/1/00
(5-year avg. annual return: 31.4%)

23

Janus Mercury Fund

Janus Investment Funds
100 Fillmore Street
Denver, CO 80206-4928
800-525-3713
www.janus.com
Ticker symbol: **JAMRX**

Fund manager: Warren Lammert
Fund objective: Aggressive growth

Performance	★ ★ ★ ★ ★
Consistency	★ ★
Fees/Services/Management	★ ★ ★ ★ ★
Total	**12 Points**

If the Internet is the backbone of the world's economic future, then owning a stake in the Janus Mercury Fund is like owning a stake in the future.

Technology stocks, particularly Internet and Internet infrastructure companies, constitute nearly half of the $17 billion portfolio. Among the leading holdings in the 80-stock portfolio are such new economy leaders as Amazon.com, i2 Technologies, Cisco Systems, and QUALCOMM.

Because of the fund's technology bias, it is not for the weak of heart, but its long-term returns have been well worth the short-term volatility. The fund has posted an average annual return of about 31 percent since it was opened in 1993.

Warren Lammert, who has managed the fund since its inception, favors a bottom-up approach to choosing investments by emphasizing large-cap companies with strong earnings growth potential. There's no better place to look for companies like that than in the Internet sector.

Other top sectors in the fund are consumer cyclicals, 21 percent; energy, 5 percent; and consumer staples, 3 percent.

The fund has had a fairly active portfolio turnover ratio of 89 percent. The fund stays at least 80 percent invested in stocks under normal circumstances.

PERFORMANCE

The fund has enjoyed outstanding growth over the past five years. Including dividends and capital gains distributions, the Janus Mercury Fund has provided an average annual return the past five years (through late 2000) of 34 percent.

A $10,000 investment in 1995 would have grown to about $43,000 five years later.

CONSISTENCY

The fund has been somewhat inconsistent, outperforming the Dow Jones Industrial Average only two of the past five years through 1999 (and was about even through most of 2000). Its biggest gain came in 1999, when it moved up 96.2 percent (compared with a 25.2 percent rise in the Dow).

FEES/SERVICES/MANAGEMENT

The fund is a pure no-load fund, with no fees to buy or sell shares. The fund's total annual expense ratio of 0.91 percent (with no 12b-1 fee) compares favorably with other funds.

The fund offers all the standard services such as retirement account availability, automatic withdrawal, and automatic checking account deduction. Its minimum initial investment of $2,500 and minimum subsequent investment of $100 are a little higher than most other funds.

The fund has been managed by Warren Lammert since its inception in 1993. The Janus fund family includes 38 funds and allows shareholders to switch from fund to fund by telephone.

Top Ten Stock Holdings

1. Nokia
2. Enron
3. AT&T-Liberty Media
4. Time Warner
5. Amazon.com

6. i2 Technologies
7. Telefonaktiebolaget LM
8. Cisco Systems
9. Vodafone AirTouch ADR
10. QUALCOMM

Fund inception: 1993
Asset mix: Common stocks, 85%; cash/equivalents, 15%
Total net assets: $17 billion

Load

Front-end load	*None*
Redemption fee (max.)	*None*

Annual Fees

12b-1 fee	*None*
Management fee	0.66%
Other expenses	0.25
Total annual expense	0.91%
Minimum initial investment	$2,500
Minimum subsequent investment	$100

Services

Telephone exchanges	*Yes*
Automatic withdrawal	*Yes*
Automatic checking deduction	*Yes*
Retirement plan/IRA	*Yes*
Instant redemption	*Yes*
Portfolio manager (years)	7
Number of funds in family	38

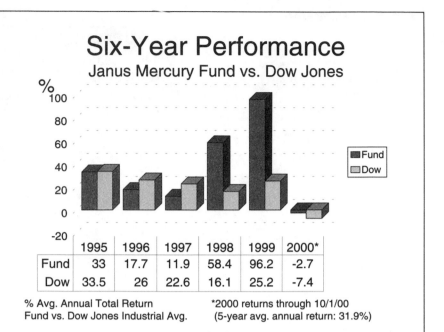

Six-Year Performance
Janus Mercury Fund vs. Dow Jones

	1995	1996	1997	1998	1999	2000*
Fund	33	17.7	11.9	58.4	96.2	-2.7
Dow	33.5	26	22.6	16.1	25.2	-7.4

% Avg. Annual Total Return   *2000 returns through 10/1/00
Fund vs. Dow Jones Industrial Avg.   (5-year avg. annual return: 31.9%)

PBHG Technology & Communications Fund

PBHG Funds
P.O. Box 419534
Kansas City, MO 64141-6534
800-433-0051
www.pbhgfunds.com
Ticker symbol: **PBTCX**

Fund manager: Jeffrey Wrona
Fund objective: Sector

Performance	★ ★ ★ ★ ★
Consistency	★ ★ ★
Fees/Services/Management	★ ★ ★ ★
Total	**12 Points**

Talk about a fund on the fast track—the PBHG Technology and Communications Fund has been setting a blistering pace since its inception in 1995. During its first five years of operation, the fund posted an average annual return of 55.7 percent.

The fund focuses on fast-growing small and midsized Internet infrastructure, computer, semiconductor, and telecommunications stocks. The $4 billion fund has about 60 stock holdings in all, including such leading holdings as InfoSpace, JDS Uniphase, Extreme Networks, E-Tek Dynamics, and Brocade Communications.

Momentum is a key quality that fund manager Jeffrey Wrona looks for in a stock. "We continually look for companies showing signs of business momentum," says Wrona. "If a company has it, we're buyers of their stock. If a company is losing momentum, we're sellers of their stock. And if business momentum is neither positive nor negative, we're holders of the stock while looking for a better replacement."

Wrona does a lot of trading in the portfolio. The fund has a 276 percent annual portfolio turnover ratio. It stays 90 to 95 percent invested in stocks under normal circumstances.

PERFORMANCE

The fund has enjoyed very outstanding growth over the past five years. Including dividends and capital gains distributions, the PBHG Technology and Communications Fund has provided an exceptional average annual return the past five years (through late 2000) of 55.7 percent.

A $10,000 investment in 1995 would have grown to about $92,000 five years later.

CONSISTENCY

The fund has been fairly consistent, outperforming or matching the Dow Jones Industrial Average three out of the past five years through 1999 (and again through most of 2000). Its biggest gain came in 1999, when it leaped up an amazing 244 percent (compared with a 25.2 percent rise in the Dow).

FEES/SERVICES/MANAGEMENT

The fund is a pure no-load fund, with no fees to buy or sell shares. The fund's total annual expense ratio of 1.19 percent (with no 12b-1 fee) is in line with other funds.

The fund offers all the standard services such as retirement account availability, automatic withdrawal, and automatic checking account deduction. Its minimum initial investment of $2,500 and minimum subsequent investment of $1 are a little higher than most other funds.

Fund manager Jeffrey Wrona has only been with the fund since 1999. The PBHG fund family includes 17 funds and allows shareholders to switch from fund to fund by telephone.

Top Ten Stock Holdings

1. InfoSpace
2. JDS Uniphase
3. Redback Net
4. GlobeSpan
5. VeriSign

6. MRV Communications
7. E-Tek Dynamics
8. Triquint Semiconductors
9. Extreme Networks
10. Brocade Communications

Fund inception: 1995
Asset mix: Common stocks, 95%; cash/equivalents, 5%
Total net assets: $3.6 billion

Load

Front-end load	*None*
Redemption fee (max.)	*None*

Annual Fees

12b-1 fee	*None*
Management fee	0.85%
Other expenses	0.34
Total annual expense	1.19%

Minimum initial investment	$2,500
Minimum subsequent investment	$1

Services

Telephone exchanges	*Yes*
Automatic withdrawal	*Yes*
Automatic checking deduction	*Yes*
Retirement plan/IRA	*Yes*
Instant redemption	*Yes*
Portfolio manager (years)	1
Number of funds in family	17

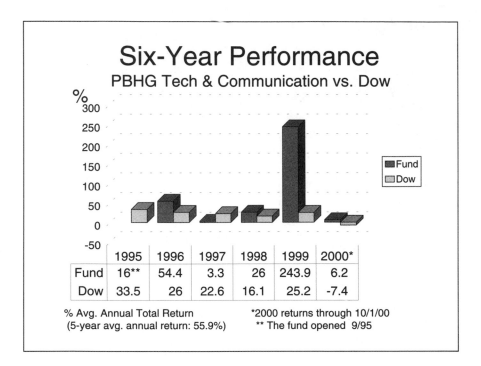

Six-Year Performance
PBHG Tech & Communication vs. Dow

	1995	1996	1997	1998	1999	2000*
Fund	16**	54.4	3.3	26	243.9	6.2
Dow	33.5	26	22.6	16.1	25.2	-7.4

% Avg. Annual Total Return   *2000 returns through 10/1/00
(5-year avg. annual return: 55.9%)   ** The fund opened 9/95

25

Gabelli Global Growth Fund

Gabelli Funds
One Corporate Center
Rye, NY 10580-1434
800-422-3554
www.gabelli.com
Ticker symbol: **GICPX**

Fund manager: Marc Gabelli
Fund objective: International equity

Performance	★ ★ ★ ★ ★
Consistency	★ ★
Fees/Services/Management	★ ★ ★ ★ ★
Total	**12 Points**

Second-generation fund manager Marc Gabelli believes that the dominant companies of tomorrow will be conducting a major portion of their business via the Internet in the next five years. As a result, his Gabelli Global Growth Fund is investing in companies that are playing leading roles in the ever-evolving communications revolution.

Gabelli isn't placing his bets strictly on telephone companies, as many specialty communications funds tend to do. The fund is also investing in global companies that are benefiting from the growing demand for information and entertainment. Communications services is the largest sector in the fund at 67 percent, followed by communications technology at 12 percent and utilities at 7 percent.

The $500 million fund invests in stocks from around the world, although its heaviest concentration is in U.S. companies. While it owns some well-known stocks, such as Cable and Wireless and Bell Atlantic, most of its holdings are less familiar names, such as Vivendi, Canal Plus, Telephone & Data Systems, and Audiofina.

Annual turnover in the 140-issue portfolio is a rather modest 63 percent. The fund was established in 1994. A $10,000 investment in the fund ten years ago would now be worth about $79,000.

PERFORMANCE

The fund has enjoyed outstanding growth over the past five years. Including dividends and capital gains distributions, the Gabelli Global Growth Fund has provided an average annual return the past five years (through late 2000) of 31.3 percent.

A $10,000 investment in 1995 would have grown to about $39,000 five years later.

CONSISTENCY

The fund has been fairly consistent, outperforming the Dow Jones Industrial Average three of the past five years through 1999 (but was trailing the Dow through most of 2000). Its biggest gain came in 1999, when it moved up 116 percent (compared with a 25.2 percent rise in the Dow).

FEES/SERVICES/MANAGEMENT

The fund is a pure no-load fund, with no fees to buy or sell shares. The fund's total annual expense ratio of 1.58 percent (with a 0.25 percent 12b-1 fee) is in line with other funds.

The fund offers all the standard services such as retirement account availability, automatic withdrawal, and automatic checking account deduction. Its minimum initial investment of $1,000 and minimum subsequent investment of $1 are in line with other funds.

The fund has been managed by Marc Gabelli since its inception in 1994. The Gabelli fund family includes 30 funds and allows shareholders to switch from fund to fund by telephone.

Top Ten Stock Holdings

1. Vivendi
2. AT&T-Liberty Media 'A'
3. Canal Plus
4. Telephone & Data Systems
5. Audiofina

6. Teleglobe
7. Nippon Broadcasting System
8. Bell Atlantic
9. Vodafone AirTouch
10. Cable & Wireless

Fund inception: 1994
Asset mix: Common stocks, 99%; preferred stocks, 1%
Total net assets: $467 million

Load

Front-end load	*None*
Redemption fee (max.)	*None*

Annual Fees

12b-1 fee	0.25%
Management fee	1.00
Other expenses	0.33
Total annual expense	1.58%
Minimum initial investment	$1,000
Minimum subsequent investment	$1

Services

Telephone exchanges	*Yes*
Automatic withdrawal	*Yes*
Automatic checking deduction	*Yes*
Retirement plan/IRA	*Yes*
Instant redemption	*Yes*
Portfolio manager (years)	6
Number of funds in family	30

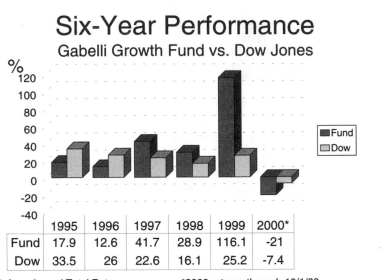

Six-Year Performance
Gabelli Growth Fund vs. Dow Jones

	1995	1996	1997	1998	1999	2000*
Fund	17.9	12.6	41.7	28.9	116.1	-21
Dow	33.5	26	22.6	16.1	25.2	-7.4

% Avg. Annual Total Return   *2000 returns through 10/1/00
Fund vs. Dow Jones Industrial Avg.   (5-year avg. annual return: 28.1%)

Value Line Special Situations Fund

Value Line Funds
220 East 42nd Street
New York, NY 10017-5891
800-223-0818
www.valueline.com
Ticker symbol: **VALSX**

Fund manager: Steven Grant
Fund objective: Long-term growth

Performance	★ ★ ★ ★
Consistency	★ ★ ★
Fees/Services/Management	★ ★ ★ ★ ★
Total	**12 Points**

Just what is a "special situation"? It could come in many forms, according to the investment goals of this Value Line offering. Traditionally, the term has referred to companies in transition—involved in a merger, liquidation, recapitalization, breakup, new management, or dramatic change in management policies.

Value Line has added one more qualifier for its Special Situations Fund—"a technological improvement or important discovery or acquisition." And from the looks of the top holdings, a "technological improvement" may as well have been the only qualifier, because the list reads like a high-tech sector fund. Microsoft, Applied Micro Circuits, PMC-Sierra, Nortel Networks, Exodus Communications, SDL, and RF Micro Devices are all among the largest holdings.

In all, technology stocks account for 57 percent of the $450 million portfolio. Health care accounts for 10 percent and communications services makes up another 9 percent. The fund also invests in consumer cyclicals, 10 percent; consumer staples, 9 percent; capital goods, 3 percent; and

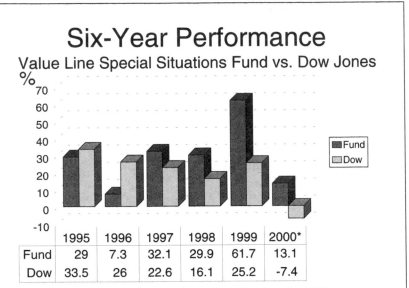

Six-Year Performance
Value Line Special Situations Fund vs. Dow Jones

	1995	1996	1997	1998	1999	2000*
Fund	29	7.3	32.1	29.9	61.7	13.1
Dow	33.5	26	22.6	16.1	25.2	-7.4

% Avg. Annual Total Return
Fund vs. Dow Jones Industrial Avg.

*2000 returns through 10/1/00
(5-year avg. annual return: 26.7%)

PBHG Select Equity Fund

PBHG Funds
P.O. Box 419534
Kansas City, MO 64141-6534
800-433-0051
www.pbhgfunds.com
Ticker symbol: **PBHEX**

Fund manager: Michael Sutton
Fund objective: Aggressive growth

Performance	★ ★ ★ ★ ★
Consistency	★ ★ ★
Fees/Services/Management	★ ★ ★ ★
Total	**12 Points**

The PBHG Select Equity Fund invests in many of the leading stocks of the new economy, such as router maker Juniper Networks, fiber-optics maker JDS Uniphase, Internet chip maker Broadcom, and Internet infrastructure manufacturers Brocade Communications and Verisign.

Fund manager Michael Sutton looks for stocks with strong business momentum, strong earnings growth potential, and solid capital appreciation potential. The fund typically limits its holdings to under 30 stocks. The fund may invest in small, midsized, and large-capitalization stocks.

The fund was launched in 1995. It is heavily weighted in technology stocks, which account for about 80 percent of the $1.8 billion portfolio. It also invests in consumer cyclicals (6 percent) and industrial stocks (2 percent). The fund stays 80 to 95 percent invested in stocks under normal circumstances.

The heavy emphasis on technology stocks has made the fund somewhat volatile for the short term but very profitable for the long term. It has posted an average annual return of 49 percent since its 1995 inception.

The fund manager is very aggressive in his trading approach, with a 200 percent annual portfolio turnover ratio.

PERFORMANCE

The fund has enjoyed very outstanding growth over the past five years. Including dividends and capital gains distributions, the PBHG Select Equity Fund has provided an exceptional average annual return the past five years (through late 2000) of 46 percent.

A $10,000 investment in 1995 would have grown to about $66,000 five years later.

CONSISTENCY

The fund has been fairly consistent, outperforming or nearly matching the Dow Jones Industrial Average four of the past five years through 1999 (and again through most of 2000). Its biggest gain came in 1999, when it jumped up 160.9 percent (compared with a 25.2 percent rise in the Dow).

FEES/SERVICES/MANAGEMENT

The fund is a pure no-load fund, with no fees to buy or sell shares. The fund's total annual expense ratio of 1.18 percent (with no 12b-1 fee) is in line with other funds.

The fund offers all the standard services such as retirement account availability, automatic withdrawal, and automatic checking account deduction. Its minimum initial investment of $2,500 and minimum subsequent investment of $1 are a little higher than most other funds.

Michael Sutton has managed the fund only since 2000. The PBHG fund family includes 17 funds and allows shareholders to switch from fund to fund by telephone.

Top Ten Stock Holdings

1. BroadVision
2. Gemstar International Group
3. Xilinx
4. RF Micro Devices
5. Juniper Networks
6. Conexant Systems
7. Legato Systems
8. Hi/fn, Inc.
9. JDS Uniphase
10. Exodus Communications

Fund inception: 1995
Asset mix: Common stocks, 87%; cash/equivalents, 13%
Total net assets: $1.8 billion

Load

Front-end load	*None*
Redemption fee (max.)	*None*

Annual Fees

12b-1 fee	*None*
Management fee	0.85%
Other expenses	0.33
Total annual expense	1.18%
Minimum initial investment	$2,500
Minimum subsequent investment	$1

Services

Telephone exchanges	*Yes*
Automatic withdrawal	*Yes*
Automatic checking deduction	*Yes*
Retirement plan/IRA	*Yes*
Instant redemption	*Yes*
Portfolio manager (years)	1
Number of funds in family	17

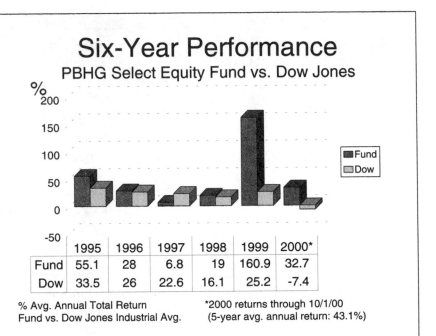

Six-Year Performance
PBHG Select Equity Fund vs. Dow Jones

	1995	1996	1997	1998	1999	2000*
Fund	55.1	28	6.8	19	160.9	32.7
Dow	33.5	26	22.6	16.1	25.2	-7.4

% Avg. Annual Total Return   *2000 returns through 10/1/00
Fund vs. Dow Jones Industrial Avg.   (5-year avg. annual return: 43.1%)

28

Fidelity Select: Electronics Portfolio

Fidelity Funds
82 Devonshire Street
Boston, MA 02109
800-544-8544
www.fidelity.com
Ticker symbol: **FSELX**

Fund manager: Brian Hanson
Fund objective: Sector

Performance	★ ★ ★ ★ ★
Consistency	★ ★ ★ ★
Fees/Services/Management	★ ★ ★
Total	**12 Points**

Companies in the high-tech sector have enjoyed unprecedented growth in recent years, fueling the explosive growth of the Fidelity Select Electronics Portfolio. A $10,000 investment in the fund ten years ago would now be worth a whopping $230,000—a 37 percent average annual return.

The fund invests in a cross section of companies in the computer and electronics arena. Most of its stock holdings are electronics components makers, electronics equipment makers, and electronics instrument and systems manufacturers and distributors. Electronics and semiconductor companies, such as Broadcom, LSI Logic, Motorola, Xilinx, Analog Devices, PMC-Sierra, and Altera dominate the portfolio, accounting for about 70 percent of total assets. Other key sectors include electronics instruments, 12 percent; computers and office equipment, 5 percent; and communications equipment, 2 percent.

The $11 billion fund has about 65 stock holdings in all. The fund was launched in 1985.

Fund manager Brian Hanson invests in both the large blue chip electronics stocks, such as Intel and Dell, and the smaller emerging companies, such as MatrixOne, Emulex, and Methode Electronics.

Hanson takes a fairly active management approach, with a 125 percent portfolio turnover ratio. The fund invests 80 to 95 percent of its assets in stocks under normal circumstances.

PERFORMANCE

The fund has enjoyed spectacular growth over the past five years. Including dividends and capital gains distributions, the Fidelity Select Electronics Portfolio has provided a load-adjusted average annual return the past five years (through late 2000) of 44 percent.

A $10,000 investment in 1995 would have grown to about $62,000 five years later.

CONSISTENCY

The fund has been very consistent, outperforming the Dow Jones Industrial Average four of the past five years through 1999 (and again through most of 2000). Its biggest gain came in 1999, when it moved up 106.6 percent (compared with a 25.2 percent rise in the Dow).

FEES/SERVICES/MANAGEMENT

The fund has a 3 percent front-end load. The fund's total annual expense ratio of 0.98 percent (with no 12b-1 fee) compares favorably with other funds.

The fund offers all the standard services such as retirement account availability, automatic withdrawal, and automatic checking account deduction. Its minimum initial investment of $2,500 and minimum subsequent investment of $250 are a little higher than most other funds.

Fund manager Brian Hanson just joined the fund in 2000, but he has been a fund manager with Fidelity since 1996. The Fidelity fund family includes more than 300 funds and allows shareholders to switch from fund to fund by telephone.

Top Ten Stock Holdings

1. Analog Devices
2. Vitesse Semiconductor
3. Micron Technology
4. PMC-Sierra
5. National Semiconductor
6. Linear Technology
7. LSI Logic
8. Intel
9. Texas Instruments
10. Altera Corp.

Fund inception: 1985
Asset mix: Common stocks, 93%; cash/equivalents, 7%
Total net assets: $11 billion

Load

Front-end load	3.00%
Redemption fee (max.)	*None*

Annual Fees

12b-1 fee	*None*
Management fee	0.58%
Other expenses	0.40
Total annual expense	0.98%
Minimum initial investment	$2,500
Minimum subsequent investment	$250

Services

Telephone exchanges	*Yes*
Automatic withdrawal	*Yes*
Automatic checking deduction	*Yes*
Retirement plan/IRA	*Yes*
Instant redemption	*Yes*
Portfolio manager (years)	1
Number of funds in family	over 300

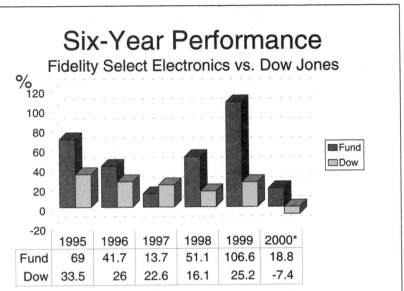

Six-Year Performance
Fidelity Select Electronics vs. Dow Jones

	1995	1996	1997	1998	1999	2000*
Fund	69	41.7	13.7	51.1	106.6	18.8
Dow	33.5	26	22.6	16.1	25.2	-7.4

% Avg. Annual Total Return   *2000 returns through 10/1/00
Fund vs. Dow Jones Industrial Avg.   (5-year avg. annual return: 39.7%)

Fidelity Select: Computers Portfolio

Fidelity Funds
82 Devonshire Street
Boston, MA 02109
800-544-8544
www.fidelity.com
Ticker symbol: **FDCPX**

Fund manager: Lawrence Rakers
Fund objective: Sector

Performance	★ ★ ★ ★ ★
Consistency	★ ★ ★ ★
Fees/Services/Management	★ ★ ★
Total	**12 Points**

The computer revolution that has swept the world during the past decade has been a very rewarding trend for shareholders of the Fidelity Select Computers Portfolio. A $10,000 investment in the fund ten years ago would now be worth about $185,000—a 34 percent average annual return. This has been one of the nation's top-performing funds during that period.

The fund invests primarily in companies that are engaged in the research, manufacturing, or distribution of computer hardware. Among the fund's holdings are computer industry leaders Cisco Systems, Hewlett-Packard, Dell Computer, EMC, Texas Instruments, and Micron Technology.

Computers and office equipment make up about 33 percent of the portfolio, followed by electronics, 31 percent; services and software, 16 percent; and communications equipment, 10 percent. In all, there are about 90 stock holdings in the $4 billion portfolio, from the very largest companies, such as Intel, Compaq, and Microsoft, to the smaller and midcap emerging companies, such as Cypress Semiconductor and Visual Networks.

The fund, which was launched in 1985, stays 80 to 95 percent invested in stocks under normal conditions. Fund manager Lawrence Rakers takes a fairly active trading approach, with a 129 percent annual portfolio turnover ratio.

PERFORMANCE

The fund has enjoyed exceptional growth over the past five years. Including dividends and capital gains distributions, the Fidelity Select Computers Portfolio has provided a load-adjusted average annual return the past five years (through late 2000) of 37.3 percent.

A $10,000 investment in 1995 would have grown to about $48,000 five years later.

CONSISTENCY

The fund has been fairly consistent, outperforming the Dow Jones Industrial Average four of the past five years through 1999 (and again through most of 2000). Its biggest gain came in 1998, when it moved up 96.4 percent (compared with a 16.1 percent rise in the Dow).

FEES/SERVICES/MANAGEMENT

The fund has a low 3 percent front-end load. The fund's total annual expense ratio of 1.05 percent (with no 12b-1 fee) is in line with other funds.

The fund offers all the standard services such as retirement account availability, automatic withdrawal, and automatic checking account deduction. Its minimum initial investment of $2,500 and minimum subsequent investment of $250 are a little higher than most other funds.

Fund manager Lawrence Rakers just joined the fund in 2000, but he has been a fund manager with Fidelity since 1993. The Fidelity fund family includes more than 300 funds and allows shareholders to switch from fund to fund by telephone.

Top Ten Stock Holdings

1. Cisco Systems
2. LSI Logic
3. EMC Corp.
4. Hewlett-Packard
5. Dell Computer

6. Network Appliance
7. Motorola
8. Analog Devices
9. Texas Instruments
10. Micron Technology

Fund inception: 1985
Asset mix: Common stocks, 95%; cash/equivalents, 5%
Total net assets: $4 billion

Load

Front-end load	3.00%
Redemption fee (max.)	*None*

Annual Fees

12b-1 fee	*None*
Management fee	0.58%
Other expenses	0.47
Total annual expense	1.05%

Minimum initial investment	$2,500
Minimum subsequent investment	$250

Services

Telephone exchanges	*Yes*
Automatic withdrawal	*Yes*
Automatic checking deduction	*Yes*
Retirement plan/IRA	*Yes*
Instant redemption	*Yes*
Portfolio manager (years)	1
Number of funds in family	over 300

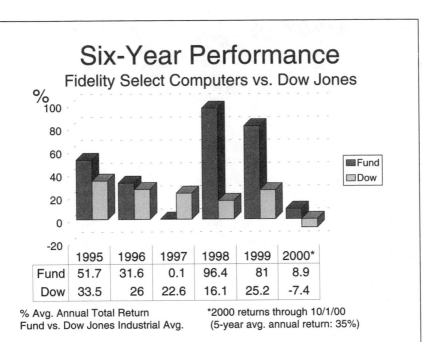

Six-Year Performance
Fidelity Select Computers vs. Dow Jones

	1995	1996	1997	1998	1999	2000*
Fund	51.7	31.6	0.1	96.4	81	8.9
Dow	33.5	26	22.6	16.1	25.2	-7.4

% Avg. Annual Total Return   *2000 returns through 10/1/00
Fund vs. Dow Jones Industrial Avg.   (5-year avg. annual return: 35%)

INVESCO Technology Fund

INVESCO Funds
7800 East Union Avenue
Denver, CO 80237
800-525-8085
www.invescofunds.com
Ticker symbol: **FTCHX**

Fund manager: William Keithler
Fund objective: Sector

Performance	★ ★ ★ ★ ★
Consistency	★ ★ ★
Fees/Services/Management	★ ★ ★ ★
Total	**12 Points**

Even in the fast-paced world of technology investing, the race isn't necessarily to the swift. Patience and diversification are the watchwords for the INVESCO Technology Fund.

William Keithler, who has managed the $5 billion fund since 1999, tends to ignore price momentum when picking stocks for the portfolio of more than 100 companies. Instead, he focuses on corporate performance and optimism for new technologies—the keys to successful technology investing over the long term.

Founded in 1984, the fund also invests in companies that have staked out solid positions in their industries. Applied Micro Circuits, which constitutes about 2 percent of the total portfolio, is a good example. The company makes a variety of chips for optical networks, which are at the core of the booming demand for wireless telecommunications products.

The 136-issue fund also keeps an eye out for smaller technology firms that are about to generate a flow of profits. In addition to Applied Micro Circuits, the other top holdings in the fund include Cisco Systems, SDL Inc., Nokia, and Oracle.

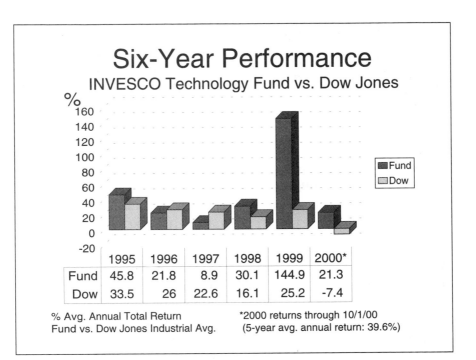

Six-Year Performance
INVESCO Technology Fund vs. Dow Jones

	1995	1996	1997	1998	1999	2000*
Fund	45.8	21.8	8.9	30.1	144.9	21.3
Dow	33.5	26	22.6	16.1	25.2	-7.4

% Avg. Annual Total Return   *2000 returns through 10/1/00
Fund vs. Dow Jones Industrial Avg.   (5-year avg. annual return: 39.6%)

31
Gabelli Global Telecommunications Fund

Gabelli Funds
One Corporate Center
Rye, NY 10580-1434
800-422-3554
www.gabelli.com
Ticker symbol: **GABTX**

Fund manager: Mario Gabelli
Fund objective: Sector

Performance	★ ★ ★ ★
Consistency	★ ★ ★
Fees/Services/Management	★ ★ ★ ★ ★
Total	**12 Points**

Telecommunications has been a growth industry the past decade, as the Internet, fax machines, and cellular phones have added exponentially to the demand. That surging demand has helped fuel the growth of phone services companies—the core holdings of the Gabelli Global Telecommunications Fund.

About 80 percent of the stocks in the $450 million fund are phone services companies. The balance are telephone equipment makers and utilities stocks. The fund, managed since its 1993 inception by Mario Gabelli, targets undervalued global telecommunications companies with strong earnings and cash flow. Its primary objective is capital appreciation. The fund has posted about a 21.5 percent average annual return since 1993.

Takeover targets within the telecommunications sector are also a focus of the fund. The top holdings of the fund comprise globally oriented U.S. and foreign stocks, including Cable & Wireless, Telephone & Data Systems, SBC Communications, and Telecom Italia.

The fund has about 250 stocks in the portfolio and stays 75 to 90 percent invested in stocks most of the time. The fund manager takes a fairly conservative investment approach, with a 60 percent annual portfolio turnover ratio.

PERFORMANCE

The fund has enjoyed solid growth over the past five years. Including dividends and capital gains distributions, the Gabelli Global Telecommunications Fund has provided an average annual return the past five years (through late 2000) of about 29 percent.

A $10,000 investment in 1995 would have grown to about $36,000 five years later.

CONSISTENCY

The fund has been fairly consistent, outperforming the Dow Jones Industrial Average three of the past five years through 1999 (and again through most of 2000). Its biggest gain came in 1999, when it moved up 80.3 percent (compared with a 25.2 percent rise in the Dow).

FEES/SERVICES/MANAGEMENT ★ ★ ★ ★ ★

The fund is a pure no-load fund, with no fees to buy or sell shares. The fund's total annual expense ratio of 1.48 percent (with a 0.25 percent 12b-1 fee) is in line with other funds.

The fund offers all the standard services such as retirement account availability, automatic withdrawal, and automatic checking account deduction. Its minimum initial investment of $1,000 and minimum subsequent investment of $1 are in line with other funds.

Mario Gabelli has been with the fund since its inception in 1993. The Gabelli fund family includes 30 funds and allows shareholders to switch from fund to fund by telephone.

Top Ten Stock Holdings

1. Telephone & Data Systems
2. Esat Telecom Group
3. Cable & Wireless
4. BCE, Inc.
5. AT&T-Liberty Media 'A'
6. NTT Mobile Communications
7. SBC Communications
8. Telecom Italia
9. GTE
10. Century Tel

Fund inception: 1993
Asset mix: Common stocks, 81%; cash/equivalents, 19%
Total net assets: $451 million

Load

Front-end load	*None*
Redemption fee (max.)	*None*

Annual Fees

12b-1 fee	0.25%
Management fee	1.00
Other expenses	0.23
Total annual expense	1.48%

Minimum initial investment	$1,000
Minimum subsequent investment	$1

Services

Telephone exchanges	*Yes*
Automatic withdrawal	*Yes*
Automatic checking deduction	*Yes*
Retirement plan/IRA	*Yes*
Instant redemption	*Yes*
Portfolio manager (years)	7
Number of funds in family	30

Technology stocks make up about 32 percent of the portfolio, followed by health care, 17 percent; consumer staples, 12 percent; consumer services, 11 percent; financial services, 8 percent; and utilities, 4 percent.

The fund stays almost 100 percent invested in stocks under normal circumstances.

PERFORMANCE

The fund has enjoyed solid growth over the past five years. Including dividends and capital gains distributions, the Vanguard U.S. Growth Fund has provided an average annual return the past five years (through late 2000) of 26 percent.

A $10,000 investment in 1995 would have grown to about $32,000 five years later.

CONSISTENCY

The fund has been fairly consistent, outperforming the Dow Jones Industrial Average four of the past five years through 1999 (and again through most of 2000). Its biggest gain came in 1998, when it moved up 40 percent (compared with a 16.1 percent rise in the Dow).

FEES/SERVICES/MANAGEMENT

The fund is a pure no-load fund, with no fees to buy or sell shares. The fund's total annual expense ratio of 0.39 percent (with no 12b-1 fee) is very low compared to most other funds.

The fund offers all the standard services such as retirement account availability, automatic withdrawal, and automatic checking account deduction. Its minimum initial investment of $3,000 and minimum subsequent investment of $100 are higher than most other funds.

The fund is managed by a team of portfolio managers, including J. Parker Hall III, since 1987, David Fowler, since 1987, and John Cole, since 1999. The Vanguard fund family includes more than 120 funds and allows shareholders to switch from fund to fund by telephone.

Top Ten Stock Holdings

1. Cisco Systems
2. General Electric
3. Microsoft
4. Intel
5. EMC

6. America Online
7. Lucent Technologies
8. Texas Instruments
9. Warner-Lambert
10. Applied Materials

Fund inception: 1959
Asset mix: Common stocks, 98%; cash/equivalents, 2%
Total net assets: $21 billion

Load

Front-end load	*None*
Redemption fee (max.)	*None*

Annual Fees

12b-1 fee	*None*
Management fee	0.37%
Other expenses	0.02
Total annual expense	0.39%
Minimum initial investment	$3,000
Minimum subsequent investment	$100

Services

Telephone exchanges	*Yes*
Automatic withdrawal	*Yes*
Automatic checking deduction	*Yes*
Retirement plan/IRA	*Yes*
Instant redemption	*Yes*
Portfolio manager (years)	13
Number of funds in family	over 120

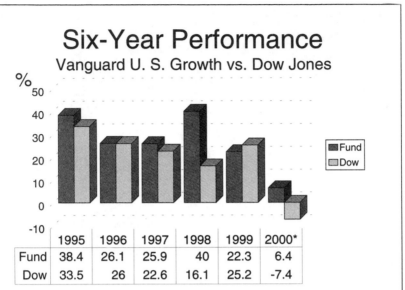

Six-Year Performance
Vanguard U. S. Growth vs. Dow Jones

	1995	1996	1997	1998	1999	2000*
Fund	38.4	26.1	25.9	40	22.3	6.4
Dow	33.5	26	22.6	16.1	25.2	-7.4

% Avg. Annual Total Return   *2000 returns through 10/1/00
Fund vs. Dow Jones Industrial Avg.   (5-year avg. annual return: 25.3%)

33

Calamos Growth Fund

Calamos Funds
1111 East Warrenville Road
Naperville, IL 60563-1493
800-323-9943
www.calamos.com
Ticker symbol: **CVGRX**

Fund managers: John Calamos and Nick Calamos
Fund objective: Aggressive growth

Performance	★ ★ ★ ★ ★
Consistency	★ ★ ★ ★
Fees/Services/Management	★ ★
Total	**11 Points**

This little-known fund has had outstanding returns throughout most of its ten-year history. In fact, the fund posted annual returns of at least 24 percent every year from 1995 through 1999.

Calamos Funds was founded by John Calamos, the son of a Greek immigrant, who comanages the funds with his son, John (Nick) Calamos, Jr.

In selecting stocks for his funds, Calamos looks for price strength, sales momentum, and earnings growth. "We're looking for companies that are growing their earnings, but whose growth has not been totally priced into the stock," explained Calamos in a recent media interview. "We're trying to gauge the companies that will be gaining Wall Street's attention."

He focuses on stocks of the fastest-growing sectors. The fund's leading sectors include technology, 41 percent of assets; consumer staples, 26 percent; consumer cyclicals, 18 percent; capital goods, 6 percent; energy, 3 percent; and utilities, 3 percent.

Many of the fund's top holdings are lesser-known technology stocks, such as Calpine, Biogen, and TriQuint Semiconductor.

The fund stays about 90 percent invested in stocks under most circumstances. Calamos takes an aggressive buy-and-sell approach, with an annual turnover ratio of about 175 percent.

PERFORMANCE

The fund has enjoyed outstanding growth over the past five years. Including dividends and capital gains distributions, the Calamos Growth Fund has provided a load-adjusted average annual return the past five years (through late 2000) of 38.7 percent.

A $10,000 investment in 1995 would have grown to about $52,000 five years later.

CONSISTENCY

The fund has been very consistent, outperforming the Dow Jones Industrial Average four of the past five years through 1999 (and again through most of 2000). Its biggest gain came in 1999, when it moved up 77.7 percent (compared with a 25.2 percent rise in the Dow).

FEES/SERVICES/MANAGEMENT

The fund has a front-end load of 4.75 percent, with a maximum back-end load of 1 percent. The fund's total annual expense ratio of 2.0 percent (with a 0.25 percent 12b-1 fee) is a little higher than most other funds.

The fund offers all the standard services such as retirement account availability, automatic withdrawal, and automatic checking account deduction. Its minimum initial investment of $500 and minimum subsequent investment of $50 compare favorably with other funds.

The fund has been managed by John Calamos since its inception in 1990. His son, Nick, serves as comanager. The Calamos fund family includes only nine funds and allows shareholders to switch from fund to fund by telephone.

Top Ten Stock Holdings

1. QUALCOMM
2. VeriSign
3. Emulex Corp.
4. PMC-Sierra
5. Calpine Corp.

6. VISX
7. Andrx Corp.
8. Comverse Technology
9. Biogen
10. TriQuint Semiconductor

Fund inception: 1990
Asset mix: Common stocks, 92%; cash/equivalents, 8%
Total net assets: $60 million

Load

Front-end load	4.75%
Redemption fee (max.)	1.00%

Annual Fees

12b-1 fee	0.25%
Management fee	0.75
Other expenses	1.00
Total annual expense	2.00%

Minimum initial investment	$500
Minimum subsequent investment	$50

Services

Telephone exchanges	*Yes*
Automatic withdrawal	*Yes*
Automatic checking deduction	*Yes*
Retirement plan/IRA	*Yes*
Instant redemption	*Yes*
Portfolio manager (years)	10
Number of funds in family	9

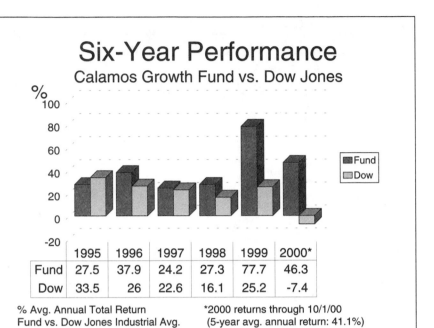

Six-Year Performance
Calamos Growth Fund vs. Dow Jones

	1995	1996	1997	1998	1999	2000*
Fund	27.5	37.9	24.2	27.3	77.7	46.3
Dow	33.5	26	22.6	16.1	25.2	-7.4

% Avg. Annual Total Return   *2000 returns through 10/1/00
Fund vs. Dow Jones Industrial Avg.   (5-year avg. annual return: 41.1%)

34
Franklin Strategic California Growth Fund

Franklin Strategic Funds
777 Mariners Island Boulevard, P.O. Box 7777
San Mateo, CA 94403-7777
800-342-5236
www.franklintempleton.com
Ticker symbol: **FKCGX**

Fund manager: Conrad B. Herrmann
Fund objective: Midcap growth

Performance	★ ★ ★ ★ ★
Consistency	★ ★ ★
Fees/Services/Management	★ ★ ★
Total	**11 Points**

I wish they all could be California . . . stocks. For those who want to cash in on California's booming business economy, this fund focuses on companies that are based in California or conduct most of their business there.

California's economy has outpaced the overall U.S. economy for five consecutive years. It is now considered the world's eighth largest economy.

The fund is packed with high-technology companies that got their start in California's Silicon Valley. Among its leading holdings are Cisco Systems, JDS Uniphase, Oracle, Xilinx, and Sun Microsystems. Most of the fund's holdings are midcap stocks, with market capitalizations of $1 billion to $10 billion.

Founded in 1991, the fund has posted an average annual return of about 27 percent since its inception. A $10,000 investment in the fund at its inception would now be worth about $67,000.

Electronics companies account for about 35 percent of the fund's total holdings, followed by technology services, which accounts for about 20 percent. Other leading sectors include financials, 9 percent; health technology, 9 percent; consumer services, 4 percent; and retail, 4 percent.

Fund manager Conrad Herrmann takes a fairly conservative trading approach, with a 53 percent annual portfolio turnover ratio. The fund generally stays about 90 percent invested in stocks.

PERFORMANCE

The fund has enjoyed outstanding growth over the past five years. Including dividends and capital gains distributions, the Franklin Strategic California Growth Fund has provided a load-adjusted average annual return the past five years (through late 2000) of 31.3 percent.

A $10,000 investment in 1995 would have grown to about $39,000 five years later.

CONSISTENCY

The fund has been very consistent, outperforming the Dow Jones Industrial Average three of the past five years through 1999 (and again through most of 2000). Its biggest gain came in 1999, when it moved up 95.2 percent (compared with a 25.2 percent rise in the Dow).

FEES/SERVICES/MANAGEMENT

The fund has a front-end load of 5.75 percent, with a maximum back-end load of 1 percent. The fund's total annual expense ratio of 1.0 percent (with a 0.25 percent 12b-1 fee) is a little lower than most funds.

The fund offers all the standard services such as retirement account availability, automatic withdrawal, and automatic checking account deduction. Its minimum initial investment of $1,000 and minimum subsequent investment of $50 are in line with other funds.

Conrad Herrmann has been managing the fund since 1993. The Franklin fund family includes more than 125 funds and allows shareholders to switch from fund to fund by telephone.

Top Ten Stock Holdings

1. JDS Uniphase
2. Cisco Systems
3. VERITAS Software
4. Applied Micro Circuits
5. Oracle Systems

6. Siebel Systems
7. Robert Half International
8. Sun Microsystems
9. Xilinx
10. Genentech

Fund inception: 1991
Asset mix: Common stocks, 91%; cash/equivalents, 9%
Total net assets: $3 billion

Load

Front-end load	5.75%
Redemption fee (max.)	1.00

Annual Fees

12b-1 fee	0.25%
Management fee	0.48
Other expenses	0.27
Total annual expense	1.00%
Minimum initial investment	$1,000
Minimum subsequent investment	$50

Services

Telephone exchanges	*Yes*
Automatic withdrawal	*Yes*
Automatic checking deduction	*Yes*
Retirement plan/IRA	*Yes*
Instant redemption	*Yes*
Portfolio manager (years)	7
Number of funds in family	over 125

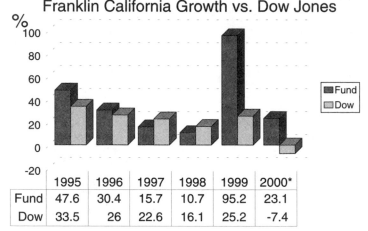

Six-Year Performance
Franklin California Growth vs. Dow Jones

	1995	1996	1997	1998	1999	2000*
Fund	47.6	30.4	15.7	10.7	95.2	23.1
Dow	33.5	26	22.6	16.1	25.2	-7.4

% Avg. Annual Total Return   *2000 returns through 10/1/00
Fund vs. Dow Jones Industrial Avg.   (5-year avg. annual return: 32.8%)

35

Dreyfus Founders Discovery Fund

Dreyfus Founders Funds
2930 East Third Avenue
Denver, CO 80206
800-645-6561
www.dreyfus.com
Ticker symbol: **FDISX**

Fund manager: Robert T. Ammann
Fund objective: Small-cap stocks

Performance	★ ★ ★ ★ ★
Consistency	★
Fees/Services/Management	★ ★ ★ ★ ★
Total	**11 Points**

While the upside potential of small-cap stocks can be exhilarating, the downside can be downright scary.

Despite the risks of banking on about 100 small-cap stocks, the Dreyfus Founders Discovery Fund has done very well over the long term. The fund has posted average annual returns of about 23 percent since its inception in 1990. A $10,000 investment in the fund ten years ago would now be worth about $78,000.

Fund manager Robert Ammann focuses on trying to uncover the hard-charging small growth companies that are headed for midcap and even large-cap success. As with every portfolio, a few of the stocks have failed to pan out, but many of his small-cap picks have been winners.

Ammann, who has managed the fund since 1997, tends to mine his picks from the technology sector, which represents about 36 percent of the portfolio. Few of the small-cap holdings have yet to achieve household-name status, but they have generated impressive earnings growth. Top holdings include such up-and-comers as Gentex Corporation, Digital Microwave, Harris Corporation, Quanta Services, and Veritas DGC.

Outside of the technology area, consumer cyclicals account for about 12 percent of the portfolio, and energy stocks make up about 5.5 percent.

Ammann is fairly aggressive in his management style, with a 157 percent annual portfolio turnover ratio. The fund stays 80 to 90 percent invested in stocks most of the time.

PERFORMANCE   ★ ★ ★ ★ ★

The fund has enjoyed outstanding growth over the past five years. Including dividends and capital gains distributions, the Dreyfus Founders Discovery Fund has provided an average annual return the past five years (through late 2000) of 32 percent.

A $10,000 investment in 1995 would have grown to about $40,000 five years later.

CONSISTENCY   ★

The fund has been very inconsistent, outperforming the Dow Jones Industrial Average only one of the five years through 1999 (and again through most of 2000). Its biggest gain came in 1999, when it moved up 94.6 percent (compared with a 25.2 percent rise in the Dow).

FEES/SERVICES/MANAGEMENT   ★ ★ ★ ★ ★

The fund is a pure no-load fund, with no fees to buy or sell shares. The fund's total annual expense ratio of 1.45 percent (with a 0.25 percent 12b-1 fee) is in line with other funds.

The fund offers all the standard services such as retirement account availability, automatic withdrawal, and automatic checking account deduction. Its minimum initial investment of $1,000 and minimum subsequent investment of $100 are in line with other funds.

The fund has been managed by Robert Ammann since 1997. The Dreyfus fund family includes more than 300 funds and allows shareholders to switch from fund to fund by telephone.

Top Ten Stock Holdings

1. Gentex Corp.
2. Veritas DGC
3. Harris Corp.
4. Quanta Services
5. National Oilwell
6. REMEC
7. Digital Microwave
8. EMCORE
9. SanDisk
10. Insight Enterprises

Fund inception: 1990
Asset mix: Common stocks, 89%; cash/equivalents, 11%
Total net assets: $187 million

Load

Front-end load	*None*
Redemption fee (max.)	*None*

Annual Fees

12b-1 fee	0.25%
Management fee	1.00
Other expenses	0.20
Total annual expense	1.45%

Minimum initial investment	$1,000
Minimum subsequent investment	$100

Services

Telephone exchanges	*Yes*
Automatic withdrawal	*Yes*
Automatic checking deduction	*Yes*
Retirement plan/IRA	*Yes*
Instant redemption	*Yes*
Portfolio manager (years)	3
Number of funds in family	over 300

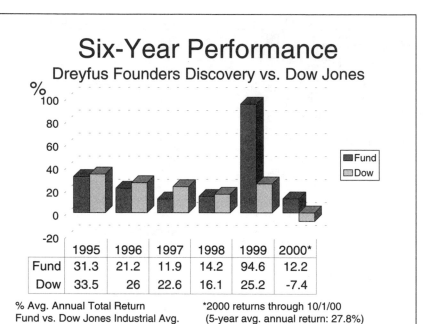

Six-Year Performance
Dreyfus Founders Discovery vs. Dow Jones

	1995	1996	1997	1998	1999	2000*
Fund	31.3	21.2	11.9	14.2	94.6	12.2
Dow	33.5	26	22.6	16.1	25.2	-7.4

% Avg. Annual Total Return   *2000 returns through 10/1/00
Fund vs. Dow Jones Industrial Avg.   (5-year avg. annual return: 27.8%)

36

Smith Barney
Aggressive Growth Fund

Smith Barney Funds
1981 North Broadway, Suite 325
Walnut Creek, CA 94596
800-451-2010
www.smithbarney.com
Ticker symbol: **SHRAX**

Fund manager: Richard Freeman
Fund objective: Aggressive growth

Performance	★ ★ ★ ★
Consistency	★ ★ ★ ★
Fees/Services/Management	★ ★ ★
Total	**11 Points**

Smith Barney Aggressive Growth Fund manager Richard Freeman packs the portfolio with small and midsized companies that stand to benefit from new products or services, technological developments, or changes in management.

The fund also invests in some larger-cap companies that are still on the fast track, such as Intel, Amgen, and Tyco International. But most are less familiar names, such as Adaptive Broadband, IDEC Pharmaceuticals, and Forest Labs.

"There are three criteria I look for in companies," says Freeman. "First, I look for firms with the potential for above-average growth; second, I look for companies whose managers may have meaningful equity stakes; third, I look for unrecognized values in the marketplace."

Freeman, who has been running the fund since its inception in 1983, takes a very conservative management approach, with just an 8 percent annual portfolio turnover ratio.

The fund has posted a 22 percent average annual increase over the past ten years. A $10,000 investment in the fund ten years ago would now be worth about $73,000.

The fund is heavily invested in health technology stocks, which make up about 33 percent of the $1.4 billion portfolio. Other leading sectors include electronics technology, 17 percent; technology services, 14 percent; computer services, 9 percent; and manufacturing, 8.5 percent.

The fund stays more than 90 percent invested in stocks under normal circumstances.

PERFORMANCE

The fund has enjoyed outstanding growth over the past five years. Including dividends and capital gains distributions, the Smith Barney Aggressive Growth Fund has provided a load-adjusted average annual return the past five years (through late 2000) of 29.9 percent.

A $10,000 investment in 1995 would have grown to about $37,000 five years later.

CONSISTENCY

The fund has been very consistent, outperforming the Dow Jones Industrial Average four of the past five years through 1999 (and again through most of 2000). Its biggest gain came in 1999, when it moved up 63.7 percent (compared with a 25.2 percent rise in the Dow).

FEES/SERVICES/MANAGEMENT

The fund has a front-end load of 5 percent, with a maximum back-end load of 1 percent. The fund's total annual expense ratio of 1.18 percent (with a 0.25 percent 12b-1 fee) is in line with other funds.

The fund offers all the standard services such as retirement account availability, automatic withdrawal, and automatic checking account deduction. Its minimum initial investment of $1,000 and minimum subsequent investment of $50 are in line with other funds.

The fund has been managed by Richard Freeman since its inception in 1983. The Smith Barney fund family includes more than 200 funds and allows shareholders to switch from fund to fund by telephone.

Top Ten Stock Holdings

1. Intel	6. Adaptive Broadband
2. Tyco International	7. IDEC Pharmaceuticals
3. Forest Labs	8. Amgen
4. America Online	9. Lehman Brother Holdings
5. Chiron	10. United Healthcare

Fund inception: 1983
Asset mix: Common stocks, 97%; cash/equivalents, 3%
Total net assets: $1.4 billion

Load

Front-end load	5.00%
Redemption fee (max.)	1.00

Annual Fees

12b-1 fee	0.25%
Management fee	0.80
Other expenses	0.13
Total annual expense	1.18%
Minimum initial investment	$1,000
Minimum subsequent investment	$50

Services

Telephone exchanges	*Yes*
Automatic withdrawal	*Yes*
Automatic checking deduction	*Yes*
Retirement plan/IRA	*Yes*
Instant redemption	*Yes*
Portfolio manager (years)	17
Number of funds in family	over 200

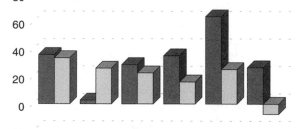

Six-Year Performance
Smith Barney Aggressive Growth vs. Dow Jones

	1995	1996	1997	1998	1999	2000*
Fund	35.8	2.7	28.6	35.1	63.7	26.6
Dow	33.5	26	22.6	16.1	25.2	-7.4

% Avg. Annual Total Return   *2000 returns through 10/1/00
Fund vs. Dow Jones Industrial Avg.   (5-year avg. annual return: 30.5%)

37

Fidelity Aggressive Growth Fund

Fidelity Funds
82 Devonshire Street
Boston, MA 02109
800-544-8544
www.fidelity.com
Ticker symbol: **FDEGX**

Fund manager: Robert Bertelson
Fund objective: Aggressive growth

Performance	★ ★ ★ ★
Consistency	★ ★ ★
Fees/Services/Management	★ ★ ★ ★
Total	**11 Points**

The Fidelity Aggressive Growth Fund invests in stocks that fund manager Robert Bertelson believes have the potential for accelerated earnings or revenue growth.

Most of the stocks in the portfolio are emerging technology companies, such as Nokia, Scientific-Atlanta, Nortel Networks, and Art Technology, although it does invest in some larger issues such as Cisco Systems and Texas Instruments.

Technology stocks account for about 59 percent of the fund's portfolio, followed by energy, 11 percent; health care, 10 percent; utilities, 6 percent; media and leisure, 3 percent; and durables, 3 percent.

Despite its size—with more than $20 billion in assets—the fund continues to perform like a young upstart. The fund was up 103.5 percent in 1999 following a 42.9 percent increase in 1998.

The fund's strong long-term returns have come at the cost of some short-term volatility, according to Bertelson. "Since we're often investing in the most rapidly growing companies within a sector, the stocks we own may be more volatile than for that industry overall, possibly resulting in much higher volatility than the average growth fund."

The fund management takes a fairly aggressive buy-and-sell approach, with a 186 percent annual turnover ratio. The fund stays more than 90 percent invested in stocks under normal circumstances.

PERFORMANCE

The fund has enjoyed outstanding growth over the past five years. Including dividends and capital gains distributions, the Fidelity Aggressive Growth Fund has provided an average annual return the past five years (through late 2000) of 29.7 percent.

A $10,000 investment in 1995 would have grown to about $37,000 five years later.

CONSISTENCY

The fund has been fairly consistent, outperforming the Dow Jones Industrial Average three of the past five years through 1999 (and was about even with the Dow through most of 2000). Its biggest gain came in 1999, when it moved up 103.5 percent (compared with a 25.2 percent rise in the Dow).

FEES/SERVICES/MANAGEMENT

The fund is a pure no-load fund, with no fees to buy or sell shares. The fund's total annual expense ratio of 0.97 percent (with no 12b-1 fee) compares favorably with other funds.

The fund offers all the standard services such as retirement account availability, automatic withdrawal, and automatic checking account deduction. Its minimum initial investment of $2,500 and minimum subsequent investment of $250 are a little high compared with other funds.

Robert Bertelsen took over management of the fund in 2000. The Fidelity fund family includes more than 300 funds and allows shareholders to switch from fund to fund by telephone.

Top Ten Stock Holdings

1. Cisco Systems	6. Amgen
2. Vodafone AirTouch	7. Dell Computer
3. Microsoft	8. Brocade Communications
4. Motorola	9. Exodus Communications
5. Ericsson Tel 'B'	10. Texas Instruments

Fund inception: 1991
Asset mix: Common stocks, 97%; cash/equivalents, 3%
Total net assets: $21 billion

Load

Front-end load	*None*
Redemption fee (max.)	*None*

Annual Fees

12b-1 fee	*None*
Management fee	0.72%
Other expenses	0.25
Total annual expense	0.97%
Minimum initial investment	$2,500
Minimum subsequent investment	$250

Services

Telephone exchanges	*Yes*
Automatic withdrawal	*Yes*
Automatic checking deduction	*Yes*
Retirement plan/IRA	*Yes*
Instant redemption	*Yes*
Portfolio manager (years)	1
Number of funds in family	over 300

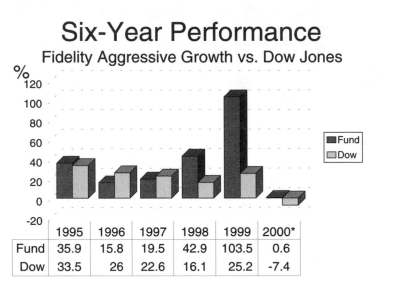

Six-Year Performance
Fidelity Aggressive Growth vs. Dow Jones

	1995	1996	1997	1998	1999	2000*
Fund	35.9	15.8	19.5	42.9	103.5	0.6
Dow	33.5	26	22.6	16.1	25.2	-7.4

% Avg. Annual Total Return   *2000 returns through 10/1/00
Fund vs. Dow Jones Industrial Avg.   (5-year avg. annual return: 30.2%)

IPS Millennium Fund

IPS Funds
625 South Gay Street
Knoxville, TN 37902
800-249-6927
www.ipsfunds.com
Ticker symbol: **IPSMX**

Fund managers: Robert Loest and Greg D'Amico
Fund objective: Aggressive growth

Performance	★ ★ ★ ★ ★
Consistency	★ ★
Fees/Services/Management	★ ★ ★ ★
Total	**11 Points**

Investors who bought shares of the IPS Millennium Fund when it was launched in 1995 would have nearly quintupled their money by the dawn of the new millennium. The handsome return on investment comes with a price, however.

Robert Loest, who has managed the 100-stock portfolio since its inception, and comanager Greg D'Amico warn investors that owning this fund can make for a wild ride, because it is heavy into the sometimes volatile technology stocks. Then again, no pain, no gain.

One of their current favorites from the technology sector is Kopin, which makes wafers for the communications industry for use in semiconductors. The company also makes high-resolution, full-color displays to browse the Internet with a cell phone or Internet appliance. Other top technology holdings include SanDisk, JDS Uniphase, Broadcom, and Cisco Systems.

Technology stocks make up about 36 percent of the portfolio, followed by utilities at 23 percent, capital goods at 16 percent, and communications services at 13 percent.

Loest prefers to buy and hold his large-cap growth stocks. The annual portfolio turnover rate is only 52 percent. The fund stays at least 90 percent invested in stocks under normal circumstances.

PERFORMANCE

The fund has enjoyed exceptional growth over the past five years. Including dividends and capital gains distributions, the IPS Millennium Fund has provided an average annual return the past five years (through late 2000) of 39 percent.

A $10,000 investment in 1995 would have grown to about $52,000 five years later.

CONSISTENCY

The fund has been fairly inconsistent, outperforming the Dow Jones Industrial Average only two of the past five years through 1999 (and again through most of 2000). Its biggest gain came in 1999, when it moved up 119.8 percent (compared with a 25.2 percent rise in the Dow).

FEES/SERVICES/MANAGEMENT

The fund is a pure no-load fund, with no fees to buy or sell shares. The fund's total annual expense ratio of 1.39 percent (with no 12b-1 fee) is in line with other funds.

The fund offers all the standard services such as retirement account availability, automatic withdrawal, and automatic checking account deduction. Its minimum initial investment of $2,500 and minimum subsequent investment of $100 are a little higher than most other funds.

Robert Loest, who manages the fund with Greg D'Amico, has been the fund manager since its inception in 1995. The IPS fund family includes only two funds.

Top Ten Stock Holdings

1. SanDisk
2. JDS Uniphase
3. Broadcom
4. Calpine
5. Duke Energy

6. Cisco Systems
7. Micromuse
8. WebMethods
9. RF Micro Devices
10. AES Corp.

Fund inception: 1995
Asset mix: Common stocks, 93%; cash/equivalents, 7%
Total net assets: $482 million

Load

Front-end load	*None*
Redemption fee (max.)	*None*

Annual Fees

12b-1 fee	*None*
Management fee	1.39%
Other expenses	0.00
Total annual expense	1.39%

Minimum initial investment	$2,500
Minimum subsequent investment	$100

Services

Telephone exchanges	*Yes*
Automatic withdrawal	*Yes*
Automatic checking deduction	*Yes*
Retirement plan/IRA	*Yes*
Instant redemption	*Yes*
Portfolio manager (years)	5
Number of funds in family	2

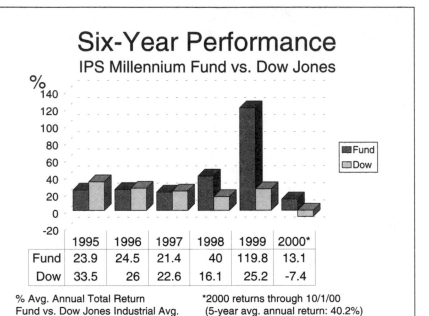

Six-Year Performance
IPS Millennium Fund vs. Dow Jones

	1995	1996	1997	1998	1999	2000*
Fund	23.9	24.5	21.4	40	119.8	13.1
Dow	33.5	26	22.6	16.1	25.2	-7.4

% Avg. Annual Total Return   *2000 returns through 10/1/00
Fund vs. Dow Jones Industrial Avg.   (5-year avg. annual return: 40.2%)

39

Fidelity OTC Portfolio Fund

Fidelity Funds
82 Devonshire Street
Boston, MA 02109
800-544-8544
www.fidelity.com
Ticker symbol: **FOCPX**

Fund manager: Jason Weiner
Fund objective: Large-cap growth

Performance	★ ★ ★ ★
Consistency	★ ★ ★
Fees/Services/Management	★ ★ ★ ★
Total	**11 Points**

The name may imply that this fund is packed with small, emerging over-the-counter stocks, but the Fidelity OTC Portfolio has plenty of bigger blue chip companies on the roster. Among its top holdings are Microsoft, Intel, Cisco Systems, Dell Computer, and Sun Microsystems.

Technology stocks dominate the portfolio, constituting about 80 percent of total assets. Utilities make up about 12 percent; media and leisure, about 3 percent; and health care, about 3 percent. The fund stays at least 90 percent invested in stocks under normal circumstances.

Normally, the fund invests at least 65 percent in stocks that are traded on the over-the-counter market. But with $15 billion in assets, the fund also has to park some of its money in larger stocks. In all, the fund holds about 100 stocks.

The fund, which has been around since 1985, has had an impressive decade. It has posted a 23 percent average annual return the past ten years. A $10,000 investment in the fund ten years ago would now be worth about $79,000.

The fund managers have been fairly aggressive in managing the fund, with a 117 percent annual turnover ratio.

PERFORMANCE

The fund has enjoyed outstanding growth over the past five years. Including dividends and capital gains distributions, the Fidelity OTC Portfolio has provided an average annual return the past five years (through late 2000) of 28.5 percent.

A $10,000 investment in 1995 would have grown to about $35,000 five years later.

CONSISTENCY

The fund has been fairly consistent, outperforming the Dow Jones Industrial Average three of the past five years through 1999 (and again through most of 2000). Its biggest gain came in 1999, when it moved up 72.5 percent (compared with a 25.2 percent rise in the Dow).

FEES/SERVICES/MANAGEMENT

The fund is a pure no-load fund, with no fees to buy or sell shares. The fund's total annual expense ratio of 0.74 percent (with no 12b-1 fee) compares favorably with other funds.

The fund offers all the standard services such as retirement account availability, automatic withdrawal, and automatic checking account deduction. Its minimum initial investment of $2,500 and minimum subsequent investment of $250 are a little high compared with other funds.

Jason Weiner took over management of the fund in 2000. The Fidelity fund family includes more than 300 funds and allows shareholders to switch from fund to fund by telephone.

Top Ten Stock Holdings

1. Cisco Systems
2. Microsoft
3. Intel
4. Sun Microsystems
5. Nortel Networks

6. Dell Computer
7. Sprint
8. Palm
9. BEA Systems
10. Ariba

Fund inception: 1985
Asset mix: Common stocks, 94%; cash/equivalents, 6%
Total net assets: $15 billion

Load

Front-end load	*None*
Redemption fee (max.)	*None*

Annual Fees

12b-1 fee	*None*
Management fee	0.50%
Other expenses	0.24
Total annual expense	0.74%
Minimum initial investment	$2,500
Minimum subsequent investment	$250

Services

Telephone exchanges	*Yes*
Automatic withdrawal	*Yes*
Automatic checking deduction	*Yes*
Retirement plan/IRA	*Yes*
Instant redemption	*Yes*
Portfolio manager (years)	1
Number of funds in family	over 300

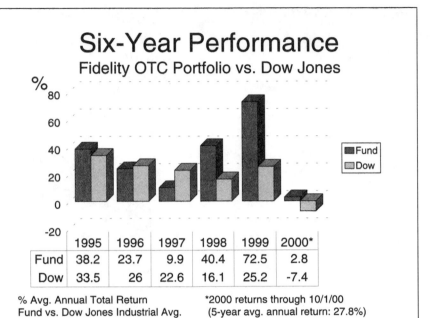

Six-Year Performance
Fidelity OTC Portfolio vs. Dow Jones

	1995	1996	1997	1998	1999	2000*
Fund	38.2	23.7	9.9	40.4	72.5	2.8
Dow	33.5	26	22.6	16.1	25.2	-7.4

% Avg. Annual Total Return   *2000 returns through 10/1/00
Fund vs. Dow Jones Industrial Avg.   (5-year avg. annual return: 27.8%)

Alger Retirement Fund: MidCap Growth

Alger Funds
4101 Pauger Street
New Orleans, LA 70122
800-992-3362
www.algerfunds.com
Ticker symbol: **ALMRX**

Fund managers: David Alger, Seilai Khoo, and Ronald Tartaro
Fund objective: Long-term growth

Performance	★ ★ ★
Consistency	★ ★ ★
Fees/Services/Management	★ ★ ★ ★ ★
Total	**11 Points**

The Alger MidCap Growth Retirement Fund invests in companies that fund founder David Alger and his team believe are destined for bigger things. Among the fund's leading holdings are such companies as Linear Technology, Waters, Forest Labs, and Teradyne—young companies that are still growing at a strong pace.

Alger, who prefers stocks "from the fastest-growing companies in America," has invested heavily in technology stocks, although retailer Best Buy and restaurant chains Outback Steakhouse and Starbucks are also among the top ten holdings.

Alger says he particularly likes "high unit growth companies," companies that sell products or services at a higher and higher rate every year. "Usually, this is the kind of company that has an imaginative and creative management, has a great product flow, is in a rapidly growing industry, or is a very creative company in a slower growing industry," explains Alger.

Technology stocks account for about 49 percent of the fund's total assets, followed by consumer cyclicals, 10 percent; energy, 8 percent; health care, 7 percent; consumer staples, 7 percent; capital goods, 4 percent; financials, 3 percent; and transportation, 3 percent. Cash and equivalents account for about 9 percent.

The fund's primary objective is long-term capital appreciation. It has about 60 issues.

The fund, created in 1993, stays at least 90 percent invested in stocks most of the time. The fund managers take an aggressive approach, with a 165 percent annual portfolio turnover ratio.

PERFORMANCE

The fund has enjoyed strong growth over the past five years. Including dividends and capital gains distributions, the Alger MidCap Growth Retirement Fund has provided an average annual return the past five years (through late 2000) of 27.3 percent.

A $10,000 investment in 1995 would have grown to about $34,000 five years later.

CONSISTENCY

The fund has been fairly consistent, outperforming the Dow Jones Industrial Average three of the past five years through 1999 (and again through most of 2000). Its biggest gain came in 1995, when it moved up 51.9 percent (compared with a 33.5 percent rise in the Dow).

FEES/SERVICES/MANAGEMENT

The fund is a true no-load fund, with no fees to buy or sell shares. It has an annual expense ratio of 1.23 percent (with no 12b-1 fee), which compares favorably with other funds.

The fund offers all the standard services such as retirement account availability, automatic withdrawal, and automatic checking account deduction. Its minimum initial investment of $1 and minimum subsequent investment of $25 compares very favorably with other funds.

The fund has been managed since its inception by David Alger, who runs the fund along with comanagers Seilai Khoo and Ronald Tartaro. The Alger fund family includes 21 funds and allows shareholders to switch from fund to fund by telephone.

Top Ten Stock Holdings

1. Best Buy	6. Microchip Technology
2. Waters Corp.	7. Kansas City South Industries
3. Outback Steakhouse	8. Teradyne
4. Altera Corp.	9. Linear Technology
5. Forest Labs	10. Starbucks

Fund inception: 1993
Asset mix: Common stocks, 94%; cash/equivalents, 6%
Total net assets: $114 million

Load

Front-end load	*None*
Redemption fee (max.)	*None*

Annual Fees

12b-1 fee	*None*
Management fee	0.80%
Other expenses	0.43
Total annual expense	1.23%

Minimum initial investment	$1
Minimum subsequent investment	$25

Services

Telephone exchanges	*Yes*
Automatic withdrawal	*Yes*
Automatic checking deduction	*Yes*
Retirement plan/IRA	*Yes*
Instant redemption	*Yes*
Portfolio manager (years)	7
Number of funds in family	21

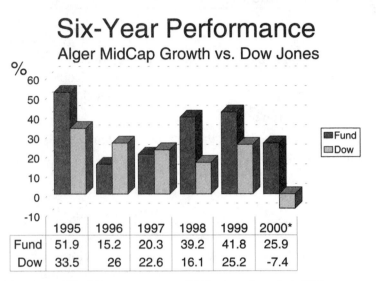

Six-Year Performance
Alger MidCap Growth vs. Dow Jones

	1995	1996	1997	1998	1999	2000*
Fund	51.9	15.2	20.3	39.2	41.8	25.9
Dow	33.5	26	22.6	16.1	25.2	-7.4

% Avg. Annual Total Return   *2000 returns through 10/1/00
Fund vs. Dow Jones Industrial Avg.   (5-year avg. annual return: 22%)

Meridian Value Fund

Meridian Funds
60 East Sir Francis Drake Boulevard
Wood Island, Suite 306
Larkspur, CA 94939
800-446-6662
Ticker symbol: **MVALX**

Fund manager: Richard Aster
Fund objective: Small-cap stocks

Performance	★ ★ ★
Consistency	★ ★ ★
Fees/Services/Management	★ ★ ★ ★ ★
Total	**11 Points**

Meridian Value Fund manager Richard Aster has a keen eye for a relatively few small-cap companies on the way up that are drawn from a diverse mix of industries.

While a number of small-cap funds rely almost exclusively on the technology sector, the Meridian Value Fund taps that sector for less than a quarter of its 42-stock portfolio. Aster, who has directed the fund since its 1994 inception, selects an almost equal number of stocks from the industrial sector. Independent oil and gas companies like Burlington Resources or Tom Brown play prominent roles in the portfolio with 2.7 percent and 2.5 percent of the total, respectively.

From the tech sector, Aster has selected electronics distributors Arrow and Avnet. From the financial sector, the fund features the stock of PartnerRe Ltd., a reinsurer of insurance companies. All told, technology stocks and industrial stocks each account for about 23 percent of the portfolio, followed by health care stocks, 13.5 percent, and financial services, 7.5 percent.

Aster is particularly interested in stocks that are undervalued relative to their long-term earning power and asset value because of market conditions, tax-loss selling, and other conditions. The $100 million fund has a portfolio turnover ratio of 124 percent. The fund stays at least 80 percent invested in stocks under normal circumstances.

PERFORMANCE

The fund has enjoyed strong growth over the past five years. Including dividends and capital gains distributions, the Meridian Value Fund has provided an average annual return the past five years (through late 2000) of 27.2 percent.

A $10,000 investment in 1995 would have grown to about $33,000 five years later.

CONSISTENCY

The fund has been fairly consistent, outperforming the Dow Jones Industrial Average three of the past five years through 1999 (and again through most of 2000). Its biggest gain came in 1999, when it moved up 38.3 percent (compared with a 25.2 percent rise in the Dow).

FEES/SERVICES/MANAGEMENT

The fund is a pure no-load fund, with no fees to buy or sell shares. The fund's total annual expense ratio of 1.63 percent (with no 12b-1 fee) is in line with other funds.

The fund offers all the standard services such as retirement account availability, automatic withdrawal, and automatic checking account deduction. Its minimum initial investment of $1,000 and minimum subsequent investment of $50 are in line with other funds.

The fund has been managed by Richard Aster since its inception in 1994. The Meridian Value Fund is one of just two Meridian funds.

Top Ten Stock Holdings

1. Arrow Electronics
2. PartnerRe
3. Burlington Resources
4. Lincare Holdings
5. REMEC

6. Belden
7. Tom Brown
8. Avnet
9. Thermo Electron
10. Healthcare Realty

Fund inception: 1994
Asset mix: Common stocks, 83%; cash/equivalents, 17%
Total net assets: $100 million

Load

Front-end load	*None*
Redemption fee (max.)	*None*

Annual Fees

12b-1 fee	*None*
Management fee	1.00%
Other expenses	0.63
Total annual expense	1.63%

Minimum initial investment	$1,000
Minimum subsequent investment	$50

Services

Telephone exchanges	*Yes*
Automatic withdrawal	*Yes*
Automatic checking deduction	*Yes*
Retirement plan/IRA	*Yes*
Instant redemption	*Yes*
Portfolio manager (years)	6
Number of funds in family	2

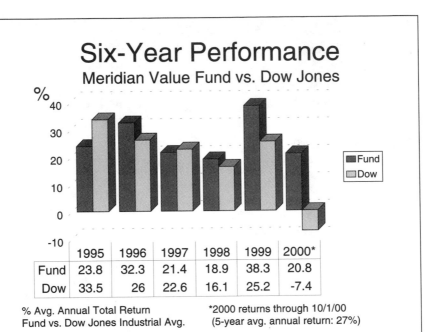

	1995	1996	1997	1998	1999	2000*
Fund	23.8	32.3	21.4	18.9	38.3	20.8
Dow	33.5	26	22.6	16.1	25.2	-7.4

% Avg. Annual Total Return   *2000 returns through 10/1/00
Fund vs. Dow Jones Industrial Avg.   (5-year avg. annual return: 27%)

Fidelity Dividend Growth Fund

Fidelity Funds
82 Devonshire Street
Boston, MA 02109
800-544-8544
www.fidelity.com
Ticker symbol: **FDGFX**

Fund manager: Charles Mangum
Fund objective: Growth and income

Performance	★ ★
Consistency	★ ★ ★ ★
Fees/Services/Management	★ ★ ★ ★ ★
Total	**11 Points**

For investors who want some cash with their capital gains, the Fidelity Dividend Growth Fund fits the bill. The fund invests at least 65 percent of its total assets in companies with growing dividends. Most of the stocks are established blue chip stocks with strong growth records, such as Cardinal Health, Schering-Plough, Eli Lilly, General Electric, and Conoco.

The $10 billion fund is broadly diversified. Technology stocks account for about 26 percent of the portfolio, followed by finance, 18 percent; health care, 17 percent; industrial machinery and equipment, 7 percent; energy, 7 percent; utilities, 5 percent; retail and wholesale, 5 percent; and media and leisure, 4 percent.

Fund manager Charles Mangum is fairly aggressive in managing the fund, with a 104 percent annual portfolio turnover ratio. The fund stays at least 90 percent invested in stocks under most circumstances. Mangum structures the portfolio with both value and growth stocks, selecting stocks based on growth potential, earnings estimates, and management.

Launched in 1993, the fund has averaged a 23.3 percent annual return. There are about 140 stocks in the portfolio.

PERFORMANCE

The fund has enjoyed strong growth over the past five years. Including dividends and capital gains distributions, the Fidelity Dividend Growth Fund has provided an average annual return the past five years (through late 2000) of 24.1 percent.

A $10,000 investment in 1995 would have grown to about $29,000 five years later.

CONSISTENCY

The fund has been very consistent, outperforming the Dow Jones Industrial Average four of the past five years through 1999 (and again through most of 2000). Its biggest gain came in 1995, when it moved up 37.5 percent (compared with a 33.5 percent rise in the Dow).

FEES/SERVICES/MANAGEMENT

The fund is a pure no-load fund, with no fees to buy or sell shares. The fund's total annual expense ratio of 0.84 percent (with no 12b-1 fee) compares very favorably with other funds.

The fund offers all the standard services such as retirement account availability, automatic withdrawal, and automatic checking account deduction. Its minimum initial investment of $2,500 and minimum subsequent investment of $250 are a little high compared with other funds.

Charles Mangum has managed the fund since 1997. The Fidelity fund family includes more than 300 funds and allows shareholders to switch from fund to fund by telephone.

Top Ten Stock Holdings

1. Cardinal Health
2. Comerica
3. Federal National Mortgage
4. Schering-Plough
5. General Electric
6. Microsoft
7. SBC Communications
8. Abbott Laboratories
9. Cisco Systems
10. Eli Lilly

Fund inception: 1993
Asset mix: Common stocks, 96%; cash/equivalents, 4%
Total net assets: $10 billion

Load

Front-end load	*None*
Redemption fee (max.)	*None*

Annual Fees

12b-1 fee	*None*
Management fee	0.65%
Other expenses	0.19
Total annual expense	0.84%
Minimum initial investment	$2,500
Minimum subsequent investment	$250

Services

Telephone exchanges	*Yes*
Automatic withdrawal	*Yes*
Automatic checking deduction	*Yes*
Retirement plan/IRA	*Yes*
Instant redemption	*Yes*
Portfolio manager (years)	3
Number of funds in family	over 300

Six-Year Performance
Fidelity Dividend Growth vs. Dow Jones

	1995	1996	1997	1998	1999	2000*
Fund	37.5	30.1	27.9	35.9	8.8	11.5
Dow	33.5	26	22.6	16.1	25.2	-7.4

% Avg. Annual Total Return
Fund vs. Dow Jones Industrial Avg.

*2000 returns through 10/1/00
(5-year avg. annual return: 23.1%)

43
Galaxy Equity Growth Fund/Trust

Galaxy Funds
4400 Computer Drive
P.O. Box 5108
Westborough, MA 01581-5108
800-299-7429
www.galaxyfunds.com
Ticker symbol: **GEGTX**

Fund manager: Robert Armknecht
Fund objective: Long-term growth

Performance	★ ★
Consistency	★ ★ ★ ★
Fees/Services/Management	★ ★ ★ ★ ★
Total	**11 Points**

Fund manager Robert Armknecht plays both sides of the stock-picking game, selecting a blend of value stocks and growth stocks for the Galaxy Equity Growth Fund/Trust. The concept has worked well for investors interested in steady, consistent returns. Although the fund has not posted any years of spectacular growth, it has done well enough to top the Dow Jones Industrial Average four of the past five years.

The fund has posted a 19 percent average annual gain since its inception in 1990. A $10,000 investment at that time would now be worth about $55,000.

The fund invests in a broad range of industries, although technology stocks constitute the largest share of the portfolio. The top holdings include both familiar old economy stocks, such as General Electric, Atlantic Richfield, Citigroup, and Texas Instruments, and emerging new economy stocks, such as Teradyne, Maxim Integrated Products, and EMC.

The $1.2 billion fund stays nearly 100 percent invested in stocks under most circumstances. Technology stocks make up about 32 percent of the portfolio, followed by consumer staples, 17 percent; consumer cyclicals, 11 percent; energy, 11 percent; capital goods, 10 percent; finance, 10 percent; and utilities, 5 percent.

Armknecht takes a fairly conservative approach in managing the fund, with a 53 percent annual portfolio turnover ratio.

PERFORMANCE

The fund has enjoyed solid growth over the past five years. Including dividends and capital gains distributions, the Galaxy Equity Growth Fund/Trust has provided an average annual return the past five years (through late 2000) of 23.8 percent.

A $10,000 investment in 1995 would have grown to about $29,000 five years later.

CONSISTENCY

The fund has been fairly consistent, outperforming the Dow Jones Industrial Average four of the past five years through 1999 (and again through most of 2000). Its biggest gain came in 1995, when it moved up 34.3 percent (compared with a 33.5 percent rise in the Dow).

FEES/SERVICES/MANAGEMENT

The fund is a pure no-load fund, with no fees to buy or sell shares. The fund's total annual expense ratio of 0.94 percent (with no 12b-1 fee) compares very favorably with other funds.

The fund offers all the standard services such as retirement account availability, automatic withdrawal, and automatic checking account deduction. Its minimum initial investment of $1 and minimum subsequent investment of $1 is very low compared with other funds.

The fund has been managed by Robert Armknecht since its inception in 1990. The Galaxy fund family includes more than 40 funds and allows shareholders to switch from fund to fund by telephone.

Top Ten Stock Holdings

1. General Electric
2. Atlantic Richfield
3. Tyco International
4. EchoStar Communications
5. Cisco Systems
6. Maxim Integrated Products
7. Citigroup
8. Teradyne
9. EMC
10. Texas Instruments

Fund inception: 1990
Asset mix: Common stocks, 98%; cash/equivalents, 2%
Total net assets: $1.2 billion

Load

Front-end load	*None*
Redemption fee (max.)	*None*

Annual Fees

12b-1 fee	*None*
Management fee	0.75%
Other expenses	0.19
Total annual expense	0.94%
Minimum initial investment	$1
Minimum subsequent investment	$1

Services

Telephone exchanges	*Yes*
Automatic withdrawal	*Yes*
Automatic checking deduction	*Yes*
Retirement plan/IRA	*Yes*
Instant redemption	*Yes*
Portfolio manager (years)	10
Number of funds in family	over 40

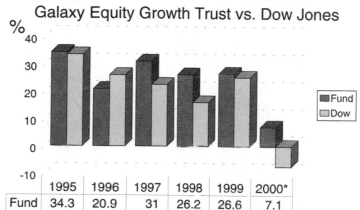

Six-Year Performance
Galaxy Equity Growth Trust vs. Dow Jones

	1995	1996	1997	1998	1999	2000*
Fund	34.3	20.9	31	26.2	26.6	7.1
Dow	33.5	26	22.6	16.1	25.2	-7.4

% Avg. Annual Total Return
Fund vs. Dow Jones Industrial Avg.

*2000 returns through 10/1/00
(5-year avg. annual return: 22.9%)

44

PIMCO Innovation Fund

PIMCO Funds
840 Newport Center Drive, Suite 360
Newport Beach, CA 92660
800-426-0107
www.pimcofunds.com
Ticker symbol: **PIVAX**

Fund manager: Dennis McKechnie
Fund objective: Aggressive growth

Performance	★ ★ ★ ★ ★
Consistency	★ ★ ★
Fees/Services/Management	★ ★ ★
Total	**11 Points**

Although technology stocks took their lumps throughout most of 2000, the manager of the PIMCO Innovation Fund remains supremely confident of its future performance.

Dennis McKechnie, who has managed the fund since 1998, believes that the earnings of technology stocks will be five to ten times higher than the broad economy over the next several years. That explains why technology stocks dominate the $1.4 billion portfolio. The fund, whose goal is capital appreciation, was established in 1994. Its portfolio consists of about 50 stocks.

McKechnie is particularly high on Internet infrastructure stocks such as JDS Uniphase, whose stock makes up 3.4 percent of the total portfolio. Other leading holdings from the networking sector include Juniper Networks, Redback Networks, and TIBCO. The fund also has large investments in other Internet and high-tech stocks, including Cisco Systems, Exodus, Intel, and Nokia.

In addition to its technology holdings, which account for more than two-thirds of the fund's assets, the fund also invests heavily in consumer cyclicals, which account for about 22 percent of the portfolio.

McKechnie is fairly aggressive in his management approach, with a 119 percent annual portfolio turnover ratio. The fund stays almost 100 percent invested in stocks most of the time.

The fund's formula for success has been working wonders. The fund has moved up 47.5 percent per year since its inception in 1994.

PERFORMANCE

The fund has enjoyed phenomenal growth over the past five years. Including dividends and capital gains distributions, the PIMCO Innovation Fund has provided a load-adjusted average annual return the past five years (through late 2000) of 44.5 percent.

A $10,000 investment in 1995 would have grown to about $63,000 five years later.

CONSISTENCY

The fund has been very consistent, outperforming the Dow Jones Industrial Average three of the past five years through 1999 (and again through most of 2000). Its biggest gain came in 1999, when it moved up 139.4 percent (compared with a 25.2 percent rise in the Dow).

FEES/SERVICES/MANAGEMENT

The fund has a front-end load of 5.5 percent, with a maximum back-end load of 1 percent. The fund's total annual expense ratio of 1.30 percent (with a 0.25 percent 12b-1 fee) is in line with other funds.

The fund offers all the standard services such as retirement account availability, automatic withdrawal, and automatic checking account deduction. Its minimum initial investment of $2,500 and minimum subsequent investment of $100 are a little high compared with other funds.

The fund has been managed by Dennis McKechnie only since 1998. The PIMCO fund family includes more than 40 funds and allows shareholders to switch from fund to fund by telephone.

Top Ten Stock Holdings

1. Cisco Systems
2. Nokia
3. Juniper Networks
4. Applied Materials
5. Siebel Systems

6. QUALCOMM
7. Sun Microsystems
8. Ketel One Spirits
9. Exodus Communications
10. Corona

Fund inception: 1994
Asset mix: Common stocks, 98%; cash/equivalents, 2%
Total net assets: $1.4 billion

Load

Front-end load	5.50%
Redemption fee (max.)	1.00

Annual Fees

12b-1 fee	0.25%
Management fee	0.65
Other expenses	0.40
Total annual expense	1.30%

Minimum initial investment	$2,500
Minimum subsequent investment	$100

Services

Telephone exchanges	*Yes*
Automatic withdrawal	*Yes*
Automatic checking deduction	*Yes*
Retirement plan/IRA	*Yes*
Instant redemption	*Yes*
Portfolio manager (years)	2
Number of funds in family	45

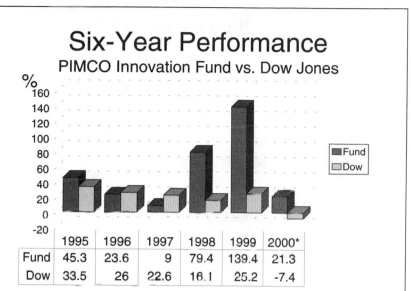

Six-Year Performance
PIMCO Innovation Fund vs. Dow Jones

	1995	1996	1997	1998	1999	2000*
Fund	45.3	23.6	9	79.4	139.4	21.3
Dow	33.5	26	22.6	16.1	25.2	-7.4

% Avg. Annual Total Return
Fund vs. Dow Jones Industrial Avg.

*2000 returns through 10/1/00
(5-year avg. annual return: 47.2%)

45

Alliance Premier Growth Fund

Alliance Funds
1345 Avenue of the Americas
New York, NY 10105
800-824-1916
www.alliancecapital.com
Ticker symbol: **APGAX**

Fund manager: Alfred Harrison
Fund objective: Long-term growth

Performance	★ ★ ★ ★
Consistency	★ ★ ★ ★
Fees/Services/Management	★ ★ ★
Total	**11 Points**

The Alliance Premier Growth Fund loads up on some of America's premier growth stocks. Cisco Systems, Home Depot, Pfizer, Intel, and Nortel Networks are all among its leading holdings. It is targeted to investors who want a stake in some of the leading blue chip growth stocks.

Fund manager Al Harrison combines fundamental research on a company-by-company basis with occasional trading of core portfolio positions to give the fund an edge in the market. He selects the portfolio from a pool of 500 large-cap stocks. His favored 25 holdings make up about two-thirds of the $6 billion portfolio.

Harrison, who has been running the fund since its inception in 1992, sometimes adds and trims core positions based on market weaknesses and strengths and on his assessment of the optimal price range for each stock.

He has been modestly active in his investment approach, with a 75 percent annual portfolio turnover ratio. The fund remains almost 100 percent invested in stocks under normal circumstances.

The fund is heavily weighted in technology stocks, which make up about 40 percent of the portfolio. Other leading sectors include consumer services, 27 percent; finance, 13 percent; health care, 6 percent; and energy, 4 percent.

PERFORMANCE

The fund has enjoyed very strong growth over the past five years. Including dividends and capital gains distributions, the Alliance Premier Growth Fund has provided a load-adjusted average annual return the past five years (through late 2000) of 28.6 percent.

A $10,000 investment in 1995 would have grown to about $35,500 five years later.

CONSISTENCY

The fund has been very consistent, outperforming the Dow Jones Industrial Average four of the past five years through 1999 (and again through most of 2000). Its biggest gain came in 1998, when it moved up 49.3 percent (compared with a 16.1 percent rise in the Dow).

FEES/SERVICES/MANAGEMENT

The fund has a front-end load of 4.25 percent, with a maximum back-end load of 1 percent. The fund's total annual expense ratio of 1.50 percent (with a 0.50 percent 12b-1 fee) is in line with other funds.

The fund offers all the standard services such as retirement account availability, automatic withdrawal, and automatic checking account deduction. Its minimum initial investment of $250 and minimum subsequent investment of $50 compare very favorably with other funds.

Alfred Harrison has managed the fund since its inception in 1992. The Alliance fund family includes 52 funds and allows shareholders to switch from fund to fund by telephone.

46
Van Kampen Emerging Growth Fund

Van Kampen Funds
1 Parkview Plaza
Oakbrook Terrace, IL 60181
800-421-5666
www.vankampen.com
Ticker symbol: **ACEGX**

Fund managers: Gary Lewis, Janet Luby, David Walker, and
Dudley Brickhouse
Fund objective: Aggressive growth

Performance	★ ★ ★ ★ ★
Consistency	★ ★ ★
Fees/Services/Management	★ ★ ★
Total	**11 Points**

As its name suggests, the Van Kampen Emerging Growth Fund gets in on the ground floor of midcap stocks whose trajectories are heading skyward.

The fund management team relies heavily on the technology sector for the midcap growth stocks that are the heart of this successful fund. Leading holdings include JDS Uniphase, VERITAS Software, Broadcom, LSI Logic, and EchoStar Communications—all of which are stars of the new economy.

Technology stocks make up nearly 70 percent of the 92-stock portfolio. The next largest sector is consumer cyclicals at about 5 percent.

The fund managers are willing to pay a premium for some of the U.S. and Canadian stocks that dominate the $10 billion fund when they're confident they will produce heady results. The fund's price-earnings ratio is a relatively high 40. Although tech-heavy funds can sometimes be volatile in the short term, this fund has produced spectacular results over the long run.

A $10,000 investment in the fund ten years ago would now be worth about $115,000—a 27.5 percent average annual return. The fund was opened in 1970.

The fund is aggressively managed, with an annual portfolio turnover ratio of 124 percent. The fund stays at least 90 percent invested in stocks under normal circumstances.

PERFORMANCE

The fund has enjoyed exceptional growth over the past five years. Including dividends and capital gains distributions, the Van Kampen Emerging Growth Fund has provided a load-adjusted average annual return the past five years (through late 2000) of 35.9 percent.

A $10,000 investment in 1995 would have grown to about $46,500 five years later.

CONSISTENCY

The fund has been fairly consistent, outperforming the Dow Jones Industrial Average three of the past five years through 1999 (and again through most of 2000). Its biggest gain came in 1999, when it moved up 103.7 percent (compared with a 25.2 percent rise in the Dow).

FEES/SERVICES/MANAGEMENT

The fund has a front-end load of 5.75 percent, with a maximum back-end load of 1 percent. The fund's total annual expense ratio of 0.97 percent (with a 0.25 percent 12b-1 fee) compares well with other funds.

The fund offers all the standard services such as retirement account availability, automatic withdrawal, and automatic checking account deduction. Its minimum initial investment of $1,000 and minimum subsequent investment of $25 are in line with other funds.

Gary Lewis, who manages the fund along with Janet Luby, David Walker, and Dudley Brickhouse, has been with the fund since 1989. The Van Kampen fund family includes more than 50 funds and allows shareholders to switch from fund to fund by telephone.

Top Ten Stock Holdings

1. JDS Uniphase
2. VERITAS Software
3. Network Appliance
4. Broadcom
5. EchoStar Communications

6. Analog Devices
7. Corning
8. Comverse Technology
9. SDL Technology
10. LSI Logic

Fund inception: 1970
Asset mix: Common stocks, 93%; cash/equivalents, 7%
Total net assets: $9.8 billion

Load

Front-end load	5.75%
Redemption fee (max.)	1.00

Annual Fees

12b-1 fee	0.25%
Management fee	0.44
Other expenses	0.28
Total annual expense	0.97%

Minimum initial investment	$1,000
Minimum subsequent investment	$25

Services

Telephone exchanges	*Yes*
Automatic withdrawal	*Yes*
Automatic checking deduction	*Yes*
Retirement plan/IRA	*Yes*
Instant redemption	*Yes*
Portfolio manager (years)	11
Number of funds in family	over 50

Six-Year Performance
Van Kampen Emerging Growth vs. Dow Jones

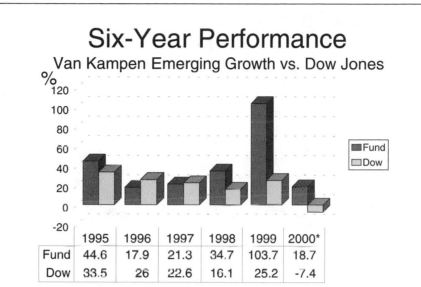

	1995	1996	1997	1998	1999	2000*
Fund	44.6	17.9	21.3	34.7	103.7	18.7
Dow	33.5	26	22.6	16.1	25.2	-7.4

% Avg. Annual Total Return   *2000 returns through 10/1/00
Fund vs. Dow Jones Industrial Avg.   (5-year avg. annual return: 37%)

47

Phoenix-Engemann Aggressive Growth Fund

Phoenix-Engemann Funds
100 Bright Meadow Boulevard, P.O. Box 2200
Enfield, CT 06083-2200
800-814-1897
www.phoenixfunds.com
Ticker symbol: **PHSKX**

Fund managers: Roger Engemann and Ned Brines
Fund objective: Aggressive growth

Performance	★ ★ ★ ★ ★
Consistency	★ ★ ★
Fees/Services/Management	★ ★ ★
Total	**11 Points**

For investors willing to endure some growing pains, the Phoenix-Engemann Aggressive Growth Fund may fit the bill.

Fund managers Roger Engemann and Ned Brines scan the horizon for dynamic, rapidly growing companies, including such high-tech leaders as JDS Uniphase, Xilinx, Brocade Communications, SDL, and Maxim Integrated Products. While the technology sector can sometimes be volatile, Engemann is willing to take the risk in exchange for above-average capital growth.

The strategy has paid off handsomely for the $625 million small-cap growth fund. A $10,000 investment in the fund ten years ago would now be worth about $67,000—a 21 percent average annual return.

Technology stocks account for about 72 percent of the 80-stock portfolio. Other leading sectors include communications services, 5.5 percent; consumer staples, 5 percent; capital goods, 5 percent; energy, 3 percent; health care, 3 percent; and consumer cyclicals, 2.5 percent.

The fund managers take a fairly aggressive management approach, with a 167 percent annual portfolio turnover ratio. Established in 1968, the fund stays about 90 percent invested in stocks most of the time.

PERFORMANCE

The fund has enjoyed outstanding growth over the past five years. Including dividends and capital gains distributions, the Phoenix-Engemann Aggressive Growth Fund has provided a load-adjusted average annual return the past five years (through late 2000) of 31 percent.

A $10,000 investment in 1995 would have grown to about $38,500 five years later.

CONSISTENCY

The fund has been fairly consistent, outperforming the Dow Jones Industrial Average three of the past five years through 1999 (and again through most of 2000). Its biggest gain came in 1999, when it moved up 84.9 percent (compared with a 25.2 percent rise in the Dow).

FEES/SERVICES/MANAGEMENT

The fund has a front-end load of 5.75 percent. The fund's total annual expense ratio of 1.19 percent (with a 0.25 percent 12b-1 fee) is in line with other funds.

The fund offers all the standard services such as retirement account availability, automatic withdrawal, and automatic checking account deduction. Its minimum initial investment of $500 and minimum subsequent investment of $25 compare favorably with other funds.

The fund has been managed by Roger Engemann and Ned Brines since 1988. The Phoenix-Engemann fund family includes 45 funds and allows shareholders to switch from fund to fund by telephone.

Top Ten Stock Holdings

1. Applied Micro Circuits
2. JDS Uniphase
3. Xilinx
4. BEA Systems
5. Brocade Communications

6. SDL, Inc.
7. Conexant Systems
8. Maxim Integrated Products
9. VERITAS Software
10. Jabil Circuit

Fund inception: 1968
Asset mix: Common stocks, 89%; cash/equivalents, 11%
Total net assets: $625 million

Load

Front-end load	5.75%
Redemption fee (max.)	*None*

Annual Fees

12b-1 fee	0.25%
Management fee	0.70
Other expenses	0.24
Total annual expense	1.19%

Minimum initial investment	$500
Minimum subsequent investment	$25

Services

Telephone exchanges	*Yes*
Automatic withdrawal	*Yes*
Automatic checking deduction	*Yes*
Retirement plan/IRA	*Yes*
Instant redemption	*Yes*
Portfolio manager (years)	12
Number of funds in family	45

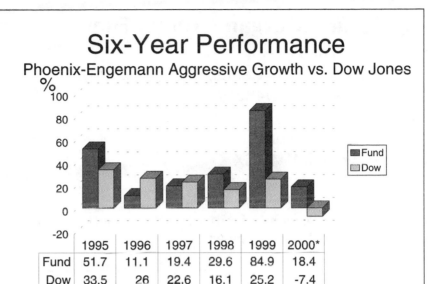

Six-Year Performance
Phoenix-Engemann Aggressive Growth vs. Dow Jones

	1995	1996	1997	1998	1999	2000*
Fund	51.7	11.1	19.4	29.6	84.9	18.4
Dow	33.5	26	22.6	16.1	25.2	-7.4

% Avg. Annual Total Return
Fund vs. Dow Jones Industrial Avg.

*2000 returns through 10/1/00
(5-year avg. annual return: 33.3%)

48

Vanguard Morgan Growth Fund

Vanguard Funds
Vanguard Financial Center, P.O. Box 2600
Valley Forge, PA 19482
800-662-2739
www.vanguard.com
Ticker symbol: **VMRGX**

Fund managers: Robert D. Rands, John S. Cone, and George U. Sauter
Fund objective: Long-term growth

Performance	★ ★
Consistency	★ ★ ★ ★
Fees/Services/Management	★ ★ ★ ★ ★
Total	**11 Points**

The Vanguard Morgan Growth Fund invests in large and midsized companies with strong records of sales and earnings growth. The fund also invests in stocks of smaller companies that appear to have strong growth potential.

The fund is managed by three portfolio managers, Robert Rands, John Cone, and George Sauter, who each select stocks for the fund using their own distinct investment strategies.

The fund was founded in 1968. A $10,000 investment in the fund ten years ago would now be worth about $52,000—an 18 percent average annual return.

The fund holds a lot of blue chip stocks from a broad range of industries, including Cisco Systems, Microsoft, Home Depot, Texas Instruments, America Online, and General Electric.

Technology stocks account for about 26 percent of the $6 billion portfolio, followed by consumer cyclicals, 24 percent; financials, 11 percent; health care, 11 percent; consumer staples, 2 percent; and energy, 2 percent.

The fund stays at least 90 percent invested in stocks under normal circumstances. The fund managers are fairly conservative in their trading approaches, with a 65 percent annual portfolio turnover ratio.

PERFORMANCE

The fund has enjoyed solid growth over the past five years. Including dividends and capital gains distributions, the Vanguard Morgan Growth Fund has provided an average annual return the past five years (through late 2000) of 24.2 percent.

A $10,000 investment in 1995 would have grown to about $29,000 five years later.

CONSISTENCY

The fund has been fairly consistent, outperforming the Dow Jones Industrial Average four of the past five years through 1999 (and again through most of 2000). Its biggest gain came in 1995, when it moved up 36 percent (compared with a 33.5 percent rise in the Dow).

FEES/SERVICES/MANAGEMENT

The fund is a pure no-load fund, with no fees to buy or sell shares. The fund's total annual expense ratio of 0.42 percent (with no 12b-1 fee) is an extremely low ratio compared with most other funds.

The fund offers all the standard services such as retirement account availability, automatic withdrawal, and automatic checking account deduction. Its minimum initial investment of $3,000 and minimum subsequent investment of $100 are higher than most other funds.

The fund is managed by a team of portfolio managers, including George Sauter, since 1993, Robert Rands, since 1994, and John Cone, since 1999. The Vanguard fund family includes over 120 funds and allows shareholders to switch from fund to fund by telephone.

Top Ten Stock Holdings

1. Cisco Systems
2. AT&T-Liberty Media
3. Microsoft
4. Citigroup
5. Corning

6. General Electric
7. Home Depot
8. Texas Instruments
9. Analog Devices
10. Pharmacia

Fund inception: 1968
Asset mix: Common stocks, 92%; cash/equivalents, 8%
Total net assets: $6 billion

Load

Front-end load	*None*
Redemption fee (max.)	*None*

Annual Fees

12b-1 fee	*None*
Management fee	0.40%
Other expenses	0.02
Total annual expense	0.42%
Minimum initial investment	$3,000
Minimum subsequent investment	$100

Services

Telephone exchanges	*Yes*
Automatic withdrawal	*Yes*
Automatic checking deduction	*Yes*
Retirement plan/IRA	*Yes*
Instant redemption	*Yes*
Portfolio manager (years)	6
Number of funds in family	over 120

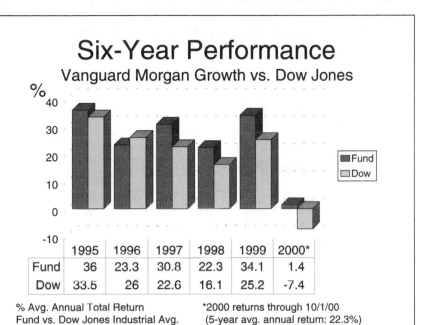

Six-Year Performance
Vanguard Morgan Growth vs. Dow Jones

	1995	1996	1997	1998	1999	2000*
Fund	36	23.3	30.8	22.3	34.1	1.4
Dow	33.5	26	22.6	16.1	25.2	-7.4

% Avg. Annual Total Return   *2000 returns through 10/1/00
Fund vs. Dow Jones Industrial Avg.   (5-year avg. annual return: 22.3%)

49
Strong Large Cap Growth Fund

Strong Funds
P.O. Box 2936
Milwaukee, WI 53201
800-368-3863
www.strongfunds.com
Ticker symbol: **STRFX**

Fund managers: Ronald Ognar and Ian Rogers
Fund objective: Aggressive growth

Performance	★ ★ ★
Consistency	★ ★ ★
Fees/Services/Management	★ ★ ★ ★ ★
Total	**11 Points**

The Strong Large Cap Growth Fund is not exactly the traditional blue chip fund that its name implies. The fund is loaded with emerging new economy stocks, such as SDL, EMC, Brocade, Juniper Group, and PMC-Sierra. It does hold a few of the traditional favorites, such as General Electric, Intel, and Microsoft, but this fund is very heavy in emerging technology stocks.

Telecommunications equipment accounts for about 13 percent of the $2 billion portfolio, followed by Internet and networking stocks, 11 percent; oil, gas, and energy, 8 percent; electronics and semiconductors, 6 percent; banks and finance, 6 percent; computer software, 5 percent; computer memory devices, 4 percent; and medical, 4 percent.

The fund's stated focus is to invest in large-cap and midcap companies with steady or growing dividends, but clearly fund managers Ronald Ognar and Ian Rogers have adopted a different approach. Very few of the fund's largest holdings pay a dividend. Instead, most of its holdings are technology companies with very rapid revenue growth that are leaders in some of the fastest-growing sectors.

The fund was opened in 1981. A $10,000 investment in the fund ten years ago would now be worth about $57,000—a 19 percent annual average return.

The fund managers take a very aggressive trading approach, with a 402 percent annual portfolio turnover ratio. The fund stays at least 90 percent invested in stocks under normal circumstances.

PERFORMANCE

The fund has enjoyed solid growth over the past five years. Including dividends and capital gains distributions, the Strong Large Cap Growth Fund has provided an average annual return the past five years (through late 2000) of 25.9 percent.

A $10,000 investment in 1995 would have grown to about $32,000 five years later.

CONSISTENCY

The fund has been fairly consistent, outperforming the Dow Jones Industrial Average three of the past five years through 1999 (and was leading the Dow through most of 2000). Its biggest gain came in 1999, when it moved up 60.3 percent (compared with a 25.2 percent rise in the Dow).

FEES/SERVICES/MANAGEMENT

The fund is a pure no-load fund, with no fees to buy or sell shares. The fund's total annual expense ratio of 1.00 percent (with no 12b-1 fee) is in line with other funds.

The fund offers all the standard services such as retirement account availability, automatic withdrawal, and automatic checking account deduction. Its minimum initial investment of $2,500 and minimum subsequent investment of $50 are a little higher than many other funds.

Ronald Ognar and Ian Rogers have been managing the fund since 1993. The Strong fund family includes 51 funds and allows shareholders to switch from fund to fund by telephone.

Top Ten Stock Holdings

1. Cisco Systems
2. General Electric
3. Intel
4. Juniper Group
5. SDL, Inc.

6. JDS Uniphase
7. Broadcom
8. EMC
9. Nokia
10. Microsoft

Fund inception: 1981
Asset mix: Common stocks, 91%; cash/equivalents, 9%
Total net assets: $1.8 billion

Load

Front-end load	*None*
Redemption fee (max.)	*None*

Annual Fees

12b-1 fee	*None*
Management fee	0.55%
Other expenses	0.45
Total annual expense	1.00%

Minimum initial investment	$2,500
Minimum subsequent investment	$50

Services

Telephone exchanges	*Yes*
Automatic withdrawal	*Yes*
Automatic checking deduction	*Yes*
Retirement plan/IRA	*Yes*
Instant redemption	*Yes*
Portfolio manager (years)	7
Number of funds in family	51

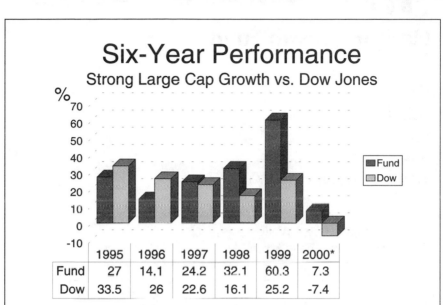

Six-Year Performance
Strong Large Cap Growth vs. Dow Jones

	1995	1996	1997	1998	1999	2000*
Fund	27	14.1	24.2	32.1	60.3	7.3
Dow	33.5	26	22.6	16.1	25.2	-7.4

% Avg. Annual Total Return
Fund vs. Dow Jones Industrial Avg.

*2000 returns through 10/1/00
(5-year avg. annual return: 27%)

50

Harbor Growth Fund

Harbor Funds
One Seagate
Toledo, OH 43666
800-422-1050
www.harborfund.com
Ticker symbol: **HAGWX**

Fund manager: Peter Welles
Fund objective: Small-cap stocks

Performance	★ ★ ★ ★
Consistency	★ ★
Fees/Services/Management	★ ★ ★ ★ ★
Total	**11 Points**

The Harbor Growth Fund invests in small companies of under $500 million in market capitalization or revenue that fund manager Peter Welles believes could be the blue chip leaders of the future.

Welles looks at several key factors in selecting stocks for the $260 million portfolio. He wants companies with capable and accessible management that is committed to above-average earnings growth. And he is looking for companies with strong financial strength and growth rates and a dominant, unrecognized, or innovative product or service with long-term growth potential.

Not all of the fund's holdings are small stocks, although most were small when the fund began buying them. Many of its top holdings have grown rapidly in recent years, including JDS Uniphase, Network Appliance, Comverse Technology, NEXTEL, EMC, and Molecular Devices.

The portfolio is dominated by technology stocks, which account for about 72 percent of total assets. Consumer staples makes up about 7 percent, and capital goods accounts for about 2 percent.

The fund was founded in 1986. A $10,000 investment in the fund ten years ago would now be worth about $57,000—a 19 percent average annual return.

The fund stays 80 to 95 percent invested in stocks under normal circumstances. Fund manager Peter Welles takes a very conservative buy-and-hold approach, with a 13 percent annual portfolio turnover ratio.

PERFORMANCE

The fund has enjoyed very strong growth over the past five years. Including dividends and capital gains distributions, the Harbor Growth Fund has provided an average annual return the past five years (through late 2000) of 29 percent.

A $10,000 investment in 1995 would have grown to about $36,000 five years later.

CONSISTENCY

The fund has been fairly inconsistent, outperforming the Dow Jones Industrial Average only two of the past five years through 1999 (but was leading the Dow through most of 2000). Its biggest gain came in 1999, when it moved up 95.4 percent (compared with a 25.2 percent rise in the Dow).

FEES/SERVICES/MANAGEMENT

The fund is a pure no-load fund, with no fees to buy or sell shares. The fund's total annual expense ratio of 0.90 percent (with no 12b-1 fee) compares favorably with other funds.

The fund offers all the standard services such as retirement account availability, automatic withdrawal, and automatic checking account deduction. Its minimum initial investment of $2,000 and minimum subsequent investment of $500 are in line with other funds.

Peter Welles has managed the fund since 1997. The Harbor fund family includes nine funds and allows shareholders to switch from fund to fund by telephone.

Top Ten Stock Holdings

1. Juniper Networks
2. Redback Networks
3. Lucent Technologies
4. Broadcom
5. Cisco Systems

6. Nortel Networks
7. Motorola
8. DoubleClick
9. Vignette
10. Microsoft

Fund inception: 1981
Asset mix: Common stocks, 94%; cash/equivalents, 6%
Total net assets: $7.4 billion

Load

Front-end load	3.00%
Redemption fee (max.)	*None*

Annual Fees

12b-1 fee	*None*
Management fee	0.59%
Other expenses	0.45
Total annual expense	1.04%
Minimum initial investment	$2,500
Minimum subsequent investment	$250

Services

Telephone exchanges	*Yes*
Automatic withdrawal	*Yes*
Automatic checking deduction	*Yes*
Retirement plan/IRA	*Yes*
Instant redemption	*Yes*
Portfolio manager (years)	1
Number of funds in family	over 300

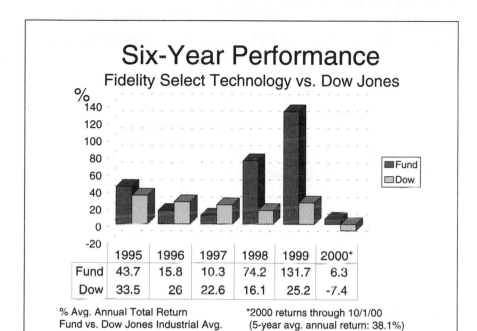

Six-Year Performance
Fidelity Select Technology vs. Dow Jones

	1995	1996	1997	1998	1999	2000*
Fund	43.7	15.8	10.3	74.2	131.7	6.3
Dow	33.5	26	22.6	16.1	25.2	-7.4

% Avg. Annual Total Return   *2000 returns through 10/1/00
Fund vs. Dow Jones Industrial Avg.   (5-year avg. annual return: 38.1%)

52

Fidelity Select: Biotechnology Portfolio

Fidelity Funds
82 Devonshire Street
Boston, MA 02109
800-544-8544
www.fidelity.com
Ticker symbol: **FBIOX**

Fund manager: Yolanda McGettigan
Fund objective: Sector

Performance	★ ★ ★ ★ ★
Consistency	★ ★ ★
Fees/Services/Management	★ ★ ★
Total	**11 Points**

Even if you don't know a monoclonal antibody from a disposable DNA probe array, you can get a stake in the biotechnology sector by picking up some shares of the Fidelity Select Biotechnology Portfolio.

Recent advances in cloning and human genome mapping have generated renewed interest in the biotech arena. This fund invests in many of the leading-edge companies in the biotech industry, such as Immunex, Millennium Pharmaceuticals, Medimmune, Genentech, and Genzyme. It also has holdings in some of the traditional pharmaceutical companies, such as Schering-Plough. The $4.4 billion fund has about 100 stock holdings in all.

The fund was founded in 1985. A $10,000 investment in the fund ten years ago would now be worth about $85,000—a 24 percent return.

Fund manager Yolanda McGettigan takes a fairly aggressive approach, with a 72 percent annual portfolio turnover ratio. The fund stays about 90 percent invested in stocks most of the time.

Because of its narrow investment focus, the fund tends to have more short-term volatility than most traditional stock funds, but it could provide superior long-term returns if the biotechnology industry continues its strong growth.

PERFORMANCE

The fund has enjoyed outstanding growth over the past five years. Including dividends and capital gains distributions, the Fidelity Select Biotechnology Portfolio has provided a load-adjusted average annual return the past five years (through late 2000) of 36.2 percent.

A $10,000 investment in 1995 would have grown to about $47,000 five years later.

CONSISTENCY

The fund has been fairly consistent, outperforming the Dow Jones Industrial Average three of the past five years through 1999 (and again through most of 2000). Its biggest gain came in 1999, when it moved up 77.7 percent (compared with a 25.2 percent rise in the Dow).

FEES/SERVICES/MANAGEMENT

The fund has a 3 percent front-end load. The fund's total annual expense ratio of 1.15 percent (with no 12b-1 fee) is in line with other funds.

The fund offers all the standard services such as retirement account availability, automatic withdrawal, and automatic checking account deduction. Its minimum initial investment of $2,500 and minimum subsequent investment of $250 are a little higher than most other funds.

Fund manager Yolanda McGettigan just joined the fund in 2000. The Fidelity fund family includes more than 300 funds and allows shareholders to switch from fund to fund by telephone.

Top Ten Stock Holdings

1. Immunex
2. Millennium Pharmaceuticals
3. Medimmune
4. Genentech
5. Schering-Plough

6. Alkermes
7. Genzyme–General Div.
8. Chiron
9. Cor Therapeutics
10. Amgen

Fund inception: 1985
Asset mix: Common stocks, 90%; cash/equivalents, 10%
Total net assets: $4.4 billion

Load

Front-end load	3.00%
Redemption fee (max.)	*None*

Annual Fees

12b-1 fee	*None*
Management fee	0.59%
Other expenses	0.56
Total annual expense	1.15%

Minimum initial investment	$2,500
Minimum subsequent investment	$250

Services

Telephone exchanges	*Yes*
Automatic withdrawal	*Yes*
Automatic checking deduction	*Yes*
Retirement plan/IRA	*Yes*
Instant redemption	*Yes*
Portfolio manager (years)	1
Number of funds in family	over 300

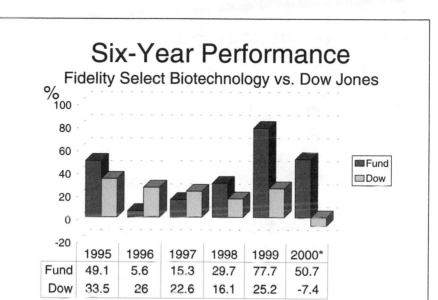

Six-Year Performance
Fidelity Select Biotechnology vs. Dow Jones

	1995	1996	1997	1998	1999	2000*
Fund	49.1	5.6	15.3	29.7	77.7	50.7
Dow	33.5	26	22.6	16.1	25.2	-7.4

% Avg. Annual Total Return   *2000 returns through 10/1/00
Fund vs. Dow Jones Industrial Avg.   (5-year avg. annual return: 36.3%)

53
Kemper Technology Fund

Kemper Funds
222 South Riverside Plaza
Chicago, IL 60606-5808
800-621-1048
www.kemper.com
Ticker symbol: **KTCAX**

Fund managers: James B. Burkhart and Deborah L. Koch
Fund objective: Sector

Performance	★ ★ ★ ★ ★
Consistency	★ ★ ★
Fees/Services/Management	★ ★ ★
Total	**11 Points**

There's more to high tech than just the Internet. Although the Kemper Technology Fund includes such new economy stalwarts as Vignette and BroadVision, the diversified tech fund also features top-performing semiconductor, data communications, and telecommunications companies.

The fund's top holdings include such large-cap technology high fliers as Oracle, Cisco Systems, Intel, Motorola, and Xilinx. The fund is high on semiconductor stocks, which constitute about 18 percent of the portfolio, because chips are the building blocks for cellular and wireless communications, networking equipment, and computers.

The fund, which has about 100 holdings, has earned an average annualized return of 22 percent over the last ten years. A $10,000 investment in the fund ten years ago would now be worth about $73,000.

Fund managers Jim Burkhart and Deborah Koch consider it their job to look beyond the technology trends and noise and instead seek companies that have the ability to generate sustainable, powerful growth. In addition, they are looking for companies with innovative management, excellent balance sheets, and large growing markets for their products or services.

Portfolio turnover of the $4 billion fund has been relatively conservative—about 59 percent. The fund stays at least 90 percent invested in stocks under normal circumstances.

PERFORMANCE

The fund has enjoyed exceptional growth over the past five years. Including dividends and capital gains distributions, the Kemper Technology Fund has provided a load-adjusted average annual return the past five years (through late 2000) of 34 percent.

A $10,000 investment in 1995 would have grown to about $43,000 five years later.

CONSISTENCY

The fund has been fairly consistent, outperforming the Dow Jones Industrial Average three of the past five years through 1999 (and again through most of 2000). Its biggest gain came in 1999, when it moved up 114.3 percent (compared with a 25.2 percent rise in the Dow).

FEES/SERVICES/MANAGEMENT

The fund has a front-end load of 5.75 percent, with a maximum back-end load of 1 percent. The fund's total annual expense ratio of 0.96 percent (with no 12b-1 fee) compares favorably with other funds.

The fund offers all the standard services such as retirement account availability, automatic withdrawal, and automatic checking account deduction. Its minimum initial investment of $1,000 and minimum subsequent investment of $100 are in line with other funds.

Jim Burkhart and Deborah Koch have been managing the fund only since 1998. The Kemper fund family includes 56 funds and allows shareholders to switch from fund to fund by telephone.

Top Ten Stock Holdings

1. Oracle	6. America Online
2. Motorola	7. Intuit
3. Cisco Systems	8. Applied Materials
4. Microsoft	9. JDS Uniphase
5. Yahoo!	10. Xilinx

Fund inception: 1948
Asset mix: Common stocks, 94%; cash/equivalents, 6%
Total net assets: $4 billion

Load

Front-end load	5.75%
Redemption fee (max.)	1.00%

Annual Fees

12b-1 fee	*None*
Management fee	0.53%
Other expenses	0.43
Total annual expense	0.96%

Minimum initial investment	$1,000
Minimum subsequent investment	$100

Services

Telephone exchanges	*Yes*
Automatic withdrawal	*Yes*
Automatic checking deduction	*Yes*
Retirement plan/IRA	*Yes*
Instant redemption	*Yes*
Portfolio manager (years)	2
Number of funds in family	56

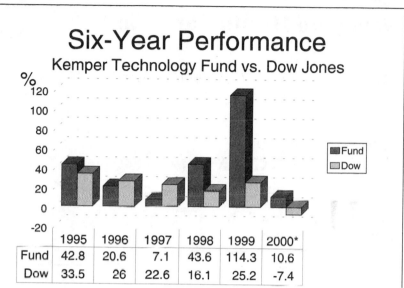

Six-Year Performance
Kemper Technology Fund vs. Dow Jones

	1995	1996	1997	1998	1999	2000*
Fund	42.8	20.6	7.1	43.6	114.3	10.6
Dow	33.5	26	22.6	16.1	25.2	-7.4

% Avg. Annual Total Return
Fund vs. Dow Jones Industrial Avg.

*2000 returns through 10/1/00
(5-year avg. annual return: 33.5%)

54

Vanguard Health Care Fund

Vanguard Funds
Vanguard Financial Center, P.O. Box 2600
Valley Forge, PA 19482
800-662-2739
www.vanguard.com
Ticker symbol: **VGHCX**

Fund manager: Edward Owens
Fund objective: Sector

Performance	★ ★ ★ ★
Consistency	★ ★ ★
Fees/Services/Management	★ ★ ★ ★
Total	**11 Points**

The Vanguard Health Care Fund invests in a cross section of traditional pharmaceutical makers, health care services companies, and young emerging biotechnology companies. The fund is geared to investors who want to cash in on the growing demand for medical products and services in the years ahead.

The fund's holdings include pharmaceutical firms, makers of medical equipment and supplies, operators of hospitals and health care facilities, and biotechnology researchers. Among the fund's largest holdings are Pfizer, Pharmacia, Abbott Labs, Immunex, UnitedHealth Group, and Merck.

Fund manager Edward Owens, who has been running the fund since its 1984 inception, looks for companies with strong financial growth, strong management, and a pipeline of products that could lead to continued earnings and revenue growth.

A $10,000 investment in the fund ten years ago would now be worth about $82,000—a 23.5 percent average annual return.

Owens is very conservative in his investment approach. He buys and holds for the long term. The fund has a 27 percent annual portfolio turnover ratio. The fund stays at least 90 percent invested in stocks under normal circumstances.

PERFORMANCE

The fund has enjoyed excellent growth over the past five years. Including dividends and capital gains distributions, the Vanguard Health Care Fund has provided an average annual return the past five years (through late 2000) of 30.3 percent.

A $10,000 investment in 1995 would have grown to about $37,000 five years later.

CONSISTENCY

The fund has been fairly consistent, outperforming the Dow Jones Industrial Average three of the past five years through 1999 (and was far ahead of the Dow through most of 2000). Its biggest gain came in 1995, when it moved up 45.2 percent (compared with a 33.5 percent rise in the Dow).

FEES/SERVICES/MANAGEMENT

The fund is a pure no-load fund, with no fees to buy or sell shares. The fund's total annual expense ratio of 0.41 percent (with no 12b-1 fee) is lower than many other funds.

The fund offers all the standard services such as retirement account availability, automatic withdrawal, and automatic checking account deduction. Its minimum initial investment of $10,000 and minimum subsequent investment of $100 are much higher than most other funds.

Fund manager Edward Owens has been with the fund since its inception in 1984. The Vanguard fund family includes over 120 funds and allows shareholders to switch from fund to fund by telephone.

Top Ten Stock Holdings

1. Pharmacia
2. Pfizer
3. American Home Products
4. McKesson HBOC
5. Immunex

6. Abbott Laboratories
7. HCA–The Healthcare Co.
8. UnitedHealth Group
9. AstraZeneca Group PLC
10. Merck

Fund inception: 1984
Asset mix: Common stocks, 91%; cash/equivalents, 9%
Total net assets: $14 billion

Load

Front-end load	*None*
Redemption fee (max.)	*None*

Annual Fees

12b-1 fee	*None*
Management fee	0.37%
Other expenses	0.04
Total annual expense	0.41%

Minimum initial investment	$10,000
Minimum subsequent investment	$100

Services

Telephone exchanges	*Yes*
Automatic withdrawal	*Yes*
Automatic checking deduction	*Yes*
Retirement plan/IRA	*Yes*
Instant redemption	*Yes*
Portfolio manager (years)	16
Number of funds in family	over 120

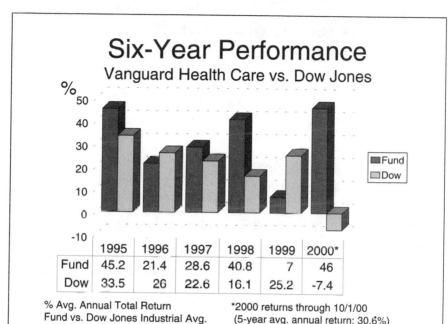

Six-Year Performance
Vanguard Health Care vs. Dow Jones

	1995	1996	1997	1998	1999	2000*
Fund	45.2	21.4	28.6	40.8	7	46
Dow	33.5	26	22.6	16.1	25.2	-7.4

% Avg. Annual Total Return
Fund vs. Dow Jones Industrial Avg.

*2000 returns through 10/1/00
(5-year avg. annual return: 30.6%)

55

Pilgrim International Small Cap Growth Fund

Pilgrim Funds
600 West Broadway, 30th Floor
San Diego, CA 92101
800-992-0180
www.pilgrimfunds.com
Ticker symbol: **NIGRX**

Fund manager: Jeffrey Bernstein (and team managed)
Fund objective: International equity

Performance	★ ★ ★ ★ ★
Consistency	★ ★
Fees/Services/Management	★ ★ ★
Total	**10 Points**

The Pilgrim International Small Cap Growth Fund offers investors a new dimension in global investing. Unlike most global funds that load up on big-name blue chips, this fund seeks out some of the most exciting young companies from the top markets around the world.

The team-managed fund, headed by Jeffrey Bernstein, invests about two-thirds of its $300 million portfolio in small companies located outside the United States. The remaining one-third of the portfolio is invested in small-cap U.S. companies. The top countries outside the United States in which the fund invests are Germany (19 percent), Great Britain (14 percent), France (11 percent), Japan (11 percent), and Sweden (7 percent).

The fund is heavily weighted in technology stocks, including electronic components and semiconductors, which make up about 7 percent of the portfolio, along with electronic components, telecommunications equipment, computer services, and telecommunications services.

The fund was launched in 1990. A $10,000 investment in the fund at that time would have been worth about $44,000 ten years later—a 16 percent average annual return.

214

In analyzing specific companies for possible investment, the fund's management team looks for such characteristics as strong research and product development savvy, strong financials, and efficient service.

Annual turnover in the 150-stock portfolio is a relatively modest 71 percent. The fund stays at least 90 percent invested in stocks under normal circumstances.

PERFORMANCE

The fund has enjoyed outstanding growth over the past five years. Including dividends and capital gains distributions, the Pilgrim International Small Cap Growth Fund has provided a load-adjusted average annual return the past five years (through late 2000) of 32 percent.

A $10,000 investment in 1995 would have grown to about $40,000 five years later.

CONSISTENCY

The fund has been somewhat inconsistent, outperforming the Dow Jones Industrial Average only two of the past five years through 1999 (and again through most of 2000). Its biggest gain came in 1999, when it moved up 121.9 percent (compared with a 25.2 percent rise in the Dow).

FEES/SERVICES/MANAGEMENT

The fund has a front-end load of 5.75 percent, with a maximum back-end load of 1 percent. The fund's total annual expense ratio of 1.84 percent (with a 0.35 percent 12b-1 fee) is in line with other funds.

The fund offers all the standard services such as retirement account availability, automatic withdrawal, and automatic checking account deduction. Its minimum initial investment of $1,000 and minimum subsequent investment of $100 compare favorably with other funds.

The fund has been managed by Jeffrey Bernstein and a team of managers since 1994. The Pilgrim fund family includes 44 funds and allows shareholders to switch from fund to fund by telephone.

Top Ten Stock Holdings

1. Marschollek Lautenschla
2. Yaskawa Electric
3. Aixtron
4. Enea Data
5. Kudelski SA Bearer
6. Vestas Wind Systems
7. Intershop Communications
8. Gruppo Editoriale L'espr
9. Pace Micro Technology
10. Metropole Television

Fund inception: 1990
Asset mix: Common stocks, 88%; cash/equivalents, 10%; preferred stocks, 2%
Total net assets: $279 million

Load

Front-end load	5.75%
Redemption fee (max.)	1.00

Annual Fees

12b-1 fee	0.35%
Management fee	1.00
Other expenses	0.49
Total annual expense	1.84%

Minimum initial investment	$1,000
Minimum subsequent investment	$100

Services

Telephone exchanges	*Yes*
Automatic withdrawal	*Yes*
Automatic checking deduction	*Yes*
Retirement plan/IRA	*Yes*
Instant redemption	*Yes*
Portfolio manager (years)	6
Number of funds in family	44

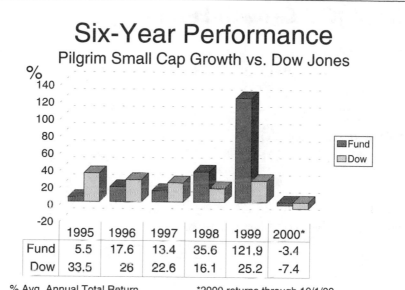

Six-Year Performance
Pilgrim Small Cap Growth vs. Dow Jones

	1995	1996	1997	1998	1999	2000*
Fund	5.5	17.6	13.4	35.6	121.9	-3.4
Dow	33.5	26	22.6	16.1	25.2	-7.4

% Avg. Annual Total Return
Fund vs. Dow Jones Industrial Avg.

*2000 returns through 10/1/00
(5-year avg. annual return: 31.1%)

56

IDEX JCC Growth Fund

IDEX Funds
201 Highland Avenue
Largo, FL 33770-2597
800-421-4339
www.idexfunds.com
Ticker symbol: **IDETX**

Fund manager: Edward Keely
Fund objective: Long-term growth

Performance	★ ★ ★ ★
Consistency	★ ★ ★
Fees/Services/Management	★ ★ ★
Total	**10 Points**

The IDEX JCC Growth Fund invests in many of the fastest-growing high-tech and Internet stocks of the market, as well as some blue chip stocks of other sectors.

Fund manager Edward Keely looks for stocks with strong earnings potential that are trading at reasonable prices relative to their future earnings growth.

The $2 billion portfolio is loaded with well-known tech stocks in both the computer and telecommunications industries, including Nokia, Cisco Systems, Microsoft, America Online, Amazon.com, and Xilinx. A few old-school companies are also in the mix, such as General Electric, Time Warner, and Texas Instruments.

Technology stocks account for about 35 percent of the portfolio, followed by communications services, 28 percent; consumer cyclicals, 15 percent; and consumer staples, 8 percent.

The fund was launched in 1986. A $10,000 investment in the fund ten years ago would now be worth about $67,000—a 21 percent annual average return.

Keely is fairly active in his investment approach, with a 71 percent annual portfolio turnover ratio. The fund stays 80 to 90 percent invested in common stocks under normal circumstances. The fund also has significant investments in preferred stocks.

PERFORMANCE

The fund has enjoyed outstanding growth over the past five years. Including dividends and capital gains distributions, the IDEX JCC Growth Fund has provided a load-adjusted average annual return the past five years (through late 2000) of 30.1 percent.

A $10,000 investment in 1995 would have grown to about $37,000 five years later.

CONSISTENCY

The fund has been fairly consistent, outperforming the Dow Jones Industrial Average three of the past five years through 1999 (and again through most of 2000). Its biggest gain came in 1998, when it moved up 64 percent (compared with a 16.1 percent rise in the Dow).

FEES/SERVICES/MANAGEMENT

The fund has a front-end load of 5.50 percent, with a maximum back-end load of 1 percent. The fund's total annual expense ratio of 1.40 percent (with a 0.35 percent 12b-1 fee) is in line with other funds.

The fund offers all the standard services such as retirement account availability, automatic withdrawal, and automatic checking account deduction. Its minimum initial investment of $500 and minimum subsequent investment of $50 compare favorably with other funds.

Edward Keely has been managing the fund since 1995. The IDEX fund family includes more than 27 funds and allows shareholders to switch from fund to fund by telephone.

Top Ten Stock Holdings

1. Nokia
2. Cisco Systems
3. Microsoft
4. General Electric
5. America Online
6. Time Warner
7. Texas Instruments
8. Xilinx
9. Enron
10. Amazon.com

Fund inception: 1986
Asset mix: Common stocks, 81%; cash/equivalents, 10%; preferred stocks, 9%
Total net assets: $2 billion

Load

Front-end load	5.50%
Redemption fee (max.)	1.00

Annual Fees

12b-1 fee	0.35%
Management fee	0.90
Other expenses	0.15
Total annual expense	1.40%

Minimum initial investment	$500
Minimum subsequent investment	$50

Services

Telephone exchanges	*Yes*
Automatic withdrawal	*Yes*
Automatic checking deduction	*Yes*
Retirement plan/IRA	*Yes*
Instant redemption	*Yes*
Portfolio manager (years)	5
Number of funds in family	over 27

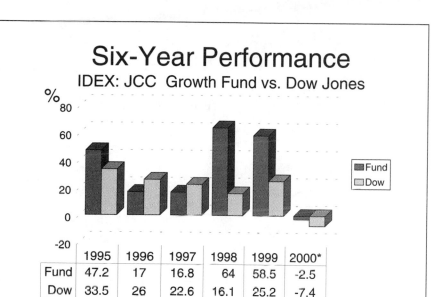

Six-Year Performance
IDEX: JCC Growth Fund vs. Dow Jones

	1995	1996	1997	1998	1999	2000*
Fund	47.2	17	16.8	64	58.5	-2.5
Dow	33.5	26	22.6	16.1	25.2	-7.4

% Avg. Annual Total Return
Fund vs. Dow Jones Industrial Avg.

*2000 returns through 10/1/00
(5-year avg. annual return: 29.5%)

57
SunAmerica Equity Growth & Income Fund

SunAmerica Equity Funds
SunAmerica Center, 733 Third Avenue
New York, NY 10017-3204
800-858-8850
www.sunamericafunds.com
Ticker symbol: **SEIAX**

Fund manager: Frank Gannon
Fund objective: Growth and income

Performance	★ ★
Consistency	★ ★ ★ ★ ★
Fees/Services/Management	★ ★ ★
Total	**10 Points**

Because of its name, the SunAmerica Equity Growth and Income Fund's stated goal is to invest in stocks of any size that show growth potential and pay dividends. But in reality, the fund comes closer to a pure growth fund. In fact, many of its top holdings don't pay dividends.

Most of the fund's leading investments are large blue chip technology stocks, such as Cisco Systems, Intel, Microsoft, EMC, and JDS Uniphase. There are also a few older stocks in the mix, such as IBM and General Electric.

Technology stocks—not known for their "income" potential—dominate the portfolio, accounting for 45 percent of total assets. Other leading sectors include health care, 11 percent; financials, 9 percent; industrial and commerce, 8 percent; energy, 7.5 percent; information and entertainment, 5 percent; consumer discretionary, 5 percent; and utilities, 2 percent.

The fund is still relatively small, with just $120 million in assets. Fund manager Frank Gannon (no ties to *Dragnet*) takes a fairly conservative approach in managing the fund, with a 63 percent annual portfolio turnover ratio. The fund stays at least 90 percent invested in stocks most of the time.

In structuring the portfolio, Gannon tries to identify the sectors with the best potential and then selects stocks from those sectors based on fundamental and technical merits.

PERFORMANCE

The fund has enjoyed strong growth over the past five years. Including dividends and capital gains distributions, the SunAmerica Equity Growth and Income Fund has provided a load-adjusted average annual return the past five years (through late 2000) of 25 percent.

A $10,000 investment in 1995 would have grown to about $30,000 five years later.

CONSISTENCY

The fund has been very consistent, outperforming the Dow Jones Industrial Average five consecutive years through 1999 (and again through most of 2000). Its biggest gain came in 1999, when it moved up 33.3 percent (compared with a 25.2 percent rise in the Dow).

FEES/SERVICES/MANAGEMENT

The fund has a front-end load of 5.75 percent, with a maximum back-end load of 1 percent. The fund's total annual expense ratio of 1.48 percent (with a 0.22 percent 12b-1 fee) is in line with other funds.

The fund offers all the standard services such as retirement account availability, automatic withdrawal, and automatic checking account deduction. Its minimum initial investment of $500 and minimum subsequent investment of $100 compare favorably with other funds.

The fund has been managed by Frank Gannon since 1997. The SunAmerica fund family includes more than 30 funds and allows shareholders to switch from fund to fund by telephone.

Top Ten Stock Holdings

1. Cisco Systems
2. Microsoft
3. General Electric
4. EMC
5. Intel

6. JDS Uniphase
7. IBM
8. Tyco International
9. Nokia
10. AT&T-Liberty Media 'A'

Fund inception: 1994
Asset mix: Common stocks, 95%; cash/equivalents, 5%
Total net assets: $119 million

Load

Front-end load	5.75%
Redemption fee (max.)	1.00

Annual Fees

12b-1 fee	0.22%
Management fee	0.75
Other expenses	0.51
Total annual expense	1.48%

Minimum initial investment	$500
Minimum subsequent investment	$100

Services

Telephone exchanges	*Yes*
Automatic withdrawal	*Yes*
Automatic checking deduction	*Yes*
Retirement plan/IRA	*Yes*
Instant redemption	*Yes*
Portfolio manager (years)	3
Number of funds in family	over 30

Six-Year Performance
SunAmerica Growth & Income vs. Dow Jones

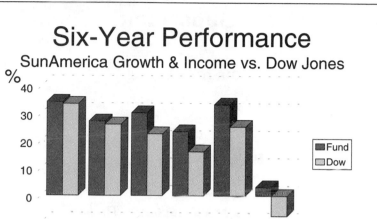

	1995	1996	1997	1998	1999	2000*
Fund	34.2	27.1	30.2	23.4	33.3	3.2
Dow	33.5	26	22.6	16.1	25.2	-7.4

% Avg. Annual Total Return
Fund vs. Dow Jones Industrial Avg.

*2000 returns through 10/1/00
(5-year avg. annual return: 25.7%)

58
Putnam New Opportunities Fund

Putnam Funds
One Post Office Square
Boston, MA 02109
800-225-1581
www.putnaminv.com
Ticker symbol: **PNOPX**

Fund managers: Daniel Miller and Jeffrey Lindsey
Fund objective: Aggressive growth

Performance	★ ★ ★
Consistency	★ ★ ★ ★
Fees/Services/Management	★ ★ ★
Total	**10 Points**

Fund managers Daniel Miller and Jeffrey Lindsey of the Putnam New Opportunities Fund are always on the lookout for the next big winners of the new economy. The fund is loaded with high-tech, Internet, and tele-communications leaders, such as VERITAS Software, Verisign, JDS Uniphase, Cisco Systems, Sun Microsystems, and Juniper Networks.

The massive $21 billion fund was launched in 1990 and has posted a 30.2 percent average annual return since then. A $10,000 investment in the fund ten years ago would now be worth about $140,000.

The fund focuses on growth stocks of the fastest-growing sectors. Stocks are also assessed based on their overall financial strength, their competitive position within their industry, their debt level, and projected earnings and cash flow.

Technology stocks make up about 57 percent of the portfolio, followed by consumer staples, 10 percent; health care, 9 percent; communications, 8 percent; consumer cyclicals, 4 percent; and financial, 3 percent.

Fund managers Daniel Miller, who has been running the fund since its inception, and Jeffrey Lindsey take a fairly active investment approach, with a 77 percent annual portfolio turnover ratio. The fund stays almost 100 percent invested in stocks under normal circumstances.

PERFORMANCE

The fund has enjoyed solid growth over the past five years. Including dividends and capital gains distributions, the Putnam New Opportunities Fund has provided a load-adjusted average annual return the past five years (through late 2000) of 27 percent.

A $10,000 investment in 1995 would have grown to about $33,000 five years later.

CONSISTENCY

The fund has been very consistent, outperforming or matching the Dow Jones Industrial Average four of the past five years through 1999 (and again through most of 2000). Its biggest gain came in 1999, when it moved up 69.7 percent (compared with a 25.2 percent rise in the Dow).

FEES/SERVICES/MANAGEMENT

The fund has a front-end load of 5.75 percent, with a maximum back-end load of 1 percent. The fund's total annual expense ratio of 0.93 percent (with a 0.35 percent 12b-1 fee) compares favorably with other funds.

The fund offers all the standard services such as retirement account availability, automatic withdrawal, and automatic checking account deduction. Its minimum initial investment of $500 and minimum subsequent investment of $50 compare favorably with other funds.

The fund managers are Daniel Miller, who has been with the fund since its inception in 1990, and Jeffrey Lindsey, since 1998. The Putnam fund family includes more than 140 funds and allows shareholders to switch from fund to fund by telephone.

Top Ten Stock Holdings

1. VERITAS Software
2. General Electric
3. Clear Channel Communications
4. VeriSign
5. JDS Uniphase

6. Cisco Systems
7. Maxim Integrated Products
8. Viacom
9. Sun Microsystems
10. Juniper Networks

Fund inception: 1990
Asset mix: Common stocks, 98%; cash/equivalents, 2%
Total net assets: $21 billion

Load

Front-end load	5.75%
Redemption fee (max.)	1.00

Annual Fees

12b-1 fee	0.35%
Management fee	0.48
Other expenses	0.10
Total annual expense	0.93%
Minimum initial investment	$500
Minimum subsequent investment	$50

Services

Telephone exchanges	*Yes*
Automatic withdrawal	*Yes*
Automatic checking deduction	*Yes*
Retirement plan/IRA	*Yes*
Instant redemption	*Yes*
Portfolio manager (years)	10
Number of funds in family	over 140

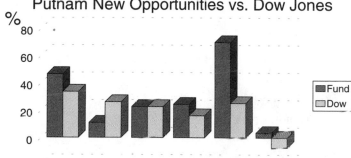

Six-Year Performance
Putnam New Opportunities vs. Dow Jones

	1995	1996	1997	1998	1999	2000*
Fund	46.3	10.9	22.6	24.4	69.7	3.5
Dow	33.5	26	22.6	16.1	25.2	-7.4

% Avg. Annual Total Return
Fund vs. Dow Jones Industrial Avg.

*2000 returns through 10/1/00
(5-year avg. annual return: 25.9%)

59

SunAmerica Growth Opportunities Fund

SunAmerica Equity Funds
SunAmerica Center, 733 Third Avenue
New York, NY 10017-3204
800-858-8850
www.sunamericafunds.com
Ticker symbol: **SGWAX**

Fund manager: Brian Clifford
Fund objective: Aggressive growth

Performance	★ ★ ★ ★
Consistency	★ ★ ★
Fees/Services/Management	★ ★ ★
Total	**10 Points**

The SunAmerica Growth Opportunities Fund focuses on midcap stocks that are market leaders in high-growth sectors. The fund management believes that midcap stocks are not followed as closely as the blue chips and may present opportunities that the larger blue chips don't.

Many of the fund's largest holdings are emerging stocks in technology sectors, such as EchoStar Communications, Atmel, Inktomi, Applied Micro Circuits, and VERITAS Software. But the fund also has its share of old economy favorites, such as Corning, Merrill Lynch, and Goldman Sachs.

Information technology stocks account for about 45 percent of the portfolio. Other leading sectors include health care, 20 percent; energy, 5 percent; financials, 4 percent; and industrial and commercial, 4 percent.

The fund, launched in 1987, is still relatively small, with just $160 million in assets. A $10,000 investment in the fund ten years ago would now be worth about $64,000—a 20.5 percent average annual increase.

Fund manager Brian Clifford takes a very aggressive management approach, with a 220 percent annual portfolio turnover ratio. The fund's ratio of cash to stocks can vary widely, depending on market conditions.

PERFORMANCE

The fund has enjoyed strong growth over the past five years. Including dividends and capital gains distributions, the SunAmerica Growth Opportunities Fund has provided a load-adjusted average annual return the past five years (through late 2000) of 28.5 percent.

A $10,000 investment in 1995 would have grown to about $35,000 five years later.

CONSISTENCY

The fund has been fairly consistent, outperforming the Dow Jones Industrial Average three of the past five years through 1999 (and again through most of 2000). Its biggest gain came in 1999, when it moved up 89 percent (compared with a 25.2 percent rise in the Dow).

FEES/SERVICES/MANAGEMENT

The fund has a front-end load of 5.75 percent, with a maximum back-end load of 1 percent. The fund's total annual expense ratio of 1.57 percent (with a 0.35 percent 12b-1 fee) is in line with other funds.

The fund offers all the standard services such as retirement account availability, automatic withdrawal, and automatic checking account deduction. Its minimum initial investment of $500 and minimum subsequent investment of $100 compare favorably with other funds.

The fund has been managed by Brian Clifford since 1997. The SunAmerica fund family includes more than 30 funds and allows shareholders to switch from fund to fund by telephone.

Top Ten Stock Holdings

1. EchoStar Communications
2. Atmel
3. Inktomi
4. Corning
5. Transocean Sedco Forex

6. Patterson Energy
7. VERITAS Software
8. Goldman Sachs Group
9. Merrill Lynch
10. Applied Micro Circuits

Fund inception: 1987
Asset mix: Common stocks, 80%; cash/equivalents, 20%
Total net assets: $159 million

Load

Front-end load	5.75%
Redemption fee (max.)	1.00

Annual Fees

12b-1 fee	0.35%
Management fee	0.75
Other expenses	0.47
Total annual expense	1.57%
Minimum initial investment	$500
Minimum subsequent investment	$100

Services

Telephone exchanges	*Yes*
Automatic withdrawal	*Yes*
Automatic checking deduction	*Yes*
Retirement plan/IRA	*Yes*
Instant redemption	*Yes*
Portfolio manager (years)	3
Number of funds in family	over 30

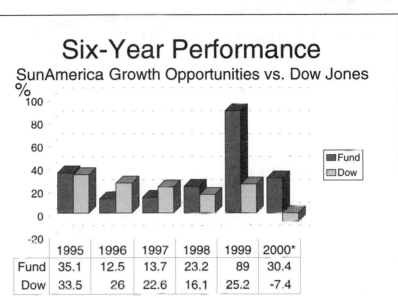

Six-Year Performance
SunAmerica Growth Opportunities vs. Dow Jones

	1995	1996	1997	1998	1999	2000*
Fund	35.1	12.5	13.7	23.2	89	30.4
Dow	33.5	26	22.6	16.1	25.2	-7.4

% Avg. Annual Total Return   *2000 returns through 10/1/00
Fund vs. Dow Jones Industrial Avg.   (5-year avg. annual return: 32.3%)

60

Putnam Voyager Fund II

Putnam Funds
One Post Office Square
Boston, MA 02109
800-225-1581
www.putnaminv.com
Ticker symbol: **PVIIX**

Fund managers: Roland W. Gillis, Jeffrey R. Lindsey, and
Charles H. Swanberg
Fund objective: Aggressive growth

Performance	★ ★ ★
Consistency	★ ★ ★ ★
Fees/Services/Management	★ ★ ★
Total	**10 Points**

The Putnam Voyager Fund II invests in some of the fastest-growing companies in America—including small, midsized, and large blue chip stocks.

The fund management team looks for stocks with strong earnings growth, financial strength, a solid competitive position within their industry, and steady cash flow.

Its leading holdings including both older tech stocks, such as Microsoft, General Electric, and Oracle, and some of the younger stocks of the new economy, such as VERITAS Software, Verisign, Juniper Networks, and i2 Technologies.

Technology stocks dominate the fund, accounting for about 58 percent of the $2 billion portfolio. Other leading sectors include health care, 9 percent; consumer cyclicals, 8 percent; consumer staples, 8 percent; communications, 5 percent; and financial, 5 percent. The fund stays nearly 100 percent invested in stocks under normal circumstances.

Launched in 1993, the fund has posted an average annual return of about 25 percent since its inception. The fund managers are fairly active in their investment approach, with a 90 percent annual portfolio turnover ratio.

PERFORMANCE

The fund has enjoyed solid growth over the past five years. Including dividends and capital gains distributions, the Putnam Voyager Fund II has provided a load-adjusted average annual return the past five years (through late 2000) of 26.7 percent.

A $10,000 investment in 1995 would have grown to about $32,600 five years later.

CONSISTENCY

The fund has been very consistent, outperforming the Dow Jones Industrial Average four of the past five years through 1999 (and was about even with the Dow through most of 2000). Its biggest gain came in 1999, when it moved up 79.9 percent (compared with a 25.2 percent rise in the Dow).

FEES/SERVICES/MANAGEMENT

The fund has a front-end load of 5.75 percent, with a maximum back-end load of 1 percent. The fund's total annual expense ratio of 1.03 percent (with a 0.35 percent 12b-1 fee) is in line with other funds.

The fund offers all the standard services such as retirement account availability, automatic withdrawal, and automatic checking account deduction. Its minimum initial investment of $500 and minimum subsequent investment of $50 compare favorably with other funds.

The fund is run by three fund managers, including Roland Gillis and Charles Swanberg, who have been with the fund since its inception in 1993, and Jeffrey Lindsey. The Putnam fund family includes more than 140 funds and allows shareholders to switch from fund to fund by telephone.

Top Ten Stock Holdings

1. VERITAS Software	6. Oracle
2. General Electric	7. Cisco Systems
3. Brocade Communications	8. QLogic
4. Microsoft	9. Metromedia Fiber
5. NEXTLINK Communications 'A'	10. Network Appliances

Fund inception: 1993
Asset mix: Common stocks, 98%; cash/equivalents, 2%
Total net assets: $2.1 billion

Load

Front-end load	5.75%
Redemption fee (max.)	1.00

Annual Fees

12b-1 fee	0.35%
Management fee	0.59
Other expenses	0.09
Total annual expense	1.03%
Minimum initial investment	$500
Minimum subsequent investment	$50

Services

Telephone exchanges	*Yes*
Automatic withdrawal	*Yes*
Automatic checking deduction	*Yes*
Retirement plan/IRA	*Yes*
Instant redemption	*Yes*
Portfolio manager (years)	7
Number of funds in family	over 140

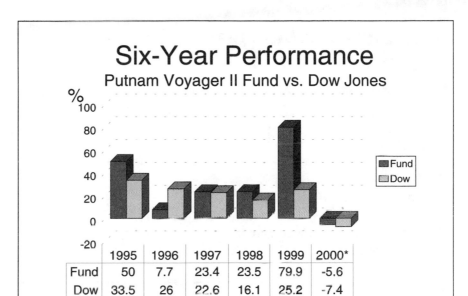

Six-Year Performance
Putnam Voyager II Fund vs. Dow Jones

	1995	1996	1997	1998	1999	2000*
Fund	50	7.7	23.4	23.5	79.9	-5.6
Dow	33.5	26	22.6	16.1	25.2	-7.4

% Avg. Annual Total Return   *2000 returns through 10/1/00
Fund vs. Dow Jones Industrial Avg.   (5-year avg. annual return: 25.3%)

61
Vanguard Tax-Managed Capital Appreciation Fund

Vanguard Funds
Vanguard Financial Center, P.O. Box 2600
Valley Forge, PA 19482
800-662-2739
www.vanguard.com
Ticker symbol: **VMCAX**

Fund manager: George U. Sauter
Fund objective: Long-term growth

Performance	★ ★
Consistency	★ ★ ★ ★
Fees/Services/Management	★ ★ ★ ★
Total	**10 Points**

The Vanguard Tax-Managed Capital Appreciation Fund is designed to increase the wealth of its shareholders without increasing their taxes.

Fund manager George Sauter, who has been with the fund since its inception in 1994, uses a variety of trading techniques to limit capital gains distributions. For instance, he prefers stocks that pay low dividends or no dividends to reduce taxable distributions, and he may sell stocks that have declined in price to offset capital gains on other stocks that have been sold at a profit. Generally speaking, however, Sauter does very little trading of the fund's holdings. The fund has just a 12 percent annual portfolio turnover ratio.

The fund invests in midsized and large-capitalization stocks from the Russell 1000 index, which represents the 1,000 largest U.S. companies. The fund is structured to match key characteristics of the index, such as industry weightings, market capitalization, and price-earnings ratios.

The fund is packed with a diversified selection of blue chip stocks, such as General Electric, Cisco Systems, Pfizer, Intel, and Exxon Mobil. Technology stocks account for about 27 percent of the $3 billion portfolio, followed by consumer services, 17 percent; health care, 12 percent; financial services, 10 percent; utilities, 9 percent; oil and energy, 5 percent; consumer staples, 5 percent; producer durables, 4 percent; materials processing, 3.5 percent; and autos and transportation, 3 percent.

The fund stays 100 percent invested in stocks under normal circumstances.

PERFORMANCE

The fund has achieved modest growth over the past five years. Including dividends and capital gains distributions, the Vanguard Tax-Managed Capital Appreciation Fund has provided an average annual return the past five years (through late 2000) of 23.5 percent.

A $10,000 investment in 1995 would have grown to about $28,500 five years later.

CONSISTENCY

The fund has been quite consistent, outperforming the Dow Jones Industrial Average four of the past five years through 1999 (and again through most of 2000). Its biggest gain came in 1995, when it moved up 34.4 percent (compared with a 33.5 percent rise in the Dow).

FEES/SERVICES/MANAGEMENT

The fund is a pure no-load fund, with no fees to buy or sell shares. The fund's total annual expense ratio of 0.19 percent (with no 12b-1 fee) is extremely low as compared with most other funds.

The fund offers all the standard services such as retirement account availability, automatic withdrawal, and automatic checking account deduction. Its minimum initial investment of $10,000 and minimum subsequent investment of $100 are much higher than most other funds.

George Sauter has managed the fund since its inception in 1994. The Vanguard fund family includes over 120 funds and allows shareholders to switch from fund to fund by telephone.

Top Ten Stock Holdings

1. General Electric
2. Cisco Systems
3. Pfizer
4. Intel
5. Citigroup

6. Microsoft
7. Exxon Mobil
8. EMC
9. IBM
10. American International Group

Fund inception: 1994
Asset mix: Common stocks, 100%
Total net assets: $3 billion

Load

Front-end load	*None*
Redemption fee (max.)	*None*

Annual Fees

12b-1 fee	*None*
Management fee	0.17%
Other expenses	0.02
Total annual expense	0.19%

Minimum initial investment	$10,000
Minimum subsequent investment	$100

Services

Telephone exchanges	*Yes*
Automatic withdrawal	*Yes*
Automatic checking deduction	*Yes*
Retirement plan/IRA	*Yes*
Instant redemption	*Yes*
Portfolio manager (years)	6
Number of funds in family	over 120

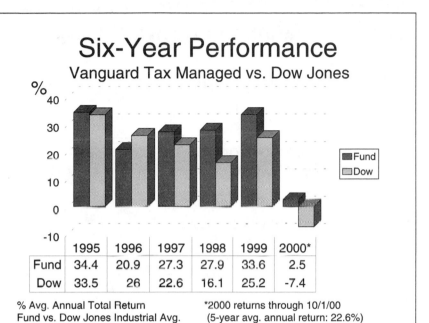

Six-Year Performance
Vanguard Tax Managed vs. Dow Jones

	1995	1996	1997	1998	1999	2000*
Fund	34.4	20.9	27.3	27.9	33.6	2.5
Dow	33.5	26	22.6	16.1	25.2	-7.4

% Avg. Annual Total Return   *2000 returns through 10/1/00
Fund vs. Dow Jones Industrial Avg.   (5-year avg. annual return: 22.6%)

62

Excelsior Value and Restructuring Fund

Excelsior Funds
73 Tremont Street
Boston, MA 02108-3913
800-446-1012
www.excelsiorfunds.com
Ticker symbol: **UMBIX**

Fund manager: David J. Williams
Fund objective: Long-term growth

Performance	★ ★
Consistency	★ ★ ★
Fees/Services/Management	★ ★ ★ ★ ★
Total	**10 Points**

Fund manager David Williams looks for diamonds in the rough.

Companies whose share prices may benefit from the restructuring or redeployment of assets and operations often find their way into the $1.3 billion portfolio. Williams is fond of stocks whose price-earnings ratios are 40 to 50 percent less than the Standard & Poor's average. For example, the Excelsior Value and Restructuring Fund owns AmeriSource Health, a drug wholesaler whose stock was selling at just 12 times its 2000 earnings.

Williams, who has managed the fund since its 1992 inception, also looks for companies that are undermanaged where there is great upside potential. The fund's top holdings include some well-managed, high performers such as QUALCOMM, Texas Instruments, and Nokia. The fund, consisting of about 70 stocks, also includes some recently hard-pressed blue chips like Xerox and Eastman Kodak. The fund is stocked with candidates for restructuring, mergers, consolidations, liquidations, spin-offs, and reorganizations.

The fund, whose goal is long-term capital appreciation, has a low portfolio turnover rate of 20 percent. Since its launch, the fund's average annual total rate of return has been 26.5 percent. A $10,000 investment in the fund ten years ago would now be worth about $30,400.

PERFORMANCE

The fund has enjoyed solid growth over the past five years. Including dividends and capital gains distributions, the Excelsior Value and Restructuring Fund has provided an average annual return the past five years (through late 2000) of about 23 percent.

A $10,000 investment in 1995 would have grown to about $28,000 five years later.

CONSISTENCY

The fund has been fairly consistent, outperforming the Dow Jones Industrial Average three of the past five years through 1999 (and again through most of 2000). Its biggest gain came in 1995, when it moved up 38.8 percent (compared with a 33.5 percent rise in the Dow).

FEES/SERVICES/MANAGEMENT

The fund is a pure no-load fund, with no fees to buy or sell shares. The fund's total annual expense ratio of 0.9 percent (with no 12b-1 fee) is very low compared with most other funds.

The fund offers all the standard services such as retirement account availability, automatic withdrawal, and automatic checking account deduction. Its minimum initial investment of $500 and minimum subsequent investment of $50 compare favorably with other funds.

The fund has been managed by David Williams since its inception in 1992. The Excelsior fund family includes 27 funds and allows shareholders to switch from fund to fund by telephone.

Top Ten Stock Holdings

1. QUALCOMM
2. Texas Instruments
3. Nokia
4. General Motors Class 'H'
5. AT&T-Liberty Media 'A'
6. Kansas City So. Industries
7. Vishay Intertechnology
8. IBM
9. Global Crossing
10. New Corp. Spons. ADR

Fund inception: 1992
Asset mix: Common stocks, 97%; cash/equivalents, 2%;
preferred stocks, 1%
Total net assets: $1.3 billion

Load

Front-end load	*None*
Redemption fee (max.)	*None*

Annual Fees

12b-1 fee	*None*
Management fee	0.60%
Other expenses	0.30
Total annual expense	0.90%
Minimum initial investment	$500
Minimum subsequent investment	$50

Services

Telephone exchanges	*Yes*
Automatic withdrawal	*Yes*
Automatic checking deduction	*Yes*
Retirement plan/IRA	*Yes*
Instant redemption	*Yes*
Portfolio manager (years)	8
Number of funds in family	27

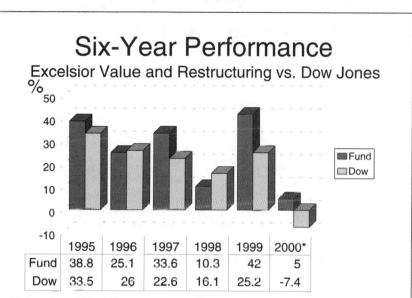

Six-Year Performance
Excelsior Value and Restructuring vs. Dow Jones

	1995	1996	1997	1998	1999	2000*
Fund	38.8	25.1	33.6	10.3	42	5
Dow	33.5	26	22.6	16.1	25.2	-7.4

% Avg. Annual Total Return
Fund vs. Dow Jones Industrial Avg.

*2000 returns through 10/1/00
(5-year avg. annual return: 23.7%)

63

Managers Special Equity Fund

Managers Funds
40 Richards Avenue
Norwalk, CT 06854-2325
800-835-3879
www.managersfunds.com
Ticker symbol: **MGSEX**

Fund managers: Andrew Knuth, Gary Pilgrim, Timothy Ebright, and
Bob Kern
Fund objective: Small-cap stocks

Performance	★ ★
Consistency	★ ★ ★
Fees/Services/Management	★ ★ ★ ★ ★
Total	**10 Points**

One fund, four approaches. Four experienced fund managers contribute their own selections to the portfolio of this $2 billion small-stock fund.

The four subadvisors include Gary Pilgrim of Pilgrim Baxter & Associates, Andrew Knuth of Westport Asset Management, Timothy Ebright of Liberty Investment Management, and Bob Kern of Kern Capital Management. Each fund manager selects a portion of the overall portfolio, using his own unique buy-and-sell strategy.

The fund invests in a wide range of small-cap stocks, such as TeleTech, Emmis Communications, Conexant Systems, and Anaren Microwave.

The fund is heavily invested in technology stocks, which account for about 40 percent of the portfolio. Other leading sectors include consumer cyclicals, 14 percent; capital goods, 10 percent; consumer staples, 8 percent; health care, 6 percent; and financials, 5 percent.

The fund was launched in 1984. A $10,000 investment in the fund ten years ago would now be worth about $62,000—a 20 percent average annual return.

The fund managers are fairly active in their approach, with an 89 percent annual portfolio turnover ratio. The fund stays 80 to 95 percent invested in stocks under most circumstances.

PERFORMANCE

The fund has enjoyed exceptional growth over the past five years. Including dividends and capital gains distributions, the Managers Special Equity Fund has provided an average annual return the past five years (through late 2000) of 23.1 percent.

A $10,000 investment in 1995 would have grown to about $28,000 five years later.

CONSISTENCY

The fund has been fairly consistent, outperforming the Dow Jones Industrial Average three of the past five years through 1999 (and again through most of 2000). Its biggest gain came in 1999, when it moved up 54.1 percent (compared with a 25.2 percent rise in the Dow).

FEES/SERVICES/MANAGEMENT

The fund is a pure no-load fund, with no fees to buy or sell shares. The fund's total annual expense ratio of 1.31 percent (with no 12b-1 fee) is in line with other funds.

The fund offers all the standard services such as retirement account availability, automatic withdrawal, and automatic checking account deduction. Its minimum initial investment of $2,000 and minimum subsequent investment of $100 are in line with other funds.

The fund is managed by four advisors, including Andrew Knuth, since 1985, Gary Pilgrim, since 1994, Timothy Ebright, since 1985, and Bob Kern, since 1997. The Managers fund family includes 13 funds and allows shareholders to switch from fund to fund by telephone.

64

Seligman Capital Fund

Seligman Funds
100 Park Avenue
New York, NY 10017
800-221-2450
www.seligman.com
Ticker symbol: **SCIFX**

Fund managers: Marion Schultheis and Jack Chang
Fund objective: Long-term growth

Performance	★ ★ ★ ★
Consistency	★ ★ ★ ★
Fees/Services/Management	★ ★
Total	**10 Points**

Seligman Capital Fund managers Marion Schultheis and Jack Chang try to stay one step ahead of Wall Street in identifying the midcap growth companies that will lead the pack in growth and earnings.

The fund, established in 1969, focuses on selecting companies with potential for significant price improvement and top risk-reward profiles. The portfolio's 75 stocks are drawn from a broad mix of sectors and companies operating primarily in the U.S. economy.

The leading sector in the $500 million portfolio is consumer cyclicals at 22 percent, followed by consumer staples at 17 percent, financials at 15 percent, capital goods at 11 percent, and technology at 9 percent.

Top stock holdings reflect the diversified nature of the fund, with retailers Circuit City and Office Depot; manufacturers Newell Rubbermaid and General Instrument; and communications and broadcasting leaders AT&T, Infinity Broadcasting, and Century Telecommunications.

A $10,000 investment in the fund ten years ago would now be worth about $67,000—a 21 percent average annual return.

The fund managers are aggressive in their approach, with an annual portfolio turnover rate of 175 percent. The fund stays at least 90 percent invested in stocks under normal circumstances.

PERFORMANCE

The fund has enjoyed very strong growth over the past five years. Including dividends and capital gains distributions, the Seligman Capital Fund has provided a load-adjusted average annual return the past five years (through late 2000) of 29.1 percent.

A $10,000 investment in 1995 would have grown to about $36,000 five years later.

CONSISTENCY

The fund has been very consistent, outperforming or matching the Dow Jones Industrial Average four of the past five years through 1999 (and again through most of 2000). Its biggest gain came in 1999, when it moved up 50.7 percent (compared with a 25.2 percent rise in the Dow).

FEES/SERVICES/MANAGEMENT

The fund has a front-end load of 4.75 percent, with a maximum back-end load of 1 percent. The fund's total annual expense ratio of 1.02 percent (with a 0.25 percent 12b-1 fee) compares well with other funds.

The fund offers all the standard services such as retirement account availability, automatic withdrawal, and automatic checking account deduction. Its minimum initial investment of $1,000 and minimum subsequent investment of $100 are in line with other funds.

Marion Schultheis, who manages the fund with Jack Chang, has only been with the fund since 1998. The Seligman fund family includes more than 40 funds and allows shareholders to switch from fund to fund by telephone.

Top Ten Stock Holdings

1. Circuit City Group
2. Century Telecommunications
3. Comdisco
4. Applied Power
5. Office Depot
6. AT&T
7. Newell Rubbermaid
8. Infinity Broadcasting
9. General Instrument
10. Dial Corp.

Fund inception: 1969
Asset mix: Common stocks, 96%; cash/equivalents, 4%
Total net assets: $509 million

Load

Front-end load	4.75%
Redemption fee (max.)	1.00%

Annual Fees

12b-1 fee	0.25%
Management fee	0.48%
Other expenses	0.29
Total annual expense	1.02%
Minimum initial investment	$1,000
Minimum subsequent investment	$100

Services

Telephone exchanges	*Yes*
Automatic withdrawal	*Yes*
Automatic checking deduction	*Yes*
Retirement plan/IRA	*Yes*
Instant redemption	*Yes*
Portfolio manager (years)	2
Number of funds in family	over 40

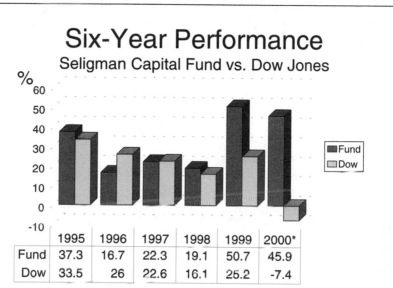

Six-Year Performance
Seligman Capital Fund vs. Dow Jones

	1995	1996	1997	1998	1999	2000*
Fund	37.3	16.7	22.3	19.1	50.7	45.9
Dow	33.5	26	22.6	16.1	25.2	-7.4

% Avg. Annual Total Return
Fund vs. Dow Jones Industrial Avg.

*2000 returns through 10/1/00
(5-year avg. annual return: 32.6%)

65
Vanguard Growth and Income Fund

Vanguard Funds
Vanguard Financial Center
P.O. Box 2600
Valley Forge, PA 19482
800-662-2739
www.vanguard.com
Ticker symbol: **VQNPX**

Fund manager: John S. Cone
Fund objective: Growth and income

Performance	★ ★
Consistency	★ ★ ★ ★
Fees/Services/Management	★ ★ ★ ★
Total	**10 Points**

Cash and capital appreciation are the goals of the Vanguard Growth and Income Fund. The fund invests primarily in large-cap stocks, many of which pay dividends.

Fund manager John Cone looks for stocks that appear to be undervalued relative to the market and that appear likely to provide higher returns than the Standard & Poor's 500 Index. In all, Cone uses more than 30 computer models to screen stocks and to rank them according to a variety of financial measures. Among the measures are current and forecast share prices and earnings, dividend yield, and future cash flow.

The $9.4 billion fund invests in a diverse selection of blue chip stocks, such as General Electric, Pfizer, Citigroup, Exxon Mobil, Merck, and Intel.

Technology stocks make up about 21 percent of the portfolio, followed by financial services, 18 percent; consumer services, 14 percent; utilities, 12 percent; health care, 9 percent; integrated oils, 6 percent; and materials and processing, 3 percent.

The fund was opened in 1986. A $10,000 investment in the fund ten years ago would now be worth about $52,000—an 18 percent average annual return.

The fund is conservatively managed, with a 54 percent annual portfolio turnover ratio. The fund stays almost 100 percent invested in stocks under normal circumstances.

PERFORMANCE

The fund has accomplished fair growth over the past five years. Including dividends and capital gains distributions, the Vanguard Growth and Income Fund has provided an average annual return the past five years (through late 2000) of 23.5 percent.

A $10,000 investment in 1995 would have grown to about $28,500 five years later.

CONSISTENCY

The fund has been very consistent, outperforming the Dow Jones Industrial Average four of the past five years through 1999 (and again through most of 2000). Its biggest gain came in 1995, when it moved up 35.9 per cent (compared with a 33.5 percent rise in the Dow).

FEES/SERVICES/MANAGEMENT

The fund is a pure no-load fund, with no fees to buy or sell shares. The fund's total annual expense ratio of 0.37 percent (with no 12b-1 fee) is very low compared with most other funds.

The fund offers all the standard services such as retirement account availability, automatic withdrawal, and automatic checking account deduction. Its minimum initial investment of $3,000 and minimum subsequent investment of $100 are higher than most other funds.

Fund manager John S. Cone has only been with the fund since 1999. The Vanguard fund family includes over 120 funds and allows shareholders to switch from fund to fund by telephone.

Top Ten Stock Holdings

1. Cisco Systems
2. Pfizer
3. General Electric
4. Citigroup
5. Exxon Mobil

6. Merck
7. Intel
8. Microsoft
9. Oracle
10. Johnson & Johnson

Fund inception: 1986
Asset mix: Common stocks, 99%; cash/equivalents, 1%
Total net assets: $9.4 billion

Load

Front-end load	*None*
Redemption fee (max.)	*None*

Annual Fees

12b-1 fee	*None*
Management fee	0.35%
Other expenses	0.02
Total annual expense	0.37%
Minimum initial investment	$3,000
Minimum subsequent investment	$100

Services

Telephone exchanges	*Yes*
Automatic withdrawal	*Yes*
Automatic checking deduction	*Yes*
Retirement plan/IRA	*Yes*
Instant redemption	*Yes*
Portfolio manager (years)	1
Number of funds in family	over 120

Six-Year Performance
Vanguard Growth & Income vs. Dow Jones

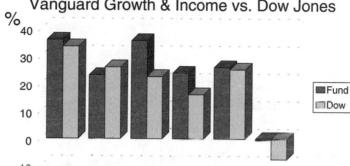

	1995	1996	1997	1998	1999	2000*
Fund	35.9	23.1	35.6	23.9	26	-0.4
Dow	33.5	26	22.6	16.1	25.2	-7.4

% Avg. Annual Total Return
Fund vs. Dow Jones Industrial Avg.

*2000 returns through 10/1/00
(5-year avg. annual return: 22.1%)

66

First American Technology Fund

First American Funds
680 East Swedesford Road
Oaks, PA 19456
800-637-2548
www.firstamericanfunds.com
Ticker symbol: **FATAX**

Fund manager: Roland Whitcomb
Fund objective: Sector

Performance	★ ★ ★ ★ ★
Consistency	★ ★ ★
Fees/Services/Management	★ ★
Total	**10 Points**

The First American Technology Fund invests in companies that are developing some of the hottest, most innovative products of the new economy.

Stocks of computer makers, software vendors, satellite communications companies, semiconductor makers, and online services are the types of companies found in this $400 million fund established in 1994. The fund's management is looking for shares in companies that have or will develop products, processes, or services that will provide or significantly benefit from technological advances.

In addition to familiar technology stalwarts like America Online, Cisco, Microsoft, Intel, and Oracle, the fund invests in some development-stage companies and small-cap companies. The fund, which has about 115 stocks, may also invest in companies launching initial public offerings, including some of the so-called hot issues that are generally traded in the aftermarket at prices exceeding their IPO prices.

As the fund's name suggests, technology is the focus of the fund. Technology stocks make up more than 90 percent of the portfolio, which has a turnover ratio of 184 percent. In 1999, the fund grew a spectacular 192 percent, although the growth rate has cooled since as investors take a harder look at technology stocks.

Fund manager Roland Whitcomb manages the portfolio aggressively, with an annual turnover ratio of 184 percent.

PERFORMANCE

The fund has enjoyed outstanding growth over the past five years. Including dividends and capital gains distributions, the First American Technology Fund has provided a load-adjusted average annual return the past five years (through late 2000) of 38 percent.

A $10,000 investment in 1995 would have grown to about $50,000 five years later.

CONSISTENCY

The fund has been fairly volatile but has still outperformed the Dow Jones Industrial Average three of the past five years through 1999 (and again through most of 2000). Its biggest gain came in 1999, when it moved up 191.8 percent (compared with a 25.2 percent rise in the Dow).

FEES/SERVICES/MANAGEMENT

The fund has a front-end load of 5.25 percent, with a maximum back-end load of 1 percent. The fund's total annual expense ratio of 1.15 percent (with a 0.25 percent 12b-1 fee) compares favorably with other funds.

The fund offers all the standard services such as retirement account availability, automatic withdrawal, and automatic checking account deduction. Its minimum initial investment of $1,000 and minimum subsequent investment of $100 are in line with other funds.

The fund has been managed by Roland Whitcomb since its inception in 1994. The First American fund family includes just three funds and allows shareholders to switch from fund to fund by telephone.

Top Ten Stock Holdings

1. Cisco Systems
2. Microsoft
3. Brocade Communications
4. Intel
5. Oracle Systems

6. eBay
7. Dell Computer
8. America Online
9. Nokia
10. Applied Materials

Fund inception: 1994
Asset mix: Common stocks, 97%; cash/equivalents, 3%
Total net assets: $400 million

Load

Front-end load	5.25%
Redemption fee (max.)	1.00

Annual Fees

12b-1 fee	0.25%
Management fee	0.70
Other expenses	0.20
Total annual expense	1.15%

Minimum initial investment	$1,000
Minimum subsequent investment	$100

Services

Telephone exchanges	*Yes*
Automatic withdrawal	*Yes*
Automatic checking deduction	*Yes*
Retirement plan/IRA	*Yes*
Instant redemption	*Yes*
Portfolio manager (years)	6
Number of funds in family	3

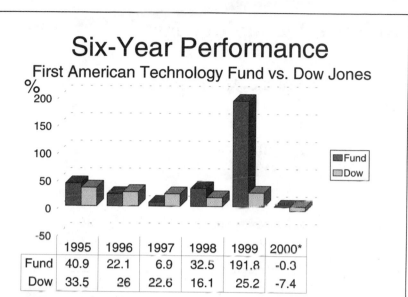

Six-Year Performance
First American Technology Fund vs. Dow Jones

	1995	1996	1997	1998	1999	2000*
Fund	40.9	22.1	6.9	32.5	191.8	-0.3
Dow	33.5	26	22.6	16.1	25.2	-7.4

% Avg. Annual Total Return
Fund vs. Dow Jones Industrial Avg.

*2000 returns through 10/1/00
(5-year avg. annual return: 36.8%)

67
Alliance Technology Fund

Alliance Funds
1345 Avenue of the Americas
New York, NY 10105
800-824-1916
www.alliancecapital.com
Ticker symbol: **ALTFX**

Fund managers: Peter Anastos and Gerald Malone
Fund objective: Sector

Performance	★ ★ ★ ★
Consistency	★ ★ ★
Fees/Services/Management	★ ★ ★
Total	**10 Points**

One of the oldest of all technology sector funds, the Alliance Technology Fund was founded in 1982—just in time for the golden age of technology. The fund has posted a 24 percent average annual return since its inception. A $10,000 investment in the fund in 1982 would have grown to about $500,000 by 2000.

The fund can be volatile in the short term, but the growth prospects in the technology area continue to be alluring for the long term.

Fund managers Gerald Malone and Peter Anastos invest in some of the leading technology stocks, such as Cisco Systems, PMC-Sierra, Nokia, Applied Materials, and Dell Computer. The fund managers say they "place strong emphasis on companies that are dominant in their industries."

The fund has about 60 stock holdings in all. The leading sectors include semiconductor components, 20 percent; computer hardware, 6 percent; computer services, 10 percent; computer software, 16 percent; contract manufacturing, 11 percent; capital equipment, 6 percent; consumer services, 3 percent; networking software, 5 percent; and communications equipment, 8 percent.

The fund managers maintain a fairly conservative trading approach, with an annual portfolio turnover ratio of 54 percent. The fund stays more than 90 percent invested in stocks under most circumstances.

PERFORMANCE

The fund has enjoyed strong growth over the past five years. Including dividends and capital gains distributions, the Alliance Technology Fund has provided a load-adjusted average annual return the past five years (through late 2000) of 29.4 percent.

A $10,000 investment in 1995 would have grown to about $36,000 five years later.

CONSISTENCY

The fund has been fairly consistent, outperforming the Dow Jones Industrial Average three of the past five years through 1999 (and again through most of 2000). Its biggest gain came in 1999, when it moved up 71.8 percent (compared with a 25.2 percent rise in the Dow).

FEES/SERVICES/MANAGEMENT

The fund has a front-end load of 4.25 percent, with a maximum back-end load of 1 percent. The fund's total annual expense ratio of 1.68 percent (with a 0.3 percent 12b-1 fee) is about average among all mutual funds.

The fund offers all the standard services such as retirement account availability, automatic withdrawal, and automatic checking account deduction. Its minimum initial investment of $250 and minimum subsequent investment of $50 compare very favorably with other funds.

The fund has been managed by Peter Anastos and Gerald Malone since 1992. The Alliance fund family includes about 52 funds and allows shareholders to switch from fund to fund by telephone.

Top Ten Stock Holdings

1. Cisco Systems
2. PMC-Sierra
3. Nokia
4. Xilinx
5. Amdocs

6. Applied Materials
7. Dell Computer
8. eBay
9. Altera Corp.
10. Sanmina Corp.

Fund inception: 1982
Asset mix: Common stocks, 96%; cash/equivalents, 4%
Total net assets: $4 billion

Load

Front-end load	4.25%
Redemption fee (max.)	1.00

Annual Fees

12b-1 fee	0.30%
Management fee	1.10
Other expenses	0.28
Total annual expense	1.68%

Minimum initial investment	$250
Minimum subsequent investment	$50

Services

Telephone exchanges	*Yes*
Automatic withdrawal	*Yes*
Automatic checking deduction	*Yes*
Retirement plan/IRA	*Yes*
Instant redemption	*Yes*
Portfolio manager (years)	8
Number of funds in family	52

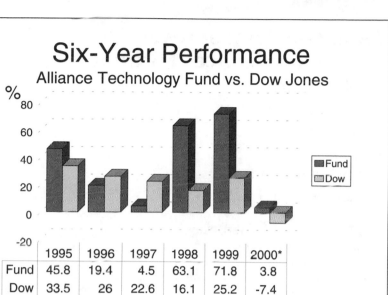

Six-Year Performance
Alliance Technology Fund vs. Dow Jones

	1995	1996	1997	1998	1999	2000*
Fund	45.8	19.4	4.5	63.1	71.8	3.8
Dow	33.5	26	22.6	16.1	25.2	-7.4

% Avg. Annual Total Return
Fund vs. Dow Jones Industrial Avg.

*2000 returns through 10/1/00
(5-year avg. annual return: 26.9%)

68

Fidelity Select: Software & Computer Services Portfolio

Fidelity Funds
82 Devonshire Street
Boston, MA 02109
800-544-8544
www.fidelity.com
Ticker symbol: **FSCSX**

Fund manager: Telis Bertsekas
Fund objective: Sector

Performance	★ ★ ★ ★ ★
Consistency	★ ★ ★
Fees/Services/Management	★ ★
Total	**10 Points**

Some of the stock market leaders of the past ten years have been software companies, including Microsoft and Oracle. The years ahead will probably bring more of the same, which is why the Fidelity Select Software and Computer Services Portfolio is loading up on the software leaders of the new economy. VERITAS Software, Checkpoint Software, BroadVision, and i2Technologies are all among the fund's 60 stock holdings.

The fund also invests in some leading computer and Internet services companies, such as America Online, Yahoo!, and eBay. And it has a stake in many other leading companies in the computer sector, such as Cisco Systems, Gateway, Compaq, and Sun Microsystems.

The fund, opened in 1985, has been one of the premier performers over the past ten years. A $10,000 investment in the fund ten years ago would now be worth about $130,000—a 29 percent average annual return.

About 87 percent of the $1.4 billion fund is invested in computer services and software stock, 3.5 percent is in computers and office equipment, and 3 percent is in communications equipment.

Fund manager Telis Bertsekas is fairly conservative in his investment approach, with a 59 percent annual portfolio turnover ratio. The fund stays about 90 percent invested in stocks under normal circumstances.

PERFORMANCE

The fund has enjoyed exceptional growth over the past five years. Including dividends and capital gains distributions, the Fidelity Select Software and Computer Services Portfolio has provided a load-adjusted average annual return the past five years (through late 2000) of 32 percent.

A $10,000 investment in 1995 would have grown to about $40,000 five years later.

CONSISTENCY

The fund has been fairly consistent, outperforming the Dow Jones Industrial Average three of the past five years through 1999 (and was about even with the Dow through most of 2000). Its biggest gain came in 1999, when it moved up 93.2 percent (compared with a 25.2 percent rise in the Dow).

FEES/SERVICES/MANAGEMENT

The fund has a 3 percent front-end load. The fund's total annual expense ratio of 1.11 percent (with no 12b-1 fee) is in line with other funds.

The fund offers all the standard services such as retirement account availability, automatic withdrawal, and automatic checking account deduction. Its minimum initial investment of $2,500 and minimum subsequent investment of $250 are a little higher than most other funds.

Telis Bertsekas became fund manager in 2000. He has been with Fidelity since 1997, but this is his first assignment as a fund manager. The Fidelity fund family includes more than 300 funds and allows shareholders to switch from fund to fund by telephone.

Top Ten Stock Holdings

1. Oracle
2. Siebel Systems
3. VERITAS Software
4. Microsoft
5. America Online
6. IBM
7. CMGI
8. Computer Associates International
9. Yahoo!
10. Sun Microsystems

Fund inception: 1985
Asset mix: Common stocks, 90%; cash/equivalents, 10%
Total net assets: $1.4 billion

Load

Front-end load	3.00%
Redemption fee (max.)	*None*

Annual Fees

12b-1 fee	*None*
Management fee	0.58%
Other expenses	0.53
Total annual expense	1.11%

Minimum initial investment	$2,500
Minimum subsequent investment	$250

Services

Telephone exchanges	*Yes*
Automatic withdrawal	*Yes*
Automatic checking deduction	*Yes*
Retirement plan/IRA	*Yes*
Instant redemption	*Yes*
Portfolio manager (years)	1
Number of funds in family	over 300

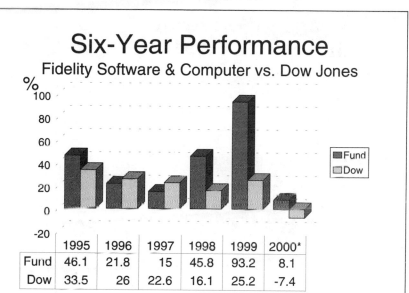

Six-Year Performance
Fidelity Software & Computer vs. Dow Jones

	1995	1996	1997	1998	1999	2000*
Fund	46.1	21.8	15	45.8	93.2	8.1
Dow	33.5	26	22.6	16.1	25.2	-7.4

% Avg. Annual Total Return
Fund vs. Dow Jones Industrial Avg.

*2000 returns through 10/1/00
(5-year avg. annual return: 34%)

69

Eaton Vance Worldwide Health Sciences Fund

Eaton Vance Funds
255 State Street
Boston, MA 02109
800-225-6265
www.eatonvancefunds.com
Ticker symbol: **ETHSX**

Fund manager: Samuel Isaly
Fund objective: Sector

Performance	★ ★ ★ ★ ★
Consistency	★ ★
Fees/Services/Management	★ ★ ★
Total	**10 Points**

The Eaton Vance Worldwide Health Sciences Fund has enjoyed healthy returns on the strength of a 40-stock portfolio that invests exclusively in the rapidly expanding global health care market.

In the United States alone, health care spending doubled between 1990 and 2000 to $1.5 trillion. And growth both in U.S. and international markets is expected to continue unabated as aging populations and other demographic factors drive demand for health sciences. In addition, medical breakthroughs will increase exponentially, and a host of new drugs will be introduced.

Against that bullish long-range backdrop, fund manager Samuel Isaly picks stocks of companies from throughout the world that he believes will play significant and profitable roles in the burgeoning global health care market. The portfolio ranges from small-cap issues to the big drug companies, such as American Home Products, Warner-Lambert, Roche Holdings, and Chiron.

A $10,000 investment in the fund ten years ago would now be worth about $86,000—an average annual return of about 24 percent.

Isaly's investment philosophy is essentially buy and hold. The average portfolio turnover rate is only 41 percent. The $350 million fund was founded in 1985 and has been under Isaly's direction since 1989.

PERFORMANCE

The fund has enjoyed outstanding growth over the past five years. Including dividends and capital gains distributions, the Eaton Vance Worldwide Heath Sciences Fund has provided a load-adjusted average annual return the past five years (through late 2000) of 32 percent.

A $10,000 investment in 1995 would have grown to about $40,000 five years later.

CONSISTENCY

The fund has been fairly inconsistent, outperforming the Dow Jones Industrial Average only two of the past five years through 1999 (but was far ahead of the Dow through most of 2000). Its biggest gain came in 1995, when it moved up 61.2 percent (compared with a 33.5 percent rise in the Dow).

FEES/SERVICES/MANAGEMENT

The fund has a front-end load of 5.75 percent, with a maximum back-end load of 1 percent. The fund's total annual expense ratio of 1.69 percent (with a 0.25 percent 12b-1 fee) is in line with other funds.

The fund offers all the standard services such as retirement account availability, automatic withdrawal, and automatic checking account deduction. Its minimum initial investment of $1,000 and minimum subsequent investment of $50 compare favorably with other funds.

The fund has been managed by Samuel Isaly since 1989. The Eaton Vance fund family includes 70 funds and allows shareholders to switch from fund to fund by telephone.

Top Ten Stock Holdings

1. Ares-Serono Group SA
2. American Home Products
3. Warner-Lambert
4. Roche Holdings
5. Sanofi Synthelabo SA

6. Atlanta AG
7. Fujisawa Pharmaceutical
8. ALZA
9. Chiron
10. Abgenix

Fund inception: 1985
Asset mix: Common stocks, 93%; cash/equivalents, 7%
Total net assets: $333 million

Load

Front-end load	5.75%
Redemption fee (max.)	1.00

Annual Fees

12b-1 fee	0.25%
Management fee	0.61
Other expenses	0.83
Total annual expense	1.69%

Minimum initial investment	$1,000
Minimum subsequent investment	$50

Services

Telephone exchanges	*Yes*
Automatic withdrawal	*Yes*
Automatic checking deduction	*Yes*
Retirement plan/IRA	*Yes*
Instant redemption	*Yes*
Portfolio manager (years)	11
Number of funds in family	70

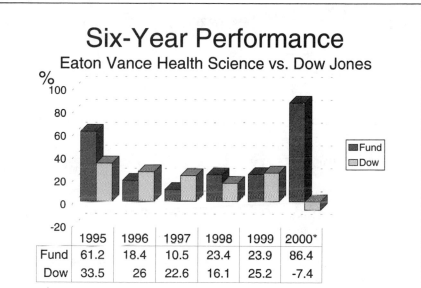

Six-Year Performance
Eaton Vance Health Science vs. Dow Jones

	1995	1996	1997	1998	1999	2000*
Fund	61.2	18.4	10.5	23.4	23.9	86.4
Dow	33.5	26	22.6	16.1	25.2	-7.4

% Avg. Annual Total Return   *2000 returns through 10/1/00
Fund vs. Dow Jones Industrial Avg.   (5-year avg. annual return: 33.8%)

70

John Hancock Technology Fund

John Hancock Global Funds
101 Huntington Avenue
Boston, MA 02199-7603
800-257-3336
www.jhfunds.com
Ticker symbol: **NTTFX**

Fund managers: Barry Gordon and Marc Klee
Fund objective: Sector

Performance	★ ★ ★ ★
Consistency	★ ★ ★
Fees/Services/Management	★ ★ ★
Total	**10 Points**

Technology is more than just the Internet. It's software, networking equipment, semiconductors, computers, and telecommunications equipment.

All of these high-tech elements are well represented in the John Hancock Technology Fund, managed by Marc Klee and Barry Gordon. Klee and Gordon are no Johnny-come-latelies to the technology game. They've been managing the fund since its inception in 1983. The fund consists of about 130 stocks.

Because of their experience, Klee and Gordon see the technology industry for the growing phenomenon that it has become. But they are not likely to swoon over each new idea that pops up on the Internet. They are able to draw on their years of industry and investment experience, using in-depth research and fundamental analysis to understand a technology company and the environment in which it operates.

Semiconductor stocks are among the biggest holdings of the $1 billion fund. These critical building blocks of the new economy have enjoyed strong growth in recent years because of their use not only in PCs, but also in such chip-dependent products as Internet appliances, cable TV, wireless phones, remote control devices, kitchen appliances, automobiles, and sophisticated medical devices.

Chipmakers such as Analog Devices, Cypress Semiconductor, Intel, Integrated Device Technology and Micron Technology are among the leading holdings of the portfolio.

A $10,000 investment in the fund ten years ago would now be worth about $110,000. The fund has a modest 61 percent annual portfolio turnover ratio.

PERFORMANCE

The fund has enjoyed outstanding growth over the past five years. Including dividends and capital gains distributions, the John Hancock Technology Fund has provided a load-adjusted average annual return the past five years (through late 2000) of 30 percent.

A $10,000 investment in 1995 would have grown to about $37,000 five years later.

CONSISTENCY

The fund has been fairly consistent, outperforming the Dow Jones Industrial Average three of the past five years through 1999 (and was about even with the Dow through most of 2000). Its biggest gain came in 1999, when it moved up a whopping 132.4 percent (compared with a 25.2 percent rise in the Dow).

FEES/SERVICES/MANAGEMENT

The fund has a front-end load of 5 percent, with a maximum back-end load of 1 percent. The fund's total annual expense ratio of 1.35 percent (with a 0.3 percent 12b-1 fee) is in line with other funds.

The fund offers all the standard services such as retirement account availability, automatic withdrawal, and automatic checking account deduction. Its minimum initial investment of $1,000 and minimum subsequent investment of $25 are in line with other funds.

The fund has been managed by Klee and Gordon since its inception in 1983. The John Hancock fund family includes 33 funds and allows shareholders to switch from fund to fund by telephone.

Top Ten Stock Holdings

1. Micron Technology
2. Exodus Communications
3. Cisco Systems
4. America Online
5. EMC Corp.

6. Oracle
7. CIENA Corp.
8. Microsoft
9. Mercury Interactive
10. Nokia

Fund inception: 1983
Asset mix: Common stocks, 93%; cash/equivalents, 7%
Total net assets: $1.1 billion

Load

Front-end load	5.00%
Redemption fee (max.)	1.00

Annual Fees

12b-1 fee	0.30%
Management fee	0.76
Other expenses	0.29
Total annual expense	1.35%

Minimum initial investment	$1,000
Minimum subsequent investment	$25

Services

Telephone exchanges	*Yes*
Automatic withdrawal	*Yes*
Automatic checking deduction	*Yes*
Retirement plan/IRA	*Yes*
Instant redemption	*Yes*
Portfolio manager (years)	17
Number of funds in family	33

Six-Year Performance
John Hancock Technology vs. Dow Jones

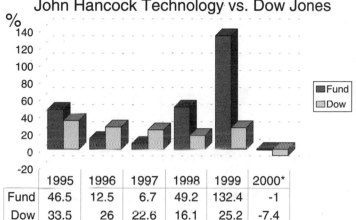

	1995	1996	1997	1998	1999	2000*
Fund	46.5	12.5	6.7	49.2	132.4	-1
Dow	33.5	26	22.6	16.1	25.2	-7.4

% Avg. Annual Total Return
Fund vs. Dow Jones Industrial Avg.

*2000 returns through 10/1/00
(5-year avg. annual return: 31.1%)

71

Calvert Large Cap Growth Fund

Calvert Funds
4550 Montgomery Avenue, Suite 1000N
Bethesda, MD 20814
800-368-2745
www.calvert.com

Fund manager: John Montgomery
Fund objective: Large-cap growth

Performance	★ ★ ★
Consistency	★ ★ ★
Fees/Services/Management	★ ★ ★
Total	**9 Points**

You can do well by doing "good" with the Calvert Large Cap Growth Fund. The socially responsible fund has provided a 26 percent average annual return since its inception in 1994—one of the best returns of all socially responsible mutual funds.

Formerly the Bridgeway Social Responsibility Portfolio, this fund was acquired by the Calvert fund family in October 2000. Calvert is known for its socially responsible mutual funds.

The fund, which has been managed by John Montgomery since its inception, focuses on companies with solid social responsibility records and good growth characteristics. The fund has no exposure to tobacco stocks and other companies that do not meet the fund's standards on corporate responsibility, pollution, hiring practices, and other social measures.

The fund invests in a diverse cross section of industries. Most of its holdings are midcap and large blue chip stocks, such as Medtronic, Nike, Digital Equipment, Compaq Computer, Merck, and Schering-Plough.

Technology stocks make up about 34 percent of this tiny $7 million portfolio. Other leading sectors include health care, 33 percent; consumer staples, 20.5 percent; communications services, 5 percent; financials, 5 percent; and utilities, 2 percent.

The fund maintains a modest 58 percent annual portfolio turnover ratio and stays at least 90 percent invested in stocks under normal circumstances.

PERFORMANCE

The fund has enjoyed strong growth over the past five years. Including dividends and capital gains distributions, the Calvert Large Cap Growth Fund has provided a load-adjusted average annual return the past five years (through late 2000) of 26.4 percent.

A $10,000 investment in 1995 would have grown to about $32,000 five years later.

CONSISTENCY

The fund has been fairly consistent, outperforming the Dow Jones Industrial Average three of the past five years through 1999 (and again through most of 2000). Its biggest gain came in 1999, when it moved up 49.4 percent (compared with a 25.2 percent rise in the Dow).

FEES/SERVICES/MANAGEMENT

The fund has a front-end load of 4.75 percent, with a maximum back-end load of 0.50 percent. The fund's total annual expense ratio of 1.50 percent (with a 1 percent 12b-1 fee) is in line with other funds.

The fund offers all the standard services such as retirement account availability, automatic withdrawal, and automatic checking account deduction. Its minimum initial investment of $2,000 and minimum subsequent investment of $250 are in line with other funds.

The fund has been managed by John Montgomery since its inception in 1994. The Calvert fund family includes 16 funds and allows shareholders to switch from fund to fund by telephone.

Top Ten Stock Holdings

1. Esterline Technologies	6. Schering-Plough
2. Medtronic	7. Compaq Computer
3. Nike	8. Merck
4. Sofamor/Danek Group	9. Safeway
5. Digital Equipment	10. Wet Seal

Fund inception: 1994
Asset mix: Common stocks, 94%; cash/equivalents, 6%
Total net assets: $7.4 million

Load

Front-end load	4.75%
Redemption fee (max.)	0.50

Annual Fees

12b-1 fee	1.00%
Management fee	0.20
Other expenses	0.30
Total annual expense	1.50%

Minimum initial investment	$2,000
Minimum subsequent investment	$250

Services

Telephone exchanges	*Yes*
Automatic withdrawal	*Yes*
Automatic checking deduction	*Yes*
Retirement plan/IRA	*Yes*
Instant redemption	*Yes*
Portfolio manager: (years)	6
Number of funds in family	16

Six-Year Performance

Calvert Large Cap Growth vs. Dow Jones

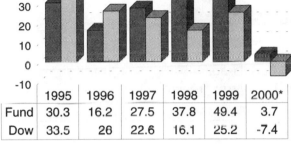

	1995	1996	1997	1998	1999	2000*
Fund	30.3	16.2	27.5	37.8	49.4	3.7
Dow	33.5	26	22.6	16.1	25.2	-7.4

% Avg. Annual Total Return   *2000 returns through 10/1/00
Fund vs. Dow Jones Industrial Avg.   (5-year avg. annual return: 26%)

72
Pilgrim Growth Opportunities Fund

Pilgrim Funds
Two Pickwick Plaza
Greenwich, CT 06830
800-992-0180
www.pilgrimfunds.com
Ticker symbol: **NGRAX**

Fund manager: Mary Lisanti
Fund objective: Long-term growth

Performance	★ ★ ★ ★
Consistency	★ ★ ★
Fees/Services/Management	★ ★
Total	**9 Points**

The telecommunications explosion, the information age, and the reengineering of American industry are major trends of the new U.S. economy. They are also among the top investment themes for the Pilgrim Growth Opportunities Fund.

Fund manager Mary Lisanti aims to invest primarily in the stocks of U.S. companies that are expected to benefit from major social, economic, and technological trends to shape the face of business over the next several years. So it's no wonder that the 140-stock fund's largest individual segment is electronic components and semiconductors, comprising about 15 percent of the portfolio. The fund's leading companies include Cisco Systems, Hewlett-Packard, and Oracle.

Other significant segments include telecommunications equipment, 9 percent; Internet software, 5 percent; computers, 4 percent; and networking products, 4 percent.

Lisanti has also tucked a few old economy stocks into the $215 million portfolio. Walt Disney and Paine Webber Group are both listed among the top holdings.

Founded in 1995, the portfolio has an aggressive annual turnover rate of 280 percent as Lisanti seeks to trade up for companies with above-average growth prospects. The fund stays more than 90 percent invested in stocks under normal circumstances.

PERFORMANCE

The fund has enjoyed outstanding growth over the past five years. Including dividends and capital gains distributions, the Pilgrim Growth Opportunities Fund has provided a load-adjusted average annual return the past five years (through late 2000) of 28.7 percent.

A $10,000 investment in 1995 would have grown to about $35,000 five years later.

CONSISTENCY

The fund has been fairly consistent, outperforming the Dow Jones Industrial Average three of the past five years through 1999 (and it was about even with the Dow through most of 2000). Its biggest gain came in 1999, when it moved up 93.3 percent (compared with a 25.2 percent rise in the Dow).

FEES/SERVICES/MANAGEMENT

The fund has a front-end load of 4.75 percent, with a maximum back-end load of 1 percent. The fund's total annual expense ratio of 1.39 percent (with a 0.3 percent 12b-1 fee) is in line with other funds.

The fund offers all the standard services such as retirement account availability, automatic withdrawal, and automatic checking account deduction. Its minimum initial investment of $1,000 and minimum subsequent investment of $100 are in line with other funds.

The fund has been managed by Mary Lisanti only since 1998. The Pilgrim fund family includes 44 funds and allows shareholders to switch from fund to fund by telephone.

Top Ten Stock Holdings

1. Cisco Systems
2. Hewlett-Packard
3. SDL, Inc.
4. Oracle
5. Adobe Systems
6. Walt Disney
7. ENSCO International
8. Paine Webber Group
9. NEXTEL Communications 'A'
10. EMC

Fund inception: 1995
Asset mix: Common stocks, 97%; cash/equivalents, 3%
Total net assets: $215 million

Load

Front-end load	4.75%
Redemption fee (max.)	1.00

Annual Fees

12b-1 fee	0.30%
Management fee	0.75
Other expenses	0.34
Total annual expense	1.39%

Minimum initial investment	$1,000
Minimum subsequent investment	$100

Services

Telephone exchanges	Yes
Automatic withdrawal	Yes
Automatic checking deduction	Yes
Retirement plan/IRA	Yes
Instant redemption	Yes
Portfolio manager (years)	2
Number of funds in family	44

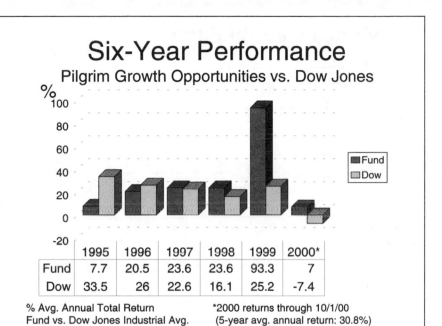

Six-Year Performance
Pilgrim Growth Opportunities vs. Dow Jones

	1995	1996	1997	1998	1999	2000*
Fund	7.7	20.5	23.6	23.6	93.3	7
Dow	33.5	26	22.6	16.1	25.2	-7.4

% Avg. Annual Total Return   *2000 returns through 10/1/00
Fund vs. Dow Jones Industrial Avg.   (5-year avg. annual return: 30.8%)

73

GAMerica Capital Fund

GAM Funds
135 East 57th Street
New York, NY 10022
800-426-4685
www.gam.com
Ticker symbol: **GCFAX**

Fund manager: Gordon Grender
Fund objective: Small-cap stocks

Performance	★ ★
Consistency	★ ★ ★ ★
Fees/Services/Management	★ ★ ★
Total	**9 Points**

Gordon Grender, manager of the GAMerica Capital Fund, prospects the field of small-cap stocks in search of attractive values to include in the 50-stock portfolio.

Grender, who has managed the fund since its inception in 1995, has established a commendable track record of picking the stocks of emerging companies that are destined for bigger and better things. The fund has posted a 23 percent average annual return since its inception.

No single sector dominates the portfolio. Financials is the largest at about 18 percent, followed by consumer staples at 12 percent, consumer cyclicals at 11.5 percent, and capital goods at 9 percent. Other sectors represented in the fund include communications services, 6 percent; basic materials, 5.5 percent; energy, 4 percent; and technology, 3 percent.

The fund's top holdings reflect a diversified cross section of the economy, including Internet supplier Power-One, Sprint, Chubb Group, Pegasus Communications, and Best Buy.

When Grender finds a stock he likes, he tends to hold on to it for the long run. The portfolio turnover ratio is a very modest 20 percent. The fund's asset mix may vary, although stock holdings usually account for at least 80 percent of the portfolio.

PERFORMANCE

The fund has enjoyed solid growth over the past five years. Including dividends and capital gains distributions, the GAMerica Capital Fund has provided a load-adjusted average annual return the past five years (through late 2000) of 24 percent.

A $10,000 investment in 1995 would have grown to about $29,000 five years later.

CONSISTENCY

The fund has been very consistent, outperforming the Dow Jones Industrial Average three of the past four years through 1999 (and again through most of 2000). (The fund opened in May 1995, so 1995 comparison is not applicable.) Its biggest gain came in 1997, when it moved up 37.3 percent (compared with a 22.6 percent rise in the Dow).

FEES/SERVICES/MANAGEMENT

The fund has a front-end load of 5 percent, with a maximum back-end load of 1 percent. The fund's total annual expense ratio of 1.84 percent (with a 0.30 percent 12b-1 fee) is in line with other funds.

The fund offers all the standard services such as retirement account availability, automatic withdrawal, and automatic checking account deduction. Its minimum initial investment of $5,000 is much higher than most other funds.

The fund has been managed by Gordon Grender since its inception in 1995. The GAM fund family includes eight funds and allows shareholders to switch from fund to fund by telephone.

Top Ten Stock Holdings

1. Power-One
2. Sprint
3. XL Capital
4. Fortune Brands
5. Chubb Group

6. Trex Company
7. Pegasus Communications
8. Delta and Pine Land
9. Best Buy
10. Foamex International

Fund inception: 1995
Asset mix: Common stocks, 80%; cash/equivalents, 19%;
corporate bonds, 1%
Total net assets: $57 million

Load

Front-end load	5.00%
Redemption fee (max.)	1.00

Annual Fees

12b-1 fee	0.30%
Management fee	1.00
Other expenses	0.54
Total annual expense	1.84%

Minimum initial investment	$5,000
Minimum subsequent investment	$100

Services

Telephone exchanges	*Yes*
Automatic withdrawal	*Yes*
Automatic checking deduction	*Yes*
Retirement plan/IRA	*Yes*
Instant redemption	*Yes*
Portfolio manager (years)	5
Number of funds in family	8

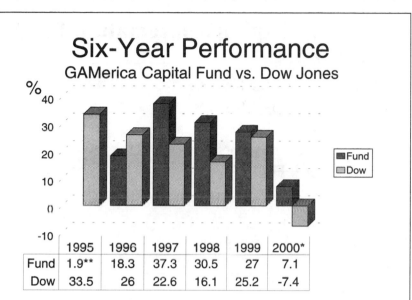

Six-Year Performance
GAMerica Capital Fund vs. Dow Jones

	1995	1996	1997	1998	1999	2000*
Fund	1.9**	18.3	37.3	30.5	27	7.1
Dow	33.5	26	22.6	16.1	25.2	-7.4

% Avg. Annual Total Return   *2000 returns through 10/1/00
(5-year avg. annual return: 25.1%)   ** Fund opened 5/12/95

74

Federated Capital Appreciation Fund

Federated Funds
Federated Investors Tower
Pittsburgh, PA 15222-3779
800-341-7400
www.federatedinvestors.com
Ticker symbol: **FEDEX**

Fund manager: Arthur Barry
Fund objective: Long-term growth

Performance	★ ★
Consistency	★ ★ ★ ★
Fees/Services/Management	★ ★ ★
Total	**9 Points**

You want diversification? The Federated Capital Appreciation Fund strikes a masterful mix between growth stocks and value stocks and between large-cap and midcap stocks.

Fund manager Arthur Barry's investment philosophy is to buy stocks of companies with superior growth prospects. Most of the holdings have a market capitalization of more than $500 million.

The lion's share of the portfolio is drawn from the technology sector, which represents about 27 percent of the 120-stock fund. Other leading sectors include financials, 11 percent; consumer staples, 7.8 percent; consumer cyclicals, 7.5 percent; health care, 7 percent; capital goods, 6 percent; communications services, 5.5 percent; energy, 5 percent; and basic materials, 5 percent.

The $420 million fund invests in established blue chips such as General Electric and Abbott Labs and such new economy stocks as Inktomi, Vitesse Semiconductor, and Broadwing.

The fund was launched in 1977. A $10,000 investment in the fund ten years ago would now be worth about $52,000—an average annual return of about 18 percent per year.

Barry takes a fairly conservative investment approach, with an annual portfolio turnover ratio of about 55 percent. The fund stays 70 to 80 percent invested in common stocks most of the time but also has investments in convertibles and preferred stocks.

PERFORMANCE

The fund has enjoyed solid growth over the past five years. Including dividends and capital gains distributions, the Federated Capital Appreciation Fund has provided a load-adjusted average annual return the past five years (through late 2000) of 24.5 percent.

A $10,000 investment in 1995 would have grown to about $30,000 five years later.

CONSISTENCY

The fund has been very consistent, outperforming the Dow Jones Industrial Average four of the past five years through 1999 (and again through most of 2000). Its biggest gain came in 1999, when it moved up 43.5 percent (compared with a 25.2 percent rise in the Dow).

FEES/SERVICES/MANAGEMENT

The fund has a front-end load of 5.50 percent, with a maximum back-end load of 0.75 percent. The fund's total annual expense ratio of 1.27 percent (with a 0.25 percent 12b-1 fee) is in line with other funds.

The fund offers all the standard services such as retirement account availability, automatic withdrawal, and automatic checking account deduction. Its minimum initial investment of $1,500 and minimum subsequent investment of $100 are in line with other funds.

The fund has been managed by Arthur Barry since 1997. The Federated fund family includes 130 funds and allows shareholders to switch from fund to fund by telephone.

Top Ten Stock Holdings

1. Microsoft
2. Cisco Systems
3. General Electric
4. Intel
5. Exxon Mobil

6. Wal-Mart
7. Oracle
8. IBM
9. Citigroup
10. Nortel Networks

Fund inception: 1985
Asset mix: Common stocks, 100%
Total net assets: $254 million

Load

Front-end load	5.25%
Redemption fee (max.)	*None*

Annual Fees

12b-1 fee	0.25%
Management fee	0.38
Other expenses	0.17
Total annual expense	0.80%
Minimum initial investment	$1,000
Minimum subsequent investment	$50

Services

Telephone exchanges	*Yes*
Automatic withdrawal	*Yes*
Automatic checking deduction	*Yes*
Retirement plan/IRA	*Yes*
Instant redemption	*Yes*
Portfolio manager (years)	3
Number of funds in family	9

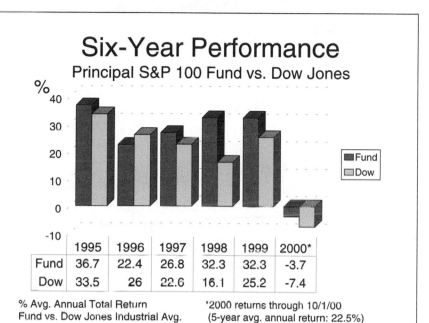

Six-Year Performance
Principal S&P 100 Fund vs. Dow Jones

	1995	1996	1997	1998	1999	2000*
Fund	36.7	22.4	26.8	32.3	32.3	-3.7
Dow	33.5	26	22.6	16.1	25.2	-7.4

% Avg. Annual Total Return   *2000 returns through 10/1/00
Fund vs. Dow Jones Industrial Avg.   (5-year avg. annual return: 22.5%)

76
Putnam Vista Fund

Putnam Funds
One Post Office Square
Boston, MA 02109
800-225-1581
www.putnaminv.com
Ticker symbol: **PVISX**

Fund managers: Team managed
Fund objective: Long-term growth

Performance	★ ★ ★
Consistency	★ ★ ★ ★
Fees/Services/Management	★ ★
Total	**9 Points**

The Putnam Vista Fund invests primarily in midsized and emerging stocks of fast-growing industries. Its stock holdings range in size from about $500 million to $6 billion in market capitalization.

The team of fund managers considers several factors in selecting stocks, such as the company's financial strength, competitive position, industry prospects, and projected future earnings.

Over the past ten years, the fund has posted an average annual return of about 22 percent. A $10,000 investment in the fund ten years ago would now be worth about $73,000.

The fund, which has been around since 1968, has about 100 stock holdings in all. Most of its leading holdings are emerging technology companies, such as VERITAS Software, LSI Logic, Comverse Technology, JDS Uniphase, and Analog Devices.

Technology stocks account for about 57 percent of the $7 billion portfolio, followed by consumer cyclicals, 14 percent; health care, 7 percent; consumer staples, 4 percent; energy, 3.5 percent; basic materials, 3 percent; and utilities, 3 percent.

The fund stays almost fully invested in stocks at all times. The fund managers take an active trading approach, with an annual portfolio turnover ratio of 155 percent.

PERFORMANCE

The fund has enjoyed outstanding growth over the past five years. Including dividends and capital gains distributions, the Putnam Vista Fund has provided a load-adjusted average annual return the past five years (through late 2000) of 26.8 percent.

A $10,000 investment in 1995 would have grown to about $33,000 five years later.

CONSISTENCY

The fund has been very consistent, outperforming the Dow Jones Industrial Average four of the past five years through 1999 (and again through most of 2000). Its biggest gain came in 1999, when it moved up 53.2 percent (compared with a 25.2 percent rise in the Dow).

FEES/SERVICES/MANAGEMENT

The fund has a front-end load of 5.75 percent, with a maximum back-end load of 1 percent. The fund's total annual expense ratio of 0.94 percent (with a 0.35 percent 12b-1 fee) compares favorably with other funds.

The fund offers all the standard services such as retirement account availability, automatic withdrawal, and automatic checking account deduction. Its minimum initial investment of $500 and minimum subsequent investment of $50 compare favorably with other funds.

The fund is managed by the team of Dana F. Clark, Margery Parker, Anthony C. Santosus, and Eric M. Wetlaufer. (Only Anthony Santosus has been with the fund for more than two years.) The Putnam fund family includes more than 140 funds and allows shareholders to switch from fund to fund by telephone.

Top Ten Stock Holdings

1. VERITAS Software
2. LSI Logic
3. Comverse Technology
4. JDS Uniphase
5. Maxim Integrated Products
6. Symbol Technologies
7. Siebel Systems
8. Immunex
9. PMC-Sierra
10. Analog Devices

Fund inception: 1968
Asset mix: Common stocks, 97%; cash/equivalents, 3%
Total net assets: $7 billion

Load

Front-end load	5.75%
Redemption fee (max.)	1.00

Annual Fees

12b-1 fee	0.35%
Management fee	0.43
Other expenses	0.16
Total annual expense	0.94%
Minimum initial investment	$500
Minimum subsequent investment	$50

Services

Telephone exchanges	*Yes*
Automatic withdrawal	*Yes*
Automatic checking deduction	*Yes*
Retirement plan/IRA	*Yes*
Instant redemption	*Yes*
Portfolio manager (years)	6
Number of funds in family	over 140

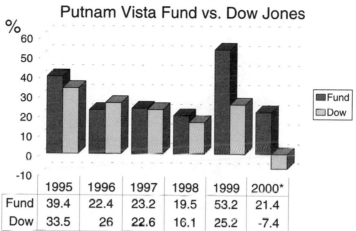

Six-Year Performance
Putnam Vista Fund vs. Dow Jones

	1995	1996	1997	1998	1999	2000*
Fund	39.4	22.4	23.2	19.5	53.2	21.4
Dow	33.5	26	22.6	16.1	25.2	-7.4

% Avg. Annual Total Return
Fund vs. Dow Jones Industrial Avg.

*2000 returns through 10/1/00
(5-year avg. annual return: 28.1%)

77

Morgan Stanley Dean Witter American Opportunities Fund

Morgan Stanley Dean Witter Funds
Two World Trade Center
New York, NY 10048
800-869-6397
www.morganstanley.com
Ticker symbol: **AMOAX**

Fund manager: Anita Kolleeny
Fund objective: Long-term growth

Performance	★ ★
Consistency	★ ★ ★ ★
Fees/Services/Management	★ ★ ★
Total	**9 Points**

Everything about the Morgan Stanley Dean Witter American Opportunities Fund is big. The stocks of some of America's corporate behemoths play prominent roles in the portfolio. And the fund's annual portfolio turnover ratio is a very aggressive 378 percent.

Yet the fund, with about 190 issues, has been nimble enough to outpace most of the other blue chip funds on the market. The growth-oriented fund uses an investment strategy, known as sector rotation, which emphasizes certain industries rather than individual companies as top prospects for capital appreciation.

The fund holds large positions in many of the most prominent stocks in the country, including Citigroup, General Electric, Chase Manhattan, Intel, Home Depot, Schlumberger, and Merrill Lynch.

Technology is the leading sector, accounting for 31 percent of the total portfolio. Other leading sectors include financial services, 9 percent; health care, 4 percent; and energy, 6 percent. The fund was founded in 1980 and has been managed since 1987 by Anita Kolleeny.

The fund has posted an average annual return of about 16.5 percent since its inception, and 20.3 percent over the past ten years. A $10,000 investment in the fund ten years ago would now be worth about $64,000.

The fund stays at least 80 percent invested in stocks under most circumstances.

This fund has been available as a back-end load fund since 1980 (under the symbol AMOBX), but was offered to individual investors in 1997 under the symbol AMOAX as an "A" fund.

PERFORMANCE

The fund has enjoyed solid growth over the past five years. Including dividends and capital gains distributions, the Morgan Stanley Dean Witter American Opportunities Fund has provided a load-adjusted average annual return the past five years (through late 2000) of 23.4 percent.

A $10,000 investment in 1995 would have grown to about $28,000 five years later.

CONSISTENCY

The fund has been very consistent, outperforming the Dow Jones Industrial Average four of the past five years through 1999 (and was about even with the Dow through most of 2000). Its biggest gain came in 1999, when it moved up 46.1 percent (compared with a 25.2 percent rise in the Dow).

FEES/SERVICES/MANAGEMENT

The fund has a front-end load of 5.25 percent. The fund's total annual expense ratio of 0.86 percent (with a 0.25 percent 12b-1 fee) compares very favorably with other funds.

The fund offers all the standard services such as retirement account availability, automatic withdrawal, and automatic checking account deduction. Its minimum initial investment of $1,000 and minimum subsequent investment of $100 are in line with other funds.

The fund has been managed by Anita Kolleeny since 1987. The Morgan Stanley fund family includes more than 50 funds and allows shareholders to switch from fund to fund by telephone.

Top Ten Stock Holdings

1. Citigroup
2. General Electric
3. Chase Manhattan
4. Schlumberger
5. Merrill Lynch

6. Home Depot
7. Cisco Systems
8. BJ Services
9. Intel
10. Micron Technology

Fund inception: 1980
Asset mix: Common stocks, 88%; cash/equivalents, 12%
Total net assets: $460 million

Load

Front-end load	5.25%
Redemption fee (max.)	*None*

Annual Fees

12b-1 fee	0.25%
Management fee	0.51
Other expenses	0.10
Total annual expense	0.86%

Minimum initial investment	$1,000
Minimum subsequent investment	$100

Services

Telephone exchanges	*Yes*
Automatic withdrawal	*Yes*
Automatic checking deduction	*Yes*
Retirement plan/IRA	*Yes*
Instant redemption	*Yes*
Portfolio manager (years)	13
Number of funds in family	over 50

Six-Year Performance

Morgan Stanley American Opportunity vs. Dow Jones

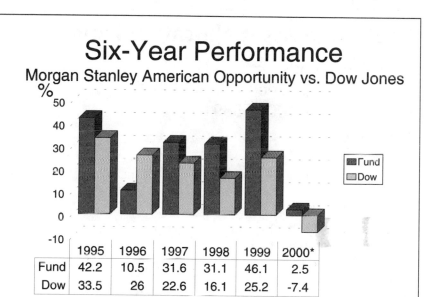

	1995	1996	1997	1998	1999	2000*
Fund	42.2	10.5	31.6	31.1	46.1	2.5
Dow	33.5	26	22.6	16.1	25.2	-7.4

% Avg. Annual Total Return
Fund vs. Dow Jones Industrial Avg.

*2000 returns through 10/1/00
(5-year avg. annual return: 24.4%)

78

Value Line Asset Allocation Fund

Value Line Funds
220 East 42nd Street
New York, NY 10017-5891
800-223-0818
www.valueline.com
Ticker symbol: **VLAAX**

Fund manager: Steven Grant
Fund objective: Balanced

Performance	★
Consistency	★ ★ ★
Fees/Services/Management	★ ★ ★ ★ ★
Total	**9 Points**

In a world where mutual fund labels don't always mean what they say, this is one fund that's true to its title. The Value Line Asset Allocation Fund divides its assets between stocks and bonds, shifting the mix as economic conditions change. This fund should appeal to conservative investors who want more diversity and stability in a fund, while still holding a stake in the stock market.

The fund's ten largest holdings are all bonds, but most of its assets are in stocks. The fund's average mix has been about 55 percent stocks, 35 percent bonds, and 10 percent cash and equivalents.

But despite the heavy weighting in bonds, the fund has been able to keep up with many of the more aggressive pure stock funds. It has posted an average annual return the past five years of about 23 percent.

Much of that growth can be attributed to its strong position in technology stocks, which account for about 35 percent of the portfolio. Other components include government bonds, 19 percent; treasuries, 11 percent; consumer cyclicals, 9 percent; health care, 6 percent; consumer staples, 6 percent; communications services, 5 percent; and capital goods, 4 percent.

Fund manager Steven Grant is fairly active in managing the fund, with a 72 percent annual portfolio turnover ratio.

PERFORMANCE

The fund has enjoyed solid growth over the past five years. Including dividends and capital gains distributions, the Value Line Asset Allocation Fund has provided an average annual return the past five years (through late 2000) of 22.8 percent.

A $10,000 investment in 1995 would have grown to about $28,000 five years later.

CONSISTENCY

The fund has been fairly consistent, outperforming the Dow Jones Industrial Average three of the past five years through 1999 (and again through most of 2000). Its biggest gain came in 1995, when it moved up 36.1 percent (compared with a 33.5 percent rise in the Dow).

FEES/SERVICES/MANAGEMENT

The fund is a pure no-load fund, with no fees to buy or sell shares. The fund's total annual expense ratio of 1.03 percent (with a 0.25 percent 12b-1 fee) compares favorably with other funds.

The fund offers all the standard services such as retirement account availability, automatic withdrawal, and automatic checking account deduction. Its minimum initial investment of $1,000 and minimum subsequent investment of $100 are in line with other funds.

The fund has been managed by Steven Grant since its inception in 1993. The Value Line fund family includes 14 funds and allows shareholders to switch from fund to fund by telephone.

Top Ten Stock Holdings

1. U.S. Treasury Bond 7.25
2. U.S. Treasury Note 6.5
3. FNMA 5.625
4. FHLMC 5
5. FNMA 6.625
6. FHLMC 6.875
7. FNMA 6.25
8. U.S. Treasury Inflation Index Note 3.875
9. International Bank Recon. & Dev. 7
10. FNMA 7.125

Fund inception: 1993
Asset mix: Common stocks, 65%; government bonds, 32%; cash/equivalents, 3%
Total net assets: $297 million

Load

Front-end load	*None*
Redemption fee (max.)	*None*

Annual Fees

12b-1 fee	0.25%
Management fee	0.65
Other expenses	0.13
Total annual expense	1.03%

Minimum initial investment	$1,000
Minimum subsequent investment	$100

Services

Telephone exchanges	*Yes*
Automatic withdrawal	*Yes*
Automatic checking deduction	*Yes*
Retirement plan/IRA	*Yes*
Instant redemption	*Yes*
Portfolio manager (years)	7
Number of funds in family	14

Six-Year Performance
Value Line Asset Allocation Fund vs. Dow Jones

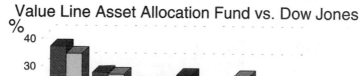

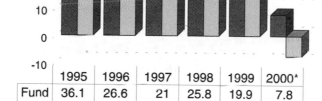

	1995	1996	1997	1998	1999	2000*
Fund	36.1	26.6	21	25.8	19.9	7.8
Dow	33.5	26	22.6	16.1	25.2	-7.4

% Avg. Annual Total Return
Fund vs. Dow Jones Industrial Avg.

*2000 returns through 10/1/00
(5-year avg. annual return: 21.4%)

79

SSgA Growth & Income Fund

SSgA Funds
Two International Place, 35th Floor
Boston, MA 02107-2291
800-647-7327
www.ssgafunds.com
Ticker symbol: **SSGWX**

Fund manager: Emerson Tuttle
Fund objective: Growth and income

Performance	★ ★
Consistency	★ ★
Fees/Services/Management	★ ★ ★ ★ ★
Total	**9 Points**

The SSgA Growth and Income Fund invests in a blend of fast-growth technology companies and established, dividend-paying blue chips.

Among the leading holdings are emerging high-tech companies such as Linear Technology, EMC, Cisco Systems, and Pharmacia. But the fund also has a diversified selection of older companies, such as IBM, General Electric, Morgan Stanley Dean Witter, Wal-Mart, and Duke Energy.

Technology stocks account for about 37 percent of the $460 million portfolio, followed by financials, 16 percent; communications services, 16 percent; health care, 9 percent; energy, 5 percent; consumer staples, 5 percent; basic materials, 4 percent; and utilities, 3 percent.

Most of the stocks in the portfolio have market caps of at least $10 billion. The fund invests in both growth stocks and value stocks.

The fund stays 100 percent invested in stocks under normal circumstances.

The fund was launched in 1993 and has posted an average annual return of about 20.5 percent since then. Fund manager Emerson Tuttle, who has been running the fund from the start, takes a fairly active management approach, with a 72 percent annual portfolio turnover ratio.

PERFORMANCE

The fund has enjoyed strong growth over the past five years. Including dividends and capital gains distributions, the SSgA Growth and Income Fund has provided an average annual return the past five years (through late 2000) of 25.1 percent.

A $10,000 investment in 1995 would have grown to about $30,000 five years later.

CONSISTENCY

The fund has been somewhat inconsistent, outperforming the Dow Jones Industrial Average only two of the past five years through 1999 (but it was beating the Dow through most of 2000). Its biggest gain came in 1997, when it moved up 37.6 percent (compared with a 22.6 percent rise in the Dow).

FEES/SERVICES/MANAGEMENT

The fund is a pure no-load fund, with no fees to buy or sell shares. The fund's total annual expense ratio of 1.10 percent (with a 0.15 percent 12b-1 fee) compares favorably with other funds.

The fund offers all the standard services such as retirement account availability, automatic withdrawal, and automatic checking account deduction. Its minimum initial investment of $1,000 and minimum subsequent investment of $100 are in line with other funds.

The fund has been managed by Emerson Tuttle since its inception in 1993. The SSgA fund family includes 24 funds and allows shareholders to switch from fund to fund by telephone.

Top Ten Stock Holdings

1. Linear Technology
2. Microsoft
3. General Electric
4. Pharmacia
5. EMC

6. Cisco Systems
7. Wal-Mart
8. Duke Energy
9. IBM
10. Morgan Stanley Dean Witter

Fund inception: 1993
Asset mix: Common stocks, 100%
Total net assets: $460 million

Load

Front-end load	*None*
Redemption fee (max.)	*None*

Annual Fees

12b-1 fee	0.15%
Management fee	0.85
Other expenses	0.10
Total annual expense	1.10%

Minimum initial investment	$1,000
Minimum subsequent investment	$100

Services

Telephone exchanges	*Yes*
Automatic withdrawal	*Yes*
Automatic checking deduction	*Yes*
Retirement plan/IRA	*Yes*
Instant redemption	*Yes*
Portfolio manager (years)	7
Number of funds in family	24

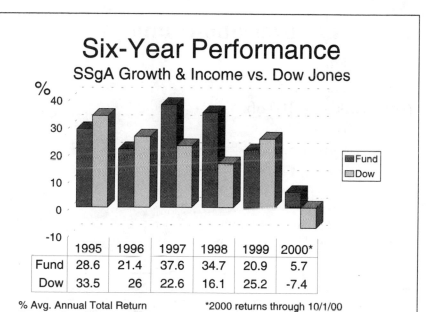

Six-Year Performance
SSgA Growth & Income vs. Dow Jones

	1995	1996	1997	1998	1999	2000*
Fund	28.6	21.4	37.6	34.7	20.9	5.7
Dow	33.5	26	22.6	16.1	25.2	-7.4

% Avg. Annual Total Return
Fund vs. Dow Jones Industrial Avg.

*2000 returns through 10/1/00
(5-year avg. annual return: 24.5%)

80

Dreyfus Appreciation Fund

Dreyfus Funds
200 Park Avenue
New York, NY 10166
800-645-6561
www.dreyfus.com
Ticker symbol: **DGAGX**

Fund manager: Fayez Sarofim
Fund objective: Long-term growth

Performance	★
Consistency	★ ★ ★
Fees/Services/Management	★ ★ ★ ★ ★
Total	**9 Points**

The Dreyfus Appreciation Fund isn't too quick to cash in its blue chips. The $4 billion fund focuses on established large-cap companies and holds on to them for the long term.

As a result, its portfolio turnover rate is a rock-bottom 12 percent. The 54-issue fund prefers companies that have sustained patterns of profitability, strong balance sheets, market dominance, an expanding global presence, and the potential to turn in steady, above-average earnings growth. The fund first identifies economic sectors it believes will expand over the next three to five years or longer.

Established in 1984, the fund has provided an average annual return the past ten years of about 17 percent. A $10,000 investment in the fund ten years ago would now be worth about $48,000.

The fund's leading holdings are all well-established mainstays of the U.S. economy, such Intel, Pfizer, General Electric, Exxon Mobil, and Cisco Systems. Technology is the fund's largest sector at 21 percent of the portfolio. Health care is second at 15 percent, and financial services is third at 13.5 percent. Other leading sectors include consumer staples, 12 percent; capital goods, 9 percent; communications services, 6 percent; and energy, 6 percent.

The fund is also alert to companies it considers undervalued in terms of earnings, assets, or growth possibilities.

PERFORMANCE

The fund has enjoyed solid growth over the past five years. Including dividends and capital gains distributions, the Dreyfus Appreciation Fund has provided an average annual return the past five years (through late 2000) of about 22 percent.

A $10,000 investment in 1995 would have grown to about $27,000 five years later.

CONSISTENCY

The fund has been fairly consistent, outperforming the Dow Jones Industrial Average three of the past five years through 1999 (and again through most of 2000). Its biggest gain came in 1995, when it moved up 37.9 percent (compared with a 33.5 percent rise in the Dow).

FEES/SERVICES/MANAGEMENT

The fund is a pure no-load fund, with no fees to buy or sell shares. The fund's total annual expense ratio of just 0.88 percent (with no 12b-1 fee) is very low compared with other funds.

The fund offers all the standard services such as retirement account availability, automatic withdrawal, and automatic checking account deduction. Its minimum initial investment of $2,500 and minimum subsequent investment of $100 is a little higher than most other funds.

The fund's management team has been headed by Fayez Sarofim for the past ten years. The Dreyfus fund family includes about 300 funds and allows shareholders to switch from fund to fund by telephone.

Top Ten Stock Holdings

1. Intel
2. Pfizer
3. General Electric
4. Cisco Systems
5. Microsoft
6. Citigroup
7. Exxon Mobil
8. Merck
9. Chase Manhattan
10. Hewlett-Packard

Fund inception: 1984
Asset mix: Common stocks, 99%; preferred stocks, 1%
Total net assets: $4 billion

Load

Front-end load	*None*
Redemption fee (max.)	*None*

Annual Fees

12b-1 fee	*None*
Management fee	0.55%
Other expenses	0.33
Total annual expense	0.88%

Minimum initial investment	$2,500
Minimum subsequent investment	$100

Services

Telephone exchanges	*Yes*
Automatic withdrawal	*Yes*
Automatic checking deduction	*Yes*
Retirement plan/IRA	*Yes*
Instant redemption	*Yes*
Portfolio manager (years)	10
Number of funds in family	300

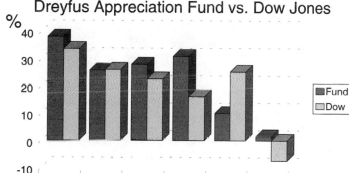

Six-Year Performance
Dreyfus Appreciation Fund vs. Dow Jones

	1995	1996	1997	1998	1999	2000*
Fund	37.9	25.7	27.9	30.8	10	1.6
Dow	33.5	26	22.6	16.1	25.2	-7.4

% Avg. Annual Total Return
Fund vs. Dow Jones Industrial Avg.

*2000 returns through 10/1/00
(5-year avg. annual return: 20.3%)

81
Massachusetts Investors Growth Stock Fund

MFS Funds
500 Boylston Street
Boston, MA 02116
800-225-2606
www.mfs.com
Ticker symbol: **MIGFX**

Fund manager: Stephen Pesek
Fund objective: Long-term growth

Performance	★ ★ ★ ★
Consistency	★ ★ ★
Fees/Services/Management	★ ★
Total	**9 Points**

This is one of the pioneers of the mutual fund industry. Opened in 1932, the Massachusetts Investors Growth Stock Fund is one of the oldest funds in the United States and remains one of the premier funds in the industry.

A $10,000 investment in the fund ten years ago would now be worth about $67,000—a 21 percent average annual return. This is one of only 16 mutual funds to beat the Standard & Poor's 500 Index over the past 1, 3, 5, 10, 15, 20, and 25 years.

The fund invests primarily in blue chip stocks across a broad range of industries, including Cisco Systems, Microsoft, Tyco International, General Electric, Oracle, and Bristol-Myers-Squibb.

Fund manager Stephen Pesek looks for companies with strong management, a successful track record, a history of consistent long-term earnings growth, and the potential for leadership in their market niche.

The fund invests heavily in technology-related stocks. Technology stocks account for about 39 percent of the $10 billion portfolio, followed by utilities and communications stocks, 12 percent; health care, 12 percent; financial services, 8.5 percent; and special products and services, 6.5 percent.

Pesek is fairly aggressive in his management approach, with a 174 percent annual portfolio turnover ratio. The fund stays almost fully invested in stocks under normal circumstances.

PERFORMANCE

The fund has enjoyed excellent growth over the past five years. Including dividends and capital gains distributions, the Massachusetts Investors Growth Stock Fund has provided a load-adjusted average annual return the past five years (through late 2000) of 30.1 percent.

A $10,000 investment in 1995 would have grown to about $37,000 five years later.

CONSISTENCY

The fund has been fairly consistent, outperforming the Dow Jones Industrial Average three of the past five years through 1999 (and again through most of 2000). Its biggest gain came in 1997, when it moved up 48.2 percent (compared with a 22.6 percent rise in the Dow).

FEES/SERVICES/MANAGEMENT

The fund has a front-end load of 5.75 percent, with a maximum back-end load of 1 percent. The fund's total annual expense ratio of 0.87 percent (with a 0.35 percent 12b-1 fee) compares favorably with other funds.

The fund offers all the standard services such as retirement account availability, automatic withdrawal, and automatic checking account deduction. Its minimum initial investment of $1,000 and minimum subsequent investment of $50 compare favorably with other funds.

Stephen Pesek has managed the fund only since 1999. The fund is part of the MFS fund family, which includes over 50 funds and allows shareholders to switch from fund to fund by telephone.

Top Ten Stock Holdings

1. Tyco International
2. Corning
3. Motorola
4. Cisco Systems
5. Nortel Networks

6. Baker Hughes
7. Microsoft
8. AES Corp.
9. Kon Kpn NV
10. Infinity Broadcasting 'A'

Fund inception: 1983
Asset mix: Common stocks, 94%; cash/equivalents, 6%
Total net assets: $3 billion

Load

Front-end load	5.75%
Redemption fee (max.)	1.00

Annual Fees

12b-1 fee	0.35%
Management fee	0.71
Other expenses	0.12
Total annual expense	1.18%

Minimum initial investment	$1,000
Minimum subsequent investment	$50

Services

Telephone exchanges	*Yes*
Automatic withdrawal	*Yes*
Automatic checking deduction	*Yes*
Retirement plan/IRA	*Yes*
Instant redemption	*Yes*
Portfolio manager (years)	1
Number of funds in family	over 50

Six-Year Performance

MFS Capital Opportunities vs. Dow Jones

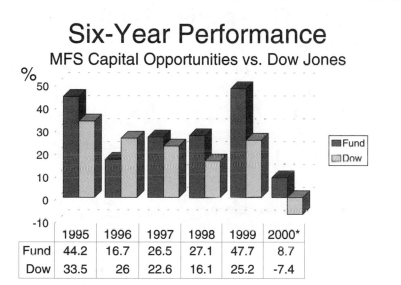

	1995	1996	1997	1998	1999	2000*
Fund	44.2	16.7	26.5	27.1	47.7	8.7
Dow	33.5	26	22.6	16.1	25.2	-7.4

% Avg. Annual Total Return   *2000 returns through 10/1/00
Fund vs. Dow Jones Industrial Avg.   (5-year avg. annual return: 26.2%)

83

Fidelity Mid Cap Stock Fund

Fidelity Funds
82 Devonshire Street
Boston, MA 02109
800-544-8544
www.fidelity.com
Ticker symbol: **FMCSX**

Fund manager: David Felman
Fund objective: Midcap growth

Performance	★ ★ ★ ★
Consistency	★ ★ ★
Fees/Services/Management	★ ★
Total	**9 Points**

The Fidelity Mid Cap Stock Fund invests in emerging companies that could become the blue chip leaders of the future. The fund is targeted to investors who want to diversify beyond the usual large-company funds or the technology-heavy aggressive growth funds.

The $5 billion fund was started in 1994 and has posted average annual returns of about 25 percent since its inception.

The fund invests across a wide range of industries, led by the health care sector, which makes up about 20 percent of total assets. Other leading sectors include technology, 16 percent; finance, 11 percent; utilities, 11 percent; energy, 10 percent; media and leisure, 4 percent; nondurables, 4 percent; and retail and wholesale, 4 percent.

Although the fund will occasionally invest in large-cap or small-cap stocks, most of its holdings are midsized companies of around $1 billion in market capitalization. Very few are household names, but someday they could grow to become blue chip market leaders. Among the fund's leading holdings are Dynergy, Calpine, Millennium Pharmaceuticals, Allegheny Energy, Vitesse Semiconductor, Freddie Mac, and Sepracor.

Fund manager David Felman is very aggressive in his trading approach, with a 205 percent annual portfolio turnover ratio. The fund stays at least 90 percent invested in stocks under most circumstances.

PERFORMANCE ★ ★ ★ ★

The fund has enjoyed solid growth over the past five years. Including dividends and capital gains distributions, the Fidelity Mid Cap Stock Fund has provided an average annual return the past five years (through late 2000) of 25.5 percent.

A $10,000 investment in 1995 would have grown to about $31,000 five years later.

CONSISTENCY ★ ★ ★

The fund has been fairly consistent, outperforming the Dow Jones Industrial Average three of the past five years through 1999 (and was leading the Dow through most of 2000). Its biggest gain came in 1999, when it moved up 39.8 percent (compared with a 25.2 percent rise in the Dow).

FEES/SERVICES/MANAGEMENT ★ ★

The fund is a pure no-load fund, with no fees to buy or sell shares. The fund's total annual expense ratio of 0.86 percent (with no 12b-1 fee) compares favorably with other funds.

The fund offers all the standard services such as retirement account availability, automatic withdrawal, and automatic checking account deduction. Its minimum initial investment of $2,500 and minimum subsequent investment of $250 are a little higher than most other funds.

Fund manager David Felman has only been with the fund since 1999. The Fidelity fund family includes over 300 funds and allows shareholders to switch from fund to fund by telephone.

Top Ten Stock Holdings

1. Freddie Mac
2. Dynergy
3. Calpine Corp.
4. Sepracor
5. Millennium Pharmaceuticals

6. Allegheny Energy
7. Devon Energy
8. Vitesse Semiconductor
9. Perkinelmer
10. Safeway

Fund inception: 1994
Asset mix: Common stocks, 91%; cash/equivalents, 9%
Total net assets: $4.7 billion

Load

Front-end load	*None*
Redemption fee (max.)	*None*

Annual Fees

12b-1 fee	*None*
Management fee	0.61%
Other expenses	0.25
Total annual expense	0.86%
Minimum initial investment	$2,500
Minimum subsequent investment	$250

Services

Telephone exchanges	*Yes*
Automatic withdrawal	*Yes*
Automatic checking deduction	*Yes*
Retirement plan/IRA	*Yes*
Instant redemption	*Yes*
Portfolio manager (years)	1
Number of funds in family	over 300

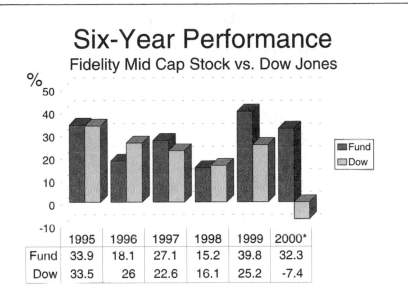

Six-Year Performance
Fidelity Mid Cap Stock vs. Dow Jones

	1995	1996	1997	1998	1999	2000*
Fund	33.9	18.1	27.1	15.2	39.8	32.3
Dow	33.5	26	22.6	16.1	25.2	-7.4

% Avg. Annual Total Return
Fund vs. Dow Jones Industrial Avg.

*2000 returns through 10/1/00
(5-year avg. annual return: 26.6%)

Top Ten Stock Holdings

1. Morgan Stanley Dean Witter
2. Credit Suisse Group
3. Charles Schwab
4. Lehman Brother Holdings
5. Kansas City South Industries

6. Citigroup
7. Waddell & Reed Financial
8. Daiwa Securities Group
9. Goldman Sachs Group
10. Merrill Lynch

Fund inception: 1985
Asset mix: Common stocks, 93%; cash/equivalents, 7%
Total net assets: $490 million

Load

Front-end load	3.00%
Redemption fee (max.)	*None*

Annual Fees

12b-1 fee	*None*
Management fee	0.58%
Other expenses	0.70
Total annual expense	1.28%

Minimum initial investment	$2,500
Minimum subsequent investment	$250

Services

Telephone exchanges	*Yes*
Automatic withdrawal	*Yes*
Automatic checking deduction	*Yes*
Retirement plan/IRA	*Yes*
Instant redemption	*Yes*
Portfolio manager (years)	1
Number of funds in family	over 300

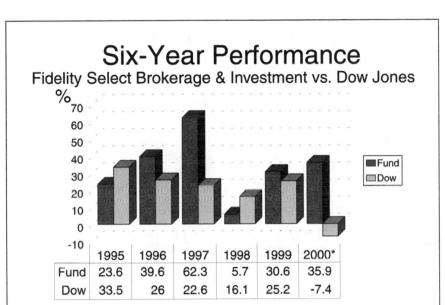

Six-Year Performance
Fidelity Select Brokerage & Investment vs. Dow Jones

	1995	1996	1997	1998	1999	2000*
Fund	23.6	39.6	62.3	5.7	30.6	35.9
Dow	33.5	26	22.6	16.1	25.2	-7.4

% Avg. Annual Total Return   *2000 returns through 10/1/00
Fund vs. Dow Jones Industrial Avg.   (5-year avg. annual return: 32%)

85

Gabelli Westwood Equity Fund

Gabelli Funds
P.O. Box 5354
Cincinnati, OH 45201-5354
800-422-3554
www.gabelli.com
Ticker symbol: **WESWX**

Fund managers: Susan Byrne and Kellie Stark
Fund objective: Long-term growth

Performance	★
Consistency	★ ★ ★
Fees/Services/Management	★ ★ ★ ★ ★
Total	**9 Points**

The Gabelli Westwood Equity Fund features a well-balanced mix of energy, retailing, financial services, health care, and high-tech stocks. The portfolio is a mirror image of the U.S. economy. Among its leading holdings are Chase Manhattan, Time Warner, Delta Air Lines, IBM, Pharmacia, Reliant Energy, and retailers The Limited and Federated Department Stores. That's diversification.

The 44-issue fund is chartered to invest primarily in the stocks of well-established large-cap companies with strong track records and above-average earnings growth. The fund's primary objective is capital appreciation. Income is a secondary consideration for the fund.

Consumer cyclical goods is the largest sector in the portfolio at about 19 percent, followed by technology at 16 percent; energy, 11 percent; health care, 9 percent; financial services, 8 percent; utilities 8 percent; and transportation, 6 percent.

A $10,000 investment in the fund ten years ago would now be worth about $44,000. The portfolio turnover ratio is a modest 67 percent. The fund stays nearly 100 percent invested in stocks under normal circumstances.

PERFORMANCE

The fund has enjoyed solid growth over the past five years. Including dividends and capital gains distributions, the Gabelli Westwood Equity Fund has provided an average annual return the past five years (through late 2000) of about 20 percent.

A $10,000 investment in 1995 would have grown to about $36,000 five years later.

CONSISTENCY

The fund has been fairly consistent, outperforming the Dow Jones Industrial Average three of the past five years through 1999 (and again through most of 2000). Its biggest gain came in 1995, when it moved up 36.9 percent (compared with a 33.5 percent rise in the Dow).

FEES/SERVICES/MANAGEMENT

The fund is a pure no-load fund, with no fees to buy or sell shares. The fund's total annual expense ratio of 1.49 percent (with a 0.25 percent 12b-1 fee) is in line with other funds.

The fund offers all the standard services such as retirement account availability, automatic withdrawal, and automatic checking account deduction. Its minimum initial investment of $1,000 and minimum subsequent investment of $1 are in line with other funds.

Susan Byrne, who manages the fund along with comanager Kellie Stark, has been with the fund since its 1987 inception. The Gabelli fund family includes 30 funds and allows shareholders to switch from fund to fund by telephone.

Top Ten Stock Holdings

1. Apache
2. The Limited
3. Federated Dept. Stores
4. PNC Financial Services Group
5. Pharmacia

6. Reliant Energy
7. Chase Manhattan
8. IBM
9. Time Warner
10. Delta Air Lines

Fund inception: 1987
Asset mix: Common stocks, 99%; cash/equivalents, 1%
Total net assets: $188 million

Load

Front-end load	*None*
Redemption fee (max.)	*None*

Annual Fees

12b-1 fee	0.25%
Management fee	1.00%
Other expenses	0.24
Total annual expense	1.49%

Minimum initial investment	$1,000
Minimum subsequent investment	$1

Services

Telephone exchanges	*Yes*
Automatic withdrawal	*Yes*
Automatic checking deduction	*Yes*
Retirement plan/IRA	*Yes*
Instant redemption	*Yes*
Portfolio manager (years)	13
Number of funds in family	30

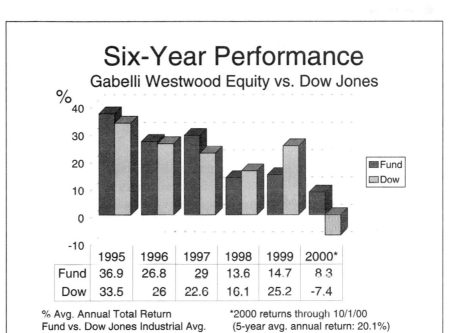

Six-Year Performance
Gabelli Westwood Equity vs. Dow Jones

	1995	1996	1997	1998	1999	2000*
Fund	36.9	26.8	29	13.6	14.7	8.3
Dow	33.5	26	22.6	16.1	25.2	-7.4

% Avg. Annual Total Return
Fund vs. Dow Jones Industrial Avg.

*2000 returns through 10/1/00
(5-year avg. annual return: 20.1%)

87

Evergreen Large Company Growth Fund

Evergreen Funds
200 Berkeley Street
Boston, MA 02116-5034
800-343-2898
www.evergreen-funds.com
Ticker symbol: **EKJAX**

Fund manager: Maureen Cullinane
Fund objective: Long-term growth

Performance	★ ★
Consistency	★ ★ ★
Fees/Services/Management	★ ★ ★
Total	**8 Points**

The Evergreen Large Company Growth Fund invests primarily in the stocks of major blue chip companies across a wide range of sectors in the United States and abroad.

Investors seeking long-term maximum growth will like what they see in this fund. Among the largest of its 60 stock holdings are such U.S. high-tech stalwarts as Cisco Systems, Intel, General Electric, IBM, and Microsoft. Leading-edge foreign stocks such as Pharmacia and Nokia also play a significant role in the portfolio.

Maureen Cullinane, who has managed the $85 million fund since 1995, mixes some old economy stocks into the portfolio, although tech stocks make up 46 percent of the portfolio. Other sectors include financial services, 9 percent; health care, 9 percent; energy, 6 percent; consumer staples, 6 percent; and consumer cyclicals, 3 percent.

The fund was established in 1935. Over the past ten years, the fund has rewarded investors with an annualized total return of about 18 percent. A $10,000 investment in the fund ten years ago would now be worth about $52,000.

Cullinane is aggressive in her management approach, with a 132 percent annual portfolio turnover ratio. The fund stays at least 90 percent invested in stocks under normal circumstances.

PERFORMANCE

The fund has enjoyed solid growth over the past five years. Including dividends and capital gains distributions, the Evergreen Large Company Growth Fund has provided a load-adjusted average annual return the past five years (through late 2000) of 23.3 percent.

A $10,000 investment in 1995 would have grown to about $28,000 five years later.

CONSISTENCY

The fund has been fairly consistent, outperforming the Dow Jones Industrial Average three of the past five years through 1999 (and again through most of 2000). Its biggest gain came in 1999, when it moved up 36.4 percent (compared with a 25.2 percent rise in the Dow).

FEES/SERVICES/MANAGEMENT

The fund has a front-end load of 4.75 percent, with a maximum back-end load of 1 percent. The fund's total annual expense ratio of 1.00 percent (with a 0.25 percent 12b-1 fee) compares well with other funds.

The fund offers all the standard services such as retirement account availability, automatic withdrawal, and automatic checking account deduction. Its minimum initial investment of $1,000 and minimum subsequent investment of $1 are in line with other funds.

The fund has been managed by Maureen Cullinane since 1995. The Evergreen fund family includes more than 90 funds and allows shareholders to switch from fund to fund by telephone.

88

John Hancock Large Cap Value Fund

John Hancock Funds
101 Huntington Avenue
Boston, MA 02199-7603
800-257-3336
www.jhfunds.com
Ticker symbol: **TAGRX**

Fund manager: Timothy Quinlisk
Fund objective: Long-term growth

Performance	★ ★
Consistency	★ ★ ★
Fees/Services/Management	★ ★ ★
Total	**8 Points**

A breakthrough technology, a popular new product, a business reorganization, or a corporate merger is the kind of catalyst that can propel the price of a stock. The challenge, of course, is recognizing the conditions that might send a stock soaring.

John Hancock Large Cap Value Fund manager Timothy Quinlisk has developed a knack for knowing when an undervalued stock is going to break out and realize its intrinsic value. Quinlisk, who has been with the fund since 1996, also looks for companies with substantial cash flows, reliable revenue streams, superior competitive positions, and strong management when selecting a stock for the $700 million, 65-stock portfolio.

The fund normally invests about two-thirds of its assets in large-cap companies, such as Corning and Citigroup. Technology stocks dominate the portfolio, accounting for about 37 percent of total assets. Other leading sectors include communications, 20 percent; financial services, 18 percent; and consumer goods, 8 percent.

A $10,000 investment in the fund ten years ago would now be worth about $53,000—an average annual return of about 17 percent.

The fund, which was established in 1949, has an annual portfolio turn-over rate of 113 percent. The fund stays 100 percent invested in stocks under normal circumstances.

PERFORMANCE

The fund has enjoyed strong growth over the past five years. Including dividends and capital gains distributions, the John Hancock Large Cap Value Fund has provided a load-adjusted average annual return the past five years (through late 2000) of 24 percent.

A $10,000 investment in 1995 would have grown to about $29,000 five years later.

CONSISTENCY

The fund has been fairly consistent, outperforming the Dow Jones Industrial Average three of the past five years through 1999 (and again through most of 2000). Its biggest gain came in 1999, when it moved up 37.9 percent (compared with a 25.2 percent rise in the Dow).

FEES/SERVICES/MANAGEMENT

The fund has a front-end load of 5 percent. The fund's total annual expense ratio of 1.17 percent (with a 0.25 percent 12b-1 fee) is in line with other funds.

The fund offers all the standard services such as retirement account availability, automatic withdrawal, and automatic checking account deduction. Its minimum initial investment of $1,000 and minimum subsequent investment of $25 compare favorably with other funds.

The fund has been managed by Timothy Quinlisk since 1996. The John Hancock fund family includes 33 funds and allows shareholders to switch from fund to fund by telephone.

Top Ten Stock Holdings

1. Corning
2. ANTEC Corp.
3. ACE Limited
4. Parametric Technology
5. AT&T-Liberty Media

6. Amphenol Corp.
7. Edwards
8. Citigroup
9. Financial Security Assurance Holdings
10. SCI Systems

Fund inception: 1949
Asset mix: Common stocks, 100%
Total net assets: $723 million

Load

Front-end load	5.00%
Redemption fee (max.)	*None*

Annual Fees

12b-1 fee	0.25%
Management fee	0.63%
Other expenses	0.29
Total annual expense	1.17%

Minimum initial investment	$1,000
Minimum subsequent investment	$25

Services

Telephone exchanges	*Yes*
Automatic withdrawal	*Yes*
Automatic checking deduction	*Yes*
Retirement plan/IRA	*Yes*
Instant redemption	*Yes*
Portfolio manager (years)	4
Number of funds in family	33

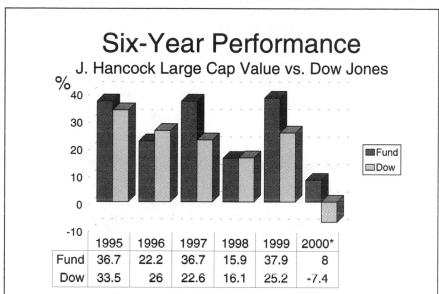

Six-Year Performance
J. Hancock Large Cap Value vs. Dow Jones

	1995	1996	1997	1998	1999	2000*
Fund	36.7	22.2	36.7	15.9	37.9	8
Dow	33.5	26	22.6	16.1	25.2	-7.4

% Avg. Annual Total Return   *2000 returns through 10/1/00
Fund vs. Dow Jones Industrial Avg.   (5-year avg. annual return: 24.9%)

89

AIM Blue Chip Fund

AIM Funds Group
11 Greenway Plaza, Suite 1919
Houston, TX 77046-1173
800-347-4246
www.aimfunds.com
Ticker symbol: **ABCAX**

Fund managers: Jonathan Schoolar and Monika Degan
Fund objective: Long-term growth

Performance	★ ★
Consistency	★ ★ ★
Fees/Services/Management	★ ★ ★
Total	**8 Points**

Contrary to its name, the AIM Blue Chip Fund is light on traditional blue chip stocks and heavy on technology. High-tech favorites such as Cisco Systems, Nortel, Intel, Microsoft, and Oracle are among the fund's leading holdings.

Jonathan Schoolar, who has been with the fund since 1996, currently comanages the fund along with Monika Degan. The $3 billion fund was launched in 1987. The fund managers look for blue chips with above-average growth that have a well-established presence in their respective industries.

The fund does have a few traditional blue chips. General Electric was recently its leading holding. It also has a large stake in such health care heavyweights as Pfizer and Warner-Lambert. In all, the fund has about 90 stocks in the portfolio.

Technology stocks constitute about 37 percent of the portfolio, followed by financial services at 11 percent; health care, 10 percent; consumer cyclicals, 9 percent; and capital goods, 8 percent.

The portfolio's turnover ratio is a conservative 22 percent. The fund stays nearly 100 percent invested in stocks under normal circumstances.

PERFORMANCE

The fund has enjoyed solid growth over the past five years. Including dividends and capital gains distributions, the AIM Blue Chip Fund has provided a load-adjusted average annual return the past five years (through late 2000) of 24.3 percent.

A $10,000 investment in 1995 would have grown to about $30,000 five years later.

CONSISTENCY

The fund has been fairly consistent, outperforming the Dow Jones Industrial Average three of the past five years through 1999 (and again through most of 2000). Its biggest gain came in 1997, when it moved up 31.9 percent (compared with a 22.6 percent rise in the Dow).

FEES/SERVICES/MANAGEMENT

The fund has a front-end load of 5.5 percent, with a maximum back-end load of 1 percent. The fund's total annual expense ratio of 1.19 percent (with a 0.35 percent 12b-1 fee) compares favorably with other funds.

The fund offers all the standard services such as retirement account availability, automatic withdrawal, and automatic checking account deduction. Its minimum initial investment of $500 and minimum subsequent investment of $50 compare favorably with other funds.

The fund managers have been with the fund since 1996. The AIM fund family includes 123 funds and allows shareholders to switch from fund to fund by telephone.

Top Ten Stock Holdings

1. General Electric
2. Cisco Systems
3. Pfizer
4. Nortel Networks
5. Intel

6. Oracle Systems
7. Microsoft
8. Tyco International
9. Sun Microsystems
10. Morgan Stanley Dean Witter

Fund inception: 1987
Asset mix: Common stocks, 97%; cash/equivalents, 3%
Total net assets: $3 billion

Load

Front-end load	5.50%
Redemption fee (max.)	1.00

Annual Fees

12b-1 fee	0.35%
Management fee	0.64
Other expenses	0.20
Total annual expense	1.19%

Minimum initial investment	$500
Minimum subsequent investment	$50

Services

Telephone exchanges	*Yes*
Automatic withdrawal	*Yes*
Automatic checking deduction	*Yes*
Retirement plan/IRA	*Yes*
Instant redemption	*Yes*
Portfolio manager (years)	4
Number of funds in family	123

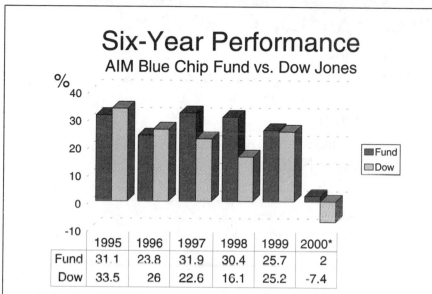

Six-Year Performance
AIM Blue Chip Fund vs. Dow Jones

	1995	1996	1997	1998	1999	2000*
Fund	31.1	23.8	31.9	30.4	25.7	2
Dow	33.5	26	22.6	16.1	25.2	-7.4

% Avg. Annual Total Return
Fund vs. Dow Jones Industrial Avg.

*2000 returns through 10/1/00
(5-year avg. annual return: 23.3%)

90

Pilgrim MidCap Growth Fund

Pilgrim Funds
600 West Broadway, 30th Floor
San Diego, CA 92101
800-992-0180
www.pilgrimfunds.com
Ticker symbol: **NCGAX**

Fund manager: Mary Lisanti
Fund objective: Small-cap stocks

Performance	★ ★ ★
Consistency	★ ★
Fees/Services/Management	★ ★ ★
Total	**8 Points**

Pilgrim MidCap Growth Fund manager Mary Lisanti looks for successful, growing companies that are managing change effectively and seem poised for solid growth.

Lisanti uses both a "bottom-up" analysis—evaluating the financial condition and competitiveness of individual companies—and a "top-down" or "thematic" approach, assessing the prospects of each industry in structuring the portfolio.

Although Lisanti just took over management of the fund in 2000, she has strong credentials. She was the *Barron's* Fund Manager of the Year in 1996 and one of the top-ranked analysts in *Institutional Investor* in 1989. She is the lead portfolio manager for several Pilgrim equity funds.

The Pilgrim MidCap Growth Fund is heavily invested in technology-related stocks, including semiconductors, 16 percent of assets; telecommunications equipment, 8 percent; electronic components, 6 percent; fiber optics, 6 percent; computer memory, 5 percent; electronic forms, 4 percent; software, 4 percent; and retail computer equipment, 4 percent.

Among its leading holdings are JDS Uniphase, VERITAS Software, Network Appliance, and NEXTEL. The fund portfolio is still relatively small, with about $160 million in assets.

A $10,000 investment in the fund ten years ago would now be worth about $67,000—a 21 percent average annual return. The fund manager takes a fairly active investment approach, with a 55 percent annual portfolio turnover ratio. The fund stays 100 percent invested in stocks under normal circumstances.

PERFORMANCE

The fund has enjoyed strong growth over the past five years. Including dividends and capital gains distributions, the Pilgrim MidCap Growth Fund has provided a load-adjusted average annual return the past five years (through late 2000) of 27.5 percent.

A $10,000 investment in 1995 would have grown to about $33,000 five years later.

CONSISTENCY

The fund has been somewhat inconsistent, outperforming the Dow Jones Industrial Average only two of the past five years through 1999 (and again through most of 2000). Its biggest gain came in 1999, when it moved up 97.6 percent (compared with a 25.2 percent rise in the Dow).

FEES/SERVICES/MANAGEMENT

The fund has a front-end load of 5.75 percent, with a maximum back-end load of 1 percent. The fund's total annual expense ratio of 1.49 percent (with a 0.35 percent 12b-1 fee) is in line with other funds.

The fund offers all the standard services such as retirement account availability, automatic withdrawal, and automatic checking account deduction. Its minimum initial investment of $1,000 and minimum subsequent investment of $100 compare favorably with other funds.

Mary Lisanti began managing the fund in 2000 but has 20 years' experience in the money management business. The Pilgrim fund family includes 44 funds and allows shareholders to switch from fund to fund by telephone.

Top Ten Stock Holdings

1. JDS Uniphase
2. VERITAS Software
3. Network Appliance
4. VoiceStream Wireless
5. CIENA

6. NEXTEL Communications
7. LSI Logic
8. Network Solutions
9. Analog Devices
10. Applied Micro Circuits

Fund inception: 1985
Asset mix: Common stocks, 100%
Total net assets: $156 million

Load

Front-end load	5.75%
Redemption fee (max.)	1.00

Annual Fees

12b-1 fee	0.35%
Management fee	0.75%
Other expenses	0.39
Total annual expense	1.49%

Minimum initial investment	$1,000
Minimum subsequent investment	$100

Services

Telephone exchanges	*Yes*
Automatic withdrawal	*Yes*
Automatic checking deduction	*Yes*
Retirement plan/IRA	*Yes*
Instant redemption	*Yes*
Portfolio manager (years)	1
Number of funds in family	44

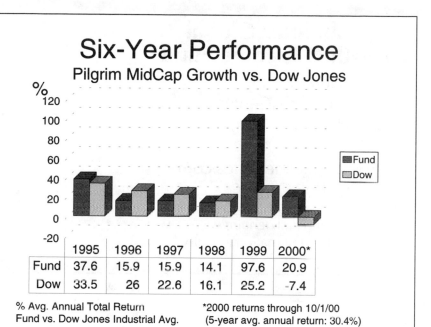

Six-Year Performance
Pilgrim MidCap Growth vs. Dow Jones

	1995	1996	1997	1998	1999	2000*
Fund	37.6	15.9	15.9	14.1	97.6	20.9
Dow	33.5	26	22.6	16.1	25.2	-7.4

% Avg. Annual Total Return   *2000 returns through 10/1/00
Fund vs. Dow Jones Industrial Avg.   (5-year avg. annual return: 30.4%)

91

Oppenheimer Global Growth & Income Fund

Oppenheimer Funds
Two World Trade Center
New York, NY 10048-0203
800-525-7048
www.oppenheimerfunds.com
Ticker symbol: **OPGIX**

Fund manager: Frank Jennings
Fund objective: International equity

Performance	★ ★ ★
Consistency	★ ★
Fees/Services/Management	★ ★ ★
Total	**8 Points**

For a diversified slice of the world of investing, the Oppenheimer Global Growth and Income Fund offers a little bit of everything. The fund has a diversified portfolio of stocks and bonds from around the world.

Opened in 1990, the fund has posted an average annual return of about 19 percent since its inception. A $10,000 investment in the fund ten years ago would now be worth about $55,000.

The fund invests primarily in blue chip and high-tech stocks, such as QUALCOMM, Toshiba, Sharp, Sybase, and National Semiconductor. The leading sectors represented in the fund include technology, 41 percent; health care, 17 percent; and durables, 12 percent.

About a third of the $1.4 billion portfolio comprises U.S. stocks. It also has significant holdings in stocks from Japan, 15 percent; United Kingdom, 13 percent; France, 4.5 percent; and the Netherlands, 4 percent.

The fund stays 75 to 80 percent invested in stocks under normal circumstances, and 15 to 20 percent in bonds, with the balance in cash and cash equivalent investments.

Fund manager Frank Jennings looks for market leaders in the fastest-growing sectors. He takes a fairly aggressive approach in managing the fund, with a 98 percent annual portfolio turnover ratio.

PERFORMANCE

The fund has enjoyed very strong growth over the past five years. Including dividends and capital gains distributions, the Oppenheimer Global Growth and Income Fund has provided a load-adjusted average annual return the past five years (through late 2000) of 27.4 percent.

A $10,000 investment in 1995 would have grown to about $33,500 five years later.

CONSISTENCY

The fund has been somewhat inconsistent, outperforming the Dow Jones Industrial Average only two of the past five years through 1999 (and again through most of 2000). Its biggest gain came in 1999, when it moved up 86.6 percent (compared with a 25.2 percent rise in the Dow).

FEES/SERVICES/MANAGEMENT

The fund has a front-end load of 5.75 percent, with a maximum back-end load of 1 percent. The fund's total annual expense ratio of 1.33 percent (with a 0.25 percent 12b-1 fee) is in line with other funds.

The fund offers all the standard services such as retirement account availability, automatic withdrawal, and automatic checking account deduction. Its minimum initial investment of $1,000 and minimum subsequent investment of $25 are in line with other funds.

The fund has been managed by Frank Jennings since 1995. The Oppenheimer fund family includes over 50 funds and allows shareholders to switch from fund to fund by telephone.

Top Ten Stock Holdings

1. QUALCOMM
2. Toshiba
3. National Semiconductor
4. Sharp
5. Coherent
6. Sybase
7. Toyo Communications Equipment
8. U.S. Treasury Strip 8/15/25
9. Bass ADS
10. U.S. Treasury Strip 11/15/27

Fund inception: 1990
Asset mix: Common stocks, 77%; bonds, 16%; cash/equivalents, 5%; other, 2%
Total net assets: $1.4 billion

Load

Front-end load	5.75%
Redemption fee (max.)	1.00

Annual Fees

12b-1 fee	0.25%
Management fee	0.78
Other expenses	0.30
Total annual expense	1.33%

Minimum initial investment	$1,000
Minimum subsequent investment	$25

Services

Telephone exchanges	*Yes*
Automatic withdrawal	*Yes*
Automatic checking deduction	*Yes*
Retirement plan/IRA	*Yes*
Instant redemption	*Yes*
Portfolio manager (years)	5
Number of funds in family	over 50

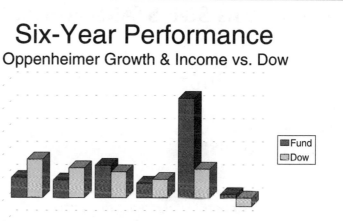

Six-Year Performance
Oppenheimer Growth & Income vs. Dow

	1995	1996	1997	1998	1999	2000*
Fund	17.4	15.3	28.3	12.8	86.6	3.1
Dow	33.5	26	22.6	16.1	25.2	-7.4

% Avg. Annual Total Return
Fund vs. Dow Jones Industrial Avg.

*2000 returns through 10/1/00
(5-year avg. annual return: 27.2%)

92

Bear Stearns S&P STARS Portfolio

Bear Stearns
245 Park Avenue
New York, NY 10167
800-766-4111
www.bearstearns.com
Ticker symbol: **BSPAX**

Fund manager: Robert Natale (team manager)
Fund objective: Long-term growth

Performance	★ ★ ★
Consistency	★ ★ ★
Fees/Services/Management	★ ★
Total	**8 Points**

It may be an odd fund name, but the Bear Stearns S&P STARS Portfolio does exactly what the name implies. The fund managers look for the star stocks of the Standard & Poor's 500 (S&P) stock index. The fund invests in about 50 stocks from the S&P that they believe will be the best performers over the next 6 to 12 months.

Most of the stocks in the portfolio are well-known companies, such as Cisco Systems, Sprint, AT&T, and General Motors. In selecting stocks, the fund managers analyze such factors as the company's management, its balance sheet, and its competitive position in its industry. In addition to the 50 S&P stocks, the fund managers may invest as much as 15 percent of assets in stocks outside of the S&P universe.

The fund invests heavily in telecommunications and other technology-related companies. The leading sectors include cable TV, 8 percent of total assets; networking products, 6 percent; electronics and electronics components, 12 percent; cellular telecommunications, 6 percent; telecommunications equipment, 5 percent; oil and gas drilling, 5 percent; commercial services, 5 percent; diversified operations, 5 percent; utilities, 15 percent; financials, 9 percent; and health care, 8 percent.

Under normal circumstances, the fund stays nearly 100 percent invested in stocks. The fund is relatively conservative in its buy-and-sell approach, with a 76 percent annual turnover ratio.

PERFORMANCE

The fund has enjoyed solid growth over the past five years. Including dividends and capital gains distributions, the Bear Stearns S&P STARS Portfolio has provided a load-adjusted average annual return the past five years (through late 2000) of 27.8 percent.

A $10,000 investment in 1995 would have grown to about $34,000 five years later.

CONSISTENCY

The fund has been fairly consistent, outperforming the Dow Jones Industrial Average three of the past five years through 1999 (and again through most of 2000). Its biggest gain came in 1998, when it moved up 39.4 percent (compared with a 16.1 percent rise in the Dow).

FEES/SERVICES/MANAGEMENT

The fund has a front-end load of 5.5 percent, with a maximum back-end load of 1 percent. The fund's total annual expense ratio of 1.5 percent (with a 0.5 percent 12b-1 fee) is about average among all funds.

The fund offers all the standard services such as retirement account availability, automatic withdrawal, and automatic checking account deduction. Its minimum initial investment of $1,000 and minimum subsequent investment of $50 are in line with most other funds.

The fund is team managed, lead by team manager Robert Natale, who has only been with the fund for two years. The Bear Stearns fund family has 37 funds and allows shareholders to switch from fund to fund by telephone.

Top Ten Stock Holdings

1. Cisco Systems
2. Global Marine
3. Comcast
4. Adobe Systems
5. Sprint

6. Tyco International
7. AT&T
8. General Motors
9. Xilinx
10. Duff & Phelps Credit Rating

Fund inception: 1995
Asset mix: Common stocks, 99%; cash/equivalents, 1%
Total net assets: $1.9 billion

Load

Front-end load	5.50%
Redemption fee (max.)	1.00%

Annual Fees

12b-1 fee	0.50%
Management fee	0.75%
Other expenses	0.25
Total annual expense	1.50%

Minimum initial investment	$1,000
Minimum subsequent investment	$50

Services

Telephone exchanges	Yes
Automatic withdrawal	Yes
Automatic checking deduction	Yes
Retirement plan/IRA	Yes
Instant redemption	Yes
Portfolio manager (years)	2
Number of funds in family	37

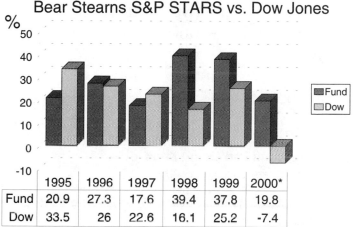

Six-Year Performance
Bear Stearns S&P STARS vs. Dow Jones

	1995	1996	1997	1998	1999	2000*
Fund	20.9	27.3	17.6	39.4	37.8	19.8
Dow	33.5	26	22.6	16.1	25.2	-7.4

% Avg. Annual Total Return   *2000 returns through 10/1/00
Fund vs. Dow Jones Industrial Avg.   (5-year avg. annual return: 28.5%)

93
PIMCO Target Fund

PIMCO Funds
840 Newport Center Drive, Suite 360
Newport Beach, CA 92660
800-426-0107
www.pimcofunds.com
Ticker symbol: **PTAAX**

Fund managers: Jeff Parker and Ken Corba
Fund objective: Aggressive growth

Performance	★ ★ ★ ★
Consistency	★ ★
Fees/Services/Management	★ ★
Total	**8 Points**

PIMCO Target Fund's managers pore through the midcap issues in search of tomorrow's large-cap leaders.

Using both qualitative and quantitative criteria, PIMCO's Ken Corba and Jeff Parker have demonstrated a keen eye for the growth stocks in the technology, consumer cyclicals, and health care sectors that have driven this fund's success. Corba and Parker like the U.S.-based midcaps, because they tend to be more nimble than the large companies and tend to have longer successful track records than the small companies.

The fund was founded in 1992 and has posted a 27 percent average annual return since then. Corba and Parker took the fund's reins in 1999.

The $300 million fund's largest holding, SDL, Inc., is an efficient manufacturer of laser pumps, a critical component in fiber-optic telecommunications networks. The fund also features several health care stocks that have historically withstood economic downturns. Other leading holdings include Comverse Technology, EchoStar Communications, JDS Uniphase, MiniMed, and Network Appliance.

The fund managers are very aggressive in their approach, with a 229 percent annual portfolio turnover ratio. The fund has about 60 stock holdings in all. The fund stays at least 90 percent invested in stocks under normal circumstances.

PERFORMANCE

The fund has enjoyed outstanding growth over the past five years. Including dividends and capital gains distributions, the PIMCO Target Fund has provided a load-adjusted average annual return the past five years (through late 2000) of 30.2 percent.

A $10,000 investment in 1995 would have grown to about $37,000 five years later.

CONSISTENCY

The fund has been somewhat inconsistent, outperforming the Dow Jones Industrial Average only two of the past five years through 1999 (and again through most of 2000). Its biggest gain came in 1999, when it moved up 66.3 percent (compared with a 25.2 percent rise in the Dow).

FEES/SERVICES/MANAGEMENT

The fund has a front-end load of 5.5 percent, with a maximum back-end load of 1 percent. The fund's total annual expense ratio of 1.21 percent (with a 0.25 percent 12b-1 fee) is in line with other funds.

The fund offers all the standard services such as retirement account availability, automatic withdrawal, and automatic checking account deduction. Its minimum initial investment of $2,500 and minimum subsequent investment of $100 are a little high compared with other funds.

The fund has been managed by Jeff Parker and Ken Corba only since 1999. The PIMCO fund family includes more than 40 funds and allows shareholders to switch from fund to fund by telephone.

Top Ten Stock Holdings

1. SDL, Inc.
2. Comverse Technology
3. PMC-Sierra
4. EchoStar Communications
5. RF Micro Devices
6. MiniMed
7. Sanmina Corp.
8. JDS Uniphase
9. Citris
10. Network Appliance

Fund inception: 1992
Asset mix: Common stocks, 94%; cash/equivalents, 6%
Total net assets: $304 million

Load

Front-end load	5.50%
Redemption fee (max.)	1.00

Annual Fees

12b-1 fee	0.25%
Management fee	0.55
Other expenses	0.41
Total annual expense	1.21%

Minimum initial investment	$2,500
Minimum subsequent investment	$100

Services

Telephone exchanges	*Yes*
Automatic withdrawal	*Yes*
Automatic checking deduction	*Yes*
Retirement plan/IRA	*Yes*
Instant redemption	*Yes*
Portfolio manager (years)	1
Number of funds in family	over 40

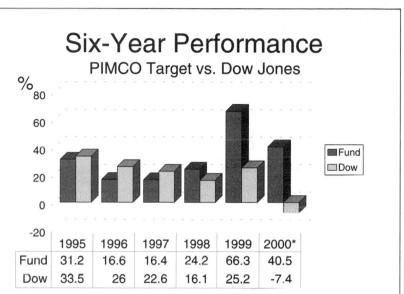

Six-Year Performance
PIMCO Target vs. Dow Jones

	1995	1996	1997	1998	1999	2000*
Fund	31.2	16.6	16.4	24.2	66.3	40.5
Dow	33.5	26	22.6	16.1	25.2	-7.4

% Avg. Annual Total Return   *2000 returns through 10/1/00
Fund vs. Dow Jones Industrial Avg.   (5-year avg. annual return: 32.3%)

Top Ten Stock Holdings

1. Hughes Electronics
2. Abbott Laboratories
3. J.P. Morgan
4. Illinois Tool Works
5. AT&T

6. USA Education
7. Tribune Company
8. Walt Disney
9. Raytheon Company
10. Boston Scientific

Fund inception: 1990
Asset mix: Common stocks, 100%
Total net assets: $2 billion

Load

Front-end load	*None*
Redemption fee (max.)	*None*

Annual Fees

12b-1 fee	*None*
Management fee	1.00%
Other expenses	0.07
Total annual expense	1.07%

Minimum initial investment	$10,000
Minimum subsequent investment	$500

Services

Telephone exchanges	*Yes*
Automatic withdrawal	*Yes*
Automatic checking deduction	*Yes*
Retirement plan/IRA	*Yes*
Instant redemption	*Yes*
Portfolio manager (years)	10
Number of funds in family	1

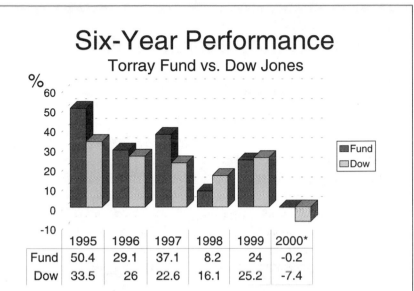

Six-Year Performance
Torray Fund vs. Dow Jones

	1995	1996	1997	1998	1999	2000*
Fund	50.4	29.1	37.1	8.2	24	-0.2
Dow	33.5	26	22.6	16.1	25.2	-7.4

% Avg. Annual Total Return   *2000 returns through 10/1/00
Fund vs. Dow Jones Industrial Avg.   (5-year avg. annual return: 21.3%)

95

Fidelity Select: Telecommunications Portfolio

Fidelity Funds
82 Devonshire Street
Boston, MA 02109
800-544-8544
www.fidelity.com
Ticker symbol: **FSTCX**

Fund manager: Peter Saperstone
Fund objective: Sector

Performance	★ ★
Consistency	★ ★ ★
Fees/Services/Management	★ ★ ★
Total	**8 Points**

For many decades, telecommunications meant one thing—a telephone. But all that has changed in the past 20 years, with the advent of fax machines, teleconferencing, videoconferencing, cellular phones, wireless devices, and the Internet.

The Fidelity Select Telecommunications Portfolio gives investors a stake in the fast-growing telecommunications sector. The fund invests in a broad cross section of telecommunications stocks, including telephone services, 36 percent; cellular, 30 percent; communications equipment, 13 percent; and computer services and software, 6 percent.

Among the fund's largest holdings are many of the most prominent blue chip stocks of the telecommunications sector, including AT&T, Nortel Networks, BellSouth, NEXTEL, Vodafone AirTouch, QUALCOMM, Motorola, and Cisco Systems.

The $1.6 billion fund was launched in 1985. Over the past ten years, the fund has had a 21.5 percent average annual return. A $10,000 investment in the fund ten years ago would now be worth about $70,000.

Fund manager Peter Saperstone is aggressive in his trading approach, with a 173 percent annual portfolio turnover ratio. The fund stays at least 90 percent invested in stocks under normal circumstances.

PERFORMANCE

The fund has enjoyed strong growth over the past five years. Including dividends and capital gains distributions, the Fidelity Select Telecommunications Portfolio has provided a load-adjusted average annual return the past five years (through late 2000) of 25 percent.

A $10,000 investment in 1995 would have grown to about $30,500 five years later.

CONSISTENCY

The fund has been fairly consistent, outperforming the Dow Jones Industrial Average three of the past five years through 1999 (and was about even with the Dow through most of 2000). Its biggest gain came in 1999, when it moved up 66.6 percent (compared with a 25.2 percent rise in the Dow).

FEES/SERVICES/MANAGEMENT

The fund has a 3 percent front-end load. The fund's total annual expense ratio of 1.09 percent (with no 12b-1 fee) is in line with other funds.

The fund offers all the standard services such as retirement account availability, automatic withdrawal, and automatic checking account deduction. Its minimum initial investment of $2,500 and minimum subsequent investment of $250 are a little higher than most other funds.

Peter Saperstone has been managing the fund since 1998 and has been a fund manager with Fidelity since 1996. The Fidelity fund family includes more than 300 funds and allows shareholders to switch from fund to fund by telephone.

Top Ten Stock Holdings

1. NEXTEL Communications
2. Vodafone AirTouch ADR
3. BellSouth
4. Sprint
5. QUALCOMM
6. Cisco Systems
7. VoiceStream Wireless
8. Motorola
9. Nortel Networks
10. AT&T

Fund inception: 1985
Asset mix: Common stocks, 95%; cash/equivalents, 5%
Total net assets: $1.6 billion

Load

Front-end load	3.00%
Redemption fee (max.)	*None*

Annual Fees

12b-1 fee	*None*
Management fee	0.58%
Other expenses	0.51
Total annual expense	1.09%
Minimum initial investment	$2,500
Minimum subsequent investment	$250

Services

Telephone exchanges	*Yes*
Automatic withdrawal	*Yes*
Automatic checking deduction	*Yes*
Retirement plan/IRA	*Yes*
Instant redemption	*Yes*
Portfolio manager (years)	2
Number of funds in family	over 300

Six-Year Performance
Fidelity Select Telecommunications vs. Dow Jones

	1995	1996	1997	1998	1999	2000*
Fund	29.7	5.4	25.8	41	66.6	-16.6
Dow	33.5	26	22.6	16.1	25.2	-7.4

% Avg. Annual Total Return
Fund vs. Dow Jones Industrial Avg.

*2000 returns through 10/1/00
(5-year avg. annual return: 20.9%)

96

Fidelity Select: Health Care Portfolio

Fidelity Funds
82 Devonshire Street
Boston, MA 02109
800-544-8544
www.fidelity.com
Ticker symbol: **FSPHX**

Fund manager: Yolanda McGettigan
Fund objective: Sector

Performance	★ ★
Consistency	★ ★ ★
Fees/Services/Management	★ ★ ★
Total	**8 Points**

Health care has been one of the steadiest sectors of the stock market for the past two decades. The Fidelity Select Health Care Portfolio, which was opened in 1981, has posted an average annual return of about 22 percent since its inception. A $10,000 investment in the fund in 1981 would have grown over 19 years to about $440,000.

The fund focuses on companies that design, manufacture, or sell health care products or services. It owns many of the world's leading pharmaceutical and medical products companies, such as Medtronic, Bristol-Myers, Schering-Plough, Amgen, Abbott, Merck, Lilly, and Johnson & Johnson.

Drugs and pharmaceuticals make up about 65 percent of the portfolio, followed by medical equipment and supplies manufacturers at 21 percent, and medical facilities management at 4 percent.

Fund manager Yolanda McGettigan is fairly conservative in managing the fund, with a 70 percent annual portfolio turnover ratio. The fund stays 80 to 95 percent invested in stocks under normal circumstances.

PERFORMANCE

The fund has enjoyed outstanding growth over the past five years. Including dividends and capital gains distributions, the Fidelity Select Health Care Portfolio has provided a load-adjusted average annual return the past five years (through late 2000) of 23.7 percent.

A $10,000 investment in 1995 would have grown to about $29,000 five years later.

CONSISTENCY

The fund has been fairly consistent, outperforming the Dow Jones Industrial Average three of the past five years through 1999 (and again through most of 2000). Its biggest gain came in 1995, when it moved up 45.9 percent (compared with a 33.5 percent rise in the Dow).

FEES/SERVICES/MANAGEMENT

The fund has a 3 percent front-end load. The fund's total annual expense ratio of 1.05 percent (with no 12b-1 fee) is in line with other funds.

The fund offers all the standard services such as retirement account availability, automatic withdrawal, and automatic checking account deduction. Its minimum initial investment of $2,500 and minimum subsequent investment of $250 are a little higher than most other funds.

Fund manager Yolanda McGettigan just joined the fund in 2000, but she has been a fund manager with Fidelity since 1997. The Fidelity fund family includes more than 300 funds and allows shareholders to switch from fund to fund by telephone.

Top Ten Stock Holdings

1. Warner-Lambert
2. Johnson & Johnson
3. Eli Lilly
4. American Home Products
5. Bristol-Myers-Squibb
6. Medtronic
7. Schering-Plough
8. Amgen
9. Abbott Laboratories
10. Merck

Fund inception: 1981
Asset mix: Common stocks, 89%; cash/equivalents, 11%
Total net assets: $2.7 billion

Load

Front-end load	3.00%
Redemption fee (max.)	*None*

Annual Fees

12b-1 fee	*None*
Management fee	0.58%
Other expenses	0.47
Total annual expense	1.05%

Minimum initial investment	$2,500
Minimum subsequent investment	$250

Services

Telephone exchanges	*Yes*
Automatic withdrawal	*Yes*
Automatic checking deduction	*Yes*
Retirement plan/IRA	*Yes*
Instant redemption	*Yes*
Portfolio manager (years)	1
Number of funds in family	over 300

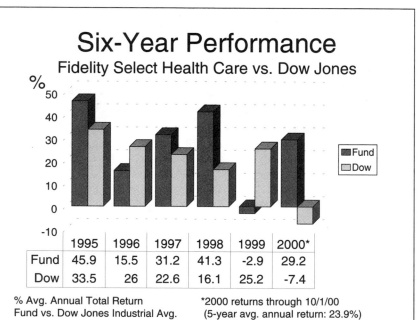

Six-Year Performance
Fidelity Select Health Care vs. Dow Jones

	1995	1996	1997	1998	1999	2000*
Fund	45.9	15.5	31.2	41.3	-2.9	29.2
Dow	33.5	26	22.6	16.1	25.2	-7.4

% Avg. Annual Total Return
Fund vs. Dow Jones Industrial Avg.

*2000 returns through 10/1/00
(5-year avg. annual return: 23.9%)

Pilgrim Worldwide Growth Fund

Pilgrim Funds
600 West Broadway, 30th Floor
San Diego, CA 92101
800-992-0180
www.pilgrimfunds.com
Ticker symbol: **NAWGX**

Fund managers: Team managed
Fund objective: International equity

Performance	★ ★ ★
Consistency	★ ★
Fees/Services/Management	★ ★
Total	**7 Points**

The management team of the Pilgrim Worldwide Growth Fund looks for successful growing companies from around the world that meet a stringent list of fundamental measures. They look for good earnings growth, a good balance sheet, strong competitive advantages, strong research and development, and experienced management.

The managers use both a "top-down" and "bottom-up" evaluation approach, searching for the leading stocks in the best industries.

Although the fund is globally oriented, many of its largest holdings are U.S. companies, such as Intel, Home Depot, Wal-Mart, and AT&T. U.S. stocks make up about 46 percent of the portfolio, followed by Japan, 8.5 percent; United Kingdom, 8 percent; France, 6 percent; and Canada, 6 percent.

Leading sectors include telecommunications equipment, 7.5 percent; semiconductors, 7 percent; fiber optics, 6 percent; telecommunications services, 4 percent; and networking products, 3 percent.

The fund has a fairly modest 57 percent annual portfolio turnover ratio. The fund stays more than 90 percent invested in stocks most of the time.

PERFORMANCE

The fund has enjoyed strong growth over the past five years. Including dividends and capital gains distributions, the Pilgrim Worldwide Growth Fund has provided a load-adjusted average annual return the past five years (through late 2000) of 26.4 percent.

A $10,000 investment in 1995 would have grown to about $32,000 five years later.

CONSISTENCY

The fund has been somewhat inconsistent, outperforming the Dow Jones Industrial Average only two of the past five years through 1999 (and it was about even with the Dow through most of 2000). Its biggest gain came in 1999, when it moved up 83.5 percent (compared with a 25.2 percent rise in the Dow).

FEES/SERVICES/MANAGEMENT

The fund has a front-end load of 5.75 percent, with a maximum back-end load of 1 percent. The fund's total annual expense ratio of 1.75 percent (with a 0.35 percent 12b-1 fee) is in line with other funds.

The fund offers all the standard services such as retirement account availability, automatic withdrawal, and automatic checking account deduction. Its minimum initial investment of $1,000 and minimum subsequent investment of $100 compare favorably with other funds.

The fund is managed by a team of portfolio managers. The subadvisor is Nicholas-Applegate Capital Management. The Pilgrim fund family includes 44 funds and allows shareholders to switch from fund to fund by telephone.

Top Ten Stock Holdings

1. Nokia
2. Nortel Networks
3. Schlumberger
4. Enron
5. Intel
6. MGM Grand
7. Wal-Mart
8. Home Depot
9. AT&T
10. Dell Computer

Fund inception: 1993
Asset mix: Common stocks, 97%; cash/equivalents, 3%
Total net assets: $235 million

Load

Front-end load	5.75%
Redemption fee (max.)	1.00

Annual Fees

12b-1 fee	0.35%
Management fee	1.00
Other expenses	0.40
Total annual expense	1.75%

Minimum initial investment	$1,000
Minimum subsequent investment	$100

Services

Telephone exchanges	*Yes*
Automatic withdrawal	*Yes*
Automatic checking deduction	*Yes*
Retirement plan/IRA	*Yes*
Instant redemption	*Yes*
Portfolio manager (years)	NA
Number of funds in family	44

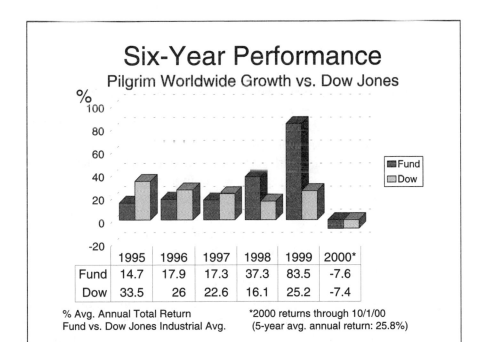

Six-Year Performance
Pilgrim Worldwide Growth vs. Dow Jones

	1995	1996	1997	1998	1999	2000*
Fund	14.7	17.9	17.3	37.3	83.5	-7.6
Dow	33.5	26	22.6	16.1	25.2	-7.4

% Avg. Annual Total Return
Fund vs. Dow Jones Industrial Avg.

*2000 returns through 10/1/00
(5-year avg. annual return: 25.8%)

98

Phoenix-Engemann Focus Growth Fund

Phoenix-Engemann Funds
Roger Engemann Management Company, Inc.
600 North Rosemead Boulevard
Pasadena, CA 91107-2133
800-814-1897
www.phoenixfunds.com
Ticker symbol: **PASGX**

Fund managers: Scott Swanson and Ned Brines
Fund objective: Aggressive growth

Performance	★ ★
Consistency	★ ★
Fees/Services/Management	★ ★ ★
Total	**7 Points**

Phoenix-Engemann Focus Growth Fund comanagers Scott Swanson and Ned Brines are very choosy in their stock selection process. The 35 stocks in the portfolio are primarily high-growth companies that are making a big splash in the early years of the 21st century.

Technology companies command nearly two-thirds of the portfolio, followed by health care, 9 percent; financial services, 8.5 percent; capital goods, 4 percent; communications services, 3 percent; and consumer staples, 3 percent.

The fund stays nearly 100 percent invested in stocks under most circumstances, although according to its charter, it may invest up to 30 percent of its assets in special situations, such as liquidations, reorganizations, mergers, or management changes. The fund was created in 1986 and has been managed since 1991 by Swanson and Brines.

The portfolio turnover rate is modest 56 percent. With a ten-year average annual return of about 18 percent, a $10,000 investment in the fund ten years ago would now be worth about $50,000.

384

PERFORMANCE

The fund has enjoyed outstanding growth over the past five years. Including dividends and capital gains distributions, the Phoenix-Engemann Focus Growth Fund has provided a load-adjusted average annual return the past five years (through late 2000) of 24.7 percent.

A $10,000 investment in 1995 would have grown to about $30,000 five years later.

CONSISTENCY

The fund has been somewhat inconsistent, outperforming the Dow Jones Industrial Average only two of the past five years through 1999 (and again through most of 2000). Its biggest gain came in 1999, when it moved up 50.6 percent (compared with a 25.2 percent rise in the Dow).

FEES/SERVICES/MANAGEMENT

The fund has a front-end load of 5.75 percent. The fund's total annual expense ratio of 1.54 percent (with a 0.25 percent 12b-1 fee) is in line with other funds.

The fund offers all the standard services such as retirement account availability, automatic withdrawal, and automatic checking account deduction. Its minimum initial investment of $500 and minimum subsequent investment of $25 compare favorably with other funds.

The fund has been managed by Scott Swanson and Ned Brines since 1991. The Phoenix-Engemann fund family includes 45 funds and allows shareholders to switch from fund to fund by telephone.

Top Ten Stock Holdings

1. Cisco Systems
2. Texas Instruments
3. JDS Uniphase
4. America Online
5. Intel
6. Microsoft
7. Tellabs
8. EMC
9. MCI WorldCom
10. General Electric

Fund inception: 1986
Asset mix: Common stocks, 97%; cash/equivalents, 3%
Total net assets: $625 million

Load

Front-end load	5.75%
Redemption fee (max.)	*None*

Annual Fees

12b-1 fee	0.25%
Management fee	0.79
Other expenses	0.50
Total annual expense	1.54%

Minimum initial investment	$500
Minimum subsequent investment	$25

Services

Telephone exchanges	*Yes*
Automatic withdrawal	*Yes*
Automatic checking deduction	*Yes*
Retirement plan/IRA	*Yes*
Instant redemption	*Yes*
Portfolio manager (years)	9
Number of funds in family	45

Six-Year Performance
Phoenix-Engemann Focus vs. Dow Jones

	1995	1996	1997	1998	1999	2000*
Fund	27.2	22.5	16	36.7	50.6	-6.1
Dow	33.5	26	22.6	16.1	25.2	-7.4

% Avg. Annual Total Return
Fund vs. Dow Jones Industrial Avg.

*2000 returns through 10/1/00
(5-year avg. annual return: 22.5%)

Fidelity Select: Energy Service Portfolio

Fidelity Funds
82 Devonshire Street
Boston, MA 02109
800-544-8544
www.fidelity.com
Ticker symbol: **FSESX**

Fund manager: Nicholas Tiller
Fund objective: Sector

Performance	★ ★
Consistency	★ ★ ★
Fees/Services/Management	★ ★
Total	**7 Points**

As the price of oil has climbed so have the share prices of the Fidelity Select Energy Service Portfolio. And every new oil crisis will help keep the fund growing. It's almost like an insurance policy against higher fuel prices.

The fund invests at least 80 percent of its assets in stocks of companies that provide services or equipment to the oil, gas, electricity, coal, nuclear, geothermal, oil shale, and solar power industries.

The fund has certainly had some ups and downs: up at least 40 percent for four of the past five years but down 49.7 percent in 1998. On average the fund was up 25 percent per year for the past five years, but only about 12 percent per year for the past ten years.

Its largest holdings include some of the leaders in the energy service industry, such as Baker Hughes, Global Marine, ENSCO, Marine Drilling, and Weatherford International. About 7 percent of the portfolio is invested in oil and gas companies.

Fund manager Nicholas Tiller takes a fairly conservative investment approach, with an annual portfolio turnover ratio of 69 percent. The fund stays at least 90 percent invested in stocks under normal circumstances.

PERFORMANCE

The fund has enjoyed outstanding growth over the past five years. Including dividends and capital gains distributions, the Fidelity Select Energy Service Portfolio has provided a load-adjusted average annual return the past five years (through late 2000) of 24.3 percent.

A $10,000 investment in 1995 would have grown to about $29,000 five years later.

CONSISTENCY

The fund has been fairly consistent, outperforming the Dow Jones Industrial Average four of the past five years through 1999 (and again through most of 2000), but it is prone to volatility—it had a 49.7 percent drop in 1998. Its biggest gain came in 1999, when it moved up 72.2 percent (compared with a 25.2 percent rise in the Dow).

FEES/SERVICES/MANAGEMENT

The fund has a 3 percent front-end load. The fund's total annual expense ratio of 1.20 percent (with no 12b-1 fee) is in line with other funds.

The fund offers all the standard services such as retirement account availability, automatic withdrawal, and automatic checking account deduction. Its minimum initial investment of $2,500 and minimum subsequent investment of $250 are a little higher than most other funds.

Fund manager Nicholas Tiller just joined the fund in 2000. He joined Fidelity in 1998, but this is his first assignment as a fund manager. The Fidelity fund family includes more than 300 funds and allows shareholders to switch from fund to fund by telephone.

Top Ten Stock Holdings

1. Weatherford International
2. Global Marine
3. Smith International
4. ENSCO International
5. Cooper Cameron
6. Nabors Industries
7. Marine Drilling
8. Baker Hughes
9. BJ Services
10. Noble Drilling

Fund inception: 1985
Asset mix: Common stocks, 95%; cash/equivalents, 5%
Total net assets: $820 million

Load

Front-end load	3.00%
Redemption fee (max.)	*None*

Annual Fees

12b-1 fee	*None*
Management fee	0.58%
Other expenses	0.62
Total annual expense	1.20%

Minimum initial investment	$2,500
Minimum subsequent investment	$250

Services

Telephone exchanges	*Yes*
Automatic withdrawal	*Yes*
Automatic checking deduction	*Yes*
Retirement plan/IRA	*Yes*
Instant redemption	*Yes*
Portfolio manager (years)	1
Number of funds in family	over 300

Six-Year Performance
Fidelity Select Energy Service vs. Dow Jones

	1995	1996	1997	1998	1999	2000*
Fund	40.9	49.1	51.9	-49.7	72.2	51.8
Dow	33.5	26	22.6	16.1	25.2	-7.4

% Avg. Annual Total Return
Fund vs. Dow Jones Industrial Avg.

*2000 returns through 10/1/00
(5-year avg. annual return: 18.6%)

100

Davis New York Venture Fund

Davis Funds
P.O. Box 1688
Santa Fe, NM 87504-1688
800-279-0279
www.davisfunds.com
Ticker symbol: **NYVTX**

Fund managers: Chris Davis and Ken Feinberg
Fund objective: Long-term growth

Performance	★
Consistency	★ ★ ★
Fees/Services/Management	★ ★ ★
Total	**7 Points**

Chris Davis, manager of the Davis New York Venture Fund, demands a lot of the companies he'll consider for inclusion in the fund's 100-stock, $9 billion portfolio. The fund's ten-point checklist includes such characteristics as first-class management, lean expense structure, proven record as an acquirer, and savvy use of technology.

Davis likes large-cap companies selling at value prices—"growth stocks in disguise," as he puts it. He then holds on to them for the long term.

Financial services are the largest sector in the portfolio at about 34 percent. Technology is hard on its heels at 31 percent, followed by consumer cyclicals at 11.5 percent.

Most of the fund's top holdings are household names, such as Hewlett-Packard, American Express, Texas Instruments, and Citigroup.

The fund, which was started in 1969, has provided an average annual return the past ten years of about 19 percent. A $10,000 investment in the fund ten years ago would now be worth about $57,000. Davis takes a very conservative trading approach, with an annual portfolio turnover ratio of just 25 percent.

PERFORMANCE

The fund has enjoyed solid growth over the past five years. Including dividends and capital gains distributions, the Davis New York Venture Fund has provided a load-adjusted average annual return the past five years (through late 2000) of 21.2 percent.

A $10,000 investment in 1995 would have grown to about $26,000 five years later.

CONSISTENCY

The fund has been fairly consistent, outperforming the Dow Jones Industrial Average three of the past five years through 1999 (and again through most of 2000). Its biggest gain came in 1995, when it moved up 40.6 percent (compared with a 33.5 percent rise in the Dow).

FEES/SERVICES/MANAGEMENT

The fund carries a maximum 4.75 percent front-end load and maximum 0.75 percent redemption fee. The fund's total annual expense ratio of 0.9 percent (with a 0.25 percent 12b-1 fee) is very low compared with other funds.

The fund offers all the standard services such as retirement account availability, automatic withdrawal, and automatic checking account deduction. Its minimum initial investment of $1,000 and minimum subsequent investment of $25 are in line with other funds.

The fund has been managed since 1997 by Chris Davis, who has been a fund manager with Davis Funds since 1989. The Davis fund family includes just nine funds and allows shareholders to switch from fund to fund by telephone.

Top Ten Stock Holdings

1. Hewlett-Packard	6. Wells Fargo
2. American Express	7. IBM
3. Texas Instruments	8. Household International
4. Citigroup	9. Tyco International
5. American Home Products	10. Intel

Fund inception: 1969
Asset mix: Common stocks, 95%; cash/equivalents, 4%; preferred stock, 1%
Total net assets: $9 billion

Load

Front-end load	4.75%
Redemption fee (max.)	0.75

Annual Fees

12b-1 fee	0.25%
Management fee	0.53
Other expenses	0.12
Total annual expense	0.90%

Minimum initial investment	$1,000
Minimum subsequent investment	$25

Services

Telephone exchanges	*Yes*
Automatic withdrawal	*Yes*
Automatic checking deduction	*Yes*
Retirement plan/IRA	*Yes*
Instant redemption	*Yes*
Portfolio manager (years)	3
Number of funds in family	9

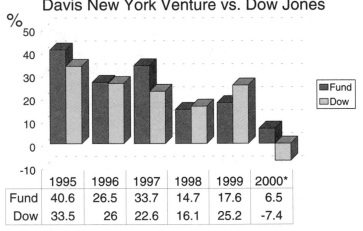

Six-Year Performance
Davis New York Venture vs. Dow Jones

	1995	1996	1997	1998	1999	2000*
Fund	40.6	26.5	33.7	14.7	17.6	6.5
Dow	33.5	26	22.6	16.1	25.2	-7.4

% Avg. Annual Total Return
Fund vs. Dow Jones Industrial Avg.

*2000 returns through 10/1/00
(5-year avg. annual return: 21.3%)

Honorable Mentions

High-Yield Bond Funds

Fund	Symbol	Load (%)	Average Annual Return (%) 3-yr.	5-yr.	Telephone
Strong Short-Term High-Yield	STHBX	None	4.58	6.51	800-368-3863
Fidelity Capital & Income	FAGIX	None	4.51	7.76	800-544-8544
Columbia High-Yield	CMHYX	None	4.42	7.30	800-547-1707
Eaton Vance Income/Boston A	EVIBX	4.75	4.14	8.63	800-225-6265
Vanguard High-Yield Corporate	VWEHX	None	3.21	6.37	800-635-1511
MainStay High-Yield Corp. A	MHCAX	4.50	3.17	8.00	800-624-6782
PIMCO High-Yield A	PHDAX	4.50	3.00	NA	800-426-0107
Lord Abbott Bond Debenture A	LBNDX	4.75	3.02	6.87	800-201-6984
T. Rowe Price High-Yield	PRHYX	None	2.81	6.89	800-225-5132
American High-Income	AHITX	3.75	2.51	6.98	800-421-0180

Long-Term Bond Funds

Fund	Symbol	Load (%)	Average Annual Return (%) 3-yr.	5-yr.	Telephone
Calvert Income A	CFICX	3.75	8.00	7.79	800-368-2745
Dreyfus Intermediate Term Inc.	DRITX	None	7.00	NA	800-645-6561
Dreyfus LifeTime Income Inv.	DLIIX	None	6.58	7.89	800-645-6561
Liberty Contrarian Income A	CHINX	4.75	6.48	6.72	800-426-3750
Advantus Mortgage Securities	ADMSX	4.50	6.17	6.66	800-665-6005
Harbor Bond	HABDX	None	6.13	6.94	800-422-1050
PIMCO Total Return A	PTTAX	4.50	8.57	5.98	800-426-0107
Vanguard Long-Term Bond Index	VBLTX	None	6.03	6.48	800-635-1511
Excelsior Managed Income	UMMGX	None	5.33	5.40	800-446-1012
Strong Corporate Bond Inv.	STCBX	None	4.92	6.83	800-368-3863

Tax-Exempt Bond Funds

Fund	Symbol	Load (%)	Average Annual Return (%) 3-yr.	5-yr.	Telephone
CitiFunds National Tax-Free Income	CFNIX	4.50	5.84	6.40	800-625-4554
Vanguard Insured Long-Term Tax	VILPX	None	4.93	5.60	800-635-1511
Fidelity Spartan Municipal Income	FHIGX	None	4.71	5.71	800-544-8544
Scudder Managed Municipal Bond	SCMBX	None	4.57	5.48	800-728-3337
Vanguard Long-Term Tax-Exempt	VWLTX	None	4.56	5.60	800-635-1511
T. Rowe Price Summit Municipal	PRINX	None	4.42	5.97	800-225-5132
Vanguard High-Yield Tax-Exempt	VWAHX	None	4.38	5.41	800-635-1511
Dreyfus Basic Municipal Bond	DRMBX	None	4.37	5.41	800-645-6561
Dreyfus Basic Intermediate Muni.	DBIMX	None	4.61	5.33	800-645-6561
Fidelity Spartan Intermediate Muni.	FLTMX	None	4.39	5.12	800-544-8544

Index

FREE OFFER!

★ ★ ★ ★ ★

Free Best 100 Online Research

Follow *The 100 Best Mutual Funds to Own in America, The 100 Best Stocks to Own in America,* and *The 100 Best Stocks to Own for Under $25* online—and read timely articles on the market by Gene Walden at **<www.allstarstocks.com>.**

Allstarstocks.com is FREE and includes a broad range of investment information and links to valuable research tools that are designed to help investors track and analyze stocks and mutual funds.